The Reputation Society

The Information Society Series
Laura DeNardis and Michael Zimmer, series editors

Interfaces on Trial 2.0, Jonathan Band and Masanobu Katoh

Opening Standards: The Global Politics of Interoperability, Laura DeNardis, editor

The Reputation Society: How Online Opinions are Reshaping the Offline World, Hassan Masum and Mark Tovey, editors

The Reputation Society

How Online Opinions Are Reshaping the Offline World

edited by Hassan Masum and Mark Tovey

The MIT Press
Cambridge, Massachusetts
London, England

For information about special quantity discounts, please email special_sales@mitpress.mit.edu.

This book was set in Stone by Graphic Composition, Inc. Printed and bound in the United States of America.

Library of Congress Cataloging-in-Publication Data

The reputation society : how online opinions are reshaping the offline world / edited by Hassan Masum and Mark Tovey ; foreword by Craig Newmark.
    p.   cm. — (The information society series)
Includes bibliographical references and index.
ISBN 978-0-262-01664-3 (hardcover : alk. paper) 1. Reputation. 2. Information society—Social aspects. 3. Internet—Social aspects. I. Masum, Hassan, 1971– II. Tovey, Mark, 1970–
HM851.R458   2012
303.48'33—dc23

                                                                              2011016661

10 9 8 7 6 5 4 3 2 1

For our parents.

Contents

Foreword: Trust, Reputation Systems, and the Immune System of Democracy

Craig Newmark

People use social networking tools to figure out whom they can trust and rely on for decision making. By the end of this decade, power and influence will have shifted largely to those people with the best reputations and trust networks and away from people with money and nominal power. That is, peer networks will confer legitimacy on people emerging from the grassroots.

This shift is already happening, gradually creating a new power and influence equilibrium with new checks and balances. It will seem dramatic when its tipping point occurs, even though we're living through it now. Everyone will get a chance to participate in large or small ways, giving a voice to what we once called "the silent majority."

When we need help with decision making, we get recommendations from people we trust; that trust is built on some combination of personal experience and reputation. That's the way humans work. We talk about reputation being one's greatest asset.

In real life, personal networks are pretty small—people numbering maybe in the hundreds. Mass media plays a role in shaping reputation for a small number of people, including celebrities and politicians. Very few people have influence in this environment.

Internet culture and technology change this dramatically. People tend to work with each other. People are normally trustworthy—and despite their large media footprint, there aren't many bad guys out there. People are finding that reputation and recommendation systems can be used to drive a lot of profit.

Reputation is contextual: you might trust someone when it comes to dry cleaners but not politics. So we want to be able to see whom we might be able to trust—maybe by seeing some explicit measurement, or maybe by seeing something implicit, like their history, and who trusts them.

We already see various forms of reputation and recommendation systems evolving, often with mixtures of preselected experts or professionals. Amazon.com and ConsumerReports.org do a good job of this. (Disclaimer: I'm on the board of Consumer Reports, since their record for integrity is close to perfect.)

Wikipedia.org does a very good job of this, mostly by having lots of people keep an eye on articles—particularly the more controversial ones. There are ongoing issues that are being addressed in good conscience as people develop new methods to address information quality and reliability.

We also see reputation and influence reflected in social networking sites. Such systems show history and context, which play into trust, as well as connections to other people.

Cory Doctorow postulates a kind of trustworthiness currency called "Whuffie." You trust someone, maybe want to reward them for something—you give them points. Turns out that there's an experimental repository of Whuffie: the Whuffie Bank. Although this sounds facetious, it's a very simple solution to the complex problem of tracking trust.

One prominent experiment in directly measuring trust is Honestly.com (formerly Unvarnished), launched in beta form in 2010. You rate what trust you have in specific individuals, and they might rate you. Honestly.com is pretty controversial and has attracted a lot of legal speculation. They're trying to address all the problems related to the trustworthiness of the information they receive, and if they can do so, they might become very successful.

This trustworthiness point raises an issue that all such systems have: they might be easy to game. Any such system is vulnerable to disinformation attacks, whereby people who are smart enough (and dishonest enough) can figure out how to fake good or bad ratings. There are numerous very successful groups that are really good at such disinformation in conventional and social media, often called "front groups," "influence peddlers," or "astroturfers." One good watchdog of such groups is the Center for Media and Democracy.

Trust is transitive—it depends on the trustworthiness of the people who trust someone. If person A trusts you, and person B trusts A, then that might affect how person B measures your trustworthiness. However, such logic gets complicated when that web of trust involves seven billion people—or even a few thousand people. It's a research problem.

How do we trust the custodians of trustworthiness? We need to have some confidence that they're not fiddling the ratings, that they're reasonably secure. After all, trust and reputation are really valuable assets.

I think the solution lies in a network of trust and reputation systems. We're seeing the evolution of a number of different ways of measuring trust, which reflects a human reality; different people think of trust in different ways.

The repositories of trust information are the banks in which we store this big asset. Like any banks, having a lot of this kind of currency confers a lot of power. Having competition provides checks and balances.

To restate the bottom line: we are already seeing a shift in power and influence, a big wave that will be significant by the end of this decade. Right now, it's like the moment before a tsunami, in which the water is drawn away from the shore. It's time to get ahead of that curve.

As you read this book, here are some questions to ask yourself:

- How might reputation help build "the immune system of democracy"?
- What "immune system disorders" would you suggest watching for?
- What opportunities do you see?

Those who are building, using, and regulating reputation systems should be thinking about what change they want to see in the world. Now is also a good time for those people to think about what unanticipated consequences their work might have.

Once the bugs are worked out, reputation and trust might be a key part of the immune system of democracy—a set of technologies and practices that help power, influence, and legitimacy to flow toward those who are willing and able to tackle the challenges that affect us all.

Acknowledgments

The editors wish to first thank Yi-Cheng Zhang (University of Fribourg), who has been a source of inspiration, ideas, and support for the better part of a decade. Yi-Cheng has a unique mind that sees to the heart of problems, and is passionate about realizing the potential of online reputation to help build a better world.

We are grateful to our two advisors, Laura DeNardis (Yale University) and Michael Zimmer (University of Wisconsin). Laura and Michael helped get this book off the ground and provided ongoing encouragement. The book germinated in a meeting with them at the 2007 Reputation Symposium held at Yale University—a seminal convergence of thinkers and doers at which organizers and participants contributed significantly to the study of reputation.

Each author included in the volume chose to spend valuable time writing a thought-provoking chapter and engaging with editorial suggestions. We acknowledge many other individuals for inspiration, help, or encouragement along the way: Dale Armstrong, Andrew Brook, Robert Barsky, Stefanie Bowles, Leslie Chan, Chris Dellarocas, Jen Dodd, Craig Eby, Chris M. Herdman, David Kaiser, David Kirsh, Paolo Laureti, Stuart Lee, Paolo Massa, Matúš Medo, Lionel Moret, Michael Nielsen, Beth Noveck, Dominic Rossi, Karl Schroeder, Angela White, and all of our other friends, family, and colleagues who have been supportive during the preparation of this volume.

Last, we owe a debt of thanks to our editor at the MIT Press, Marguerite Avery, and her colleagues Mel Goldsipe, Nancy Kotary, Katie Persons, and Johna Picco, for their cheerful and sympathetic guidance throughout the project.

Introduction: Building the Reputation Society

Hassan Masum, Mark Tovey, and Yi-Cheng Zhang

The principal office of history I take to be this: to prevent virtuous actions from being forgotten, and that evil words and deeds should fear an infamous reputation with posterity.

—Tacitus, Roman historian

The Rise and Importance of Online Reputation

Since the dawn of history, humans have faced the necessity of deciding whom to trust and what to believe. Yet a dramatic intensification of the scope and speed of interactions in our modern society is driving an increasing need to distinguish what is true, useful, and relevant from what is not. So how can people decide whom to trust, what to choose, and which leaders and ideas to support?

In day-to-day life, we can usually make decisions and judgments based on firsthand experience. We can also obtain information from others in our immediate circle. However, personally obtained information is not always enough to make good decisions, or come to appropriate judgments.

Historically, in order to share judgments effectively, various forms of *reputation* arose. In times past, in villages and clans, gossip and gatherings spread information about local conditions and the character of particular people (Bailey 1971). More recently, the media—often in concert with state and religious power—promulgated and shaped opinions over large territories. To facilitate mutually beneficial exchange, trading guilds and certification agencies developed reputational mechanisms (Klein 1997), as did sovereign nations borrowing internationally (Tomz 2007). Reputation has always operated within networks of relationships (Craik 2009). It still does, even as these networks grow in complexity and speed, and spawn new online forms of trust and reputation (Golbeck 2009; Jøsang, Ismail, and Boyd 2007).

In today's world, reliable advice from others' experiences is often unavailable, whether for buying products, choosing a service, or judging a policy. One promising solution is to bring to reputation a similar kind of systematization as currencies, laws, and accounting brought to primitive barter economies. Properly designed reputation systems have the potential to reshape society for the better by shining the light of accountability into dark places, through the mediated judgments of billions of people worldwide, to create what we call the *Reputation Society* (Masum and Zhang 2004).

A key concern of the Reputation Society is the need to deal with information overload. When anything can be broadcast and accessed, filtering becomes essential (Shenk 1997). Worse yet, long-term civic issues can become lost in a constant stream of short-term distractions. How do we find what is relevant and worth acting on?

The effective use of reputation has implications for many of our daily activities. In the marketplace, being able to judge which products are worth buying ensures value for money and provides sellers incentive to improve. Medically, the difference between the worst and best treatment can be the difference between life and death. Politically, the ability to distinguish between truth and falsehood determines the shape of our democracies and the trustworthiness of our leaders.

Buoyed by the successes of human ingenuity to date, some optimists see no need for systematic efforts to tackle such challenges, believing that the right solutions will naturally emerge from inquisitive minds and competitive markets. Others—skeptics and pessimists—have resigned themselves to the failings of the human race, and so also do not see value in systematic efforts for improvement.

We differ with both the optimists and the pessimists. We believe that determined effort can create institutions and mechanisms that can stand as examples for the world. A realistic understanding of human nature, combined with wise rules, can guard liberties and pave the way for future progress—as the Constitutions of the United States and other democracies have done for so long by protecting and improving social welfare.

What Kind of World Might Online Reputation Lead To?

To make the potential of online reputation clearer, we offer some examples of what the development of online reputation might accomplish.

Buying Wisely

Each day, people decide which goods and services to purchase. Many of these decisions are made with inadequate information about the quality of the products. Our information about products is obtained largely through image-based advertising, with little reliable quality assessment.

However, information about product quality is increasingly available through certification agencies, which rate products for safety (Underwriters Laboratories), quality (Consumer Reports), sustainability (ForestEthics) and other factors. What if such systems could also incorporate evaluations from a global population, using information from services similar to Epinions.com? Being able to make most buying decisions as if a team of expert advisors were at your side could significantly improve the quality of goods and services across the economy, and increase collective satisfaction (Zhang 2005).

In fact, online reputation has been adopted by many well-known e-commerce sites, such as Amazon.com, eBay.com, and TripAdvisor.com. These sites may assign reputation explicitly (e.g., using five-star rating scales) or implicitly (e.g., displaying how many helpful contributions a user has made). Such reputations may be used to assess objects (GoodGuide.com), people (RateMyProfessors.com), or even ideas (WhyNot .net). The design of these reputation systems requires a combination of technical and social knowledge, along with practical experience (Farmer and Glass 2010).

Achieving Sustainability

Evolving a society based on *sustainable prosperity*—that is, achieving continuing human advancement while using resources in a way that keeps them viable for our children and their descendants—is one of the great challenges of the twenty-first century (Brown 2009). Sharing goods and services more effectively could be part of the solution. Car-sharing services, for example, are rapidly gaining in popularity in urban areas. Botsman and Rogers (2010) document examples of people sharing everything from power tools to office space. Reputation systems are essential to making such sharing work. We might be ready to lend a drill to a neighbor who has been highly rated by other neighbors, but be wary of a neighbor with a reputation for carelessness. More broadly, putting trusted ratings for products and investments at our fingertips might make it easier to choose more ecologically friendly options (Goleman 2010).

Upgrading Politics

Unlike previous generations, it may no longer be necessary for us to choose between populism and rulership by elites. Consider a project like TheyWorkForYou.com (one of a group of web projects created by MySociety.org, a nonpartisan group in the United Kingdom). On this website, the performance of each UK member of parliament (MP) is tracked in various ways. This information includes the number of votes and debates in parliament in which the MP has participated, the readability of their parliamentary speeches, and the number of annotations that the public has made on those speeches.

Tools for rating policies (Gürkan et al. 2010) and for tracking performance and corruption (Picci 2011) might enable the public to make politicians more accountable. The political process itself could expand to include citizens as co-equal partners in "collaborative democracy" (Lathrop and Ruma 2010; Noveck 2009), if facilitated by tools that allow participation that is both inclusive and effective (Tovey 2008).

There is also a dark side to online reputation systems. Exploring possible negative scenarios can suggest futures we may want to avoid.

Avoiding Mobocracy Online

In many instances, citizens have cooperated online to expose or punish what they consider to be repugnant behavior (Solove 2007). If a woman is captured on YouTube.com refusing to pick up her dog's excrement on the subway, some degree of sanction may be appropriate. But what if her name, picture, address, and place of work are publicized online? There are documented instances in which digital vigilantes take it upon themselves to harass a person by phone or complain to that person's place of employment, resulting in the person losing his or her job (Downey 2010). How far can community sanction go before the sanction causes unwarranted shame, fear, and economic harm?

Although the Internet has been a source of much progress, it has also been a platform for significant personal harms (Levmore and Nussbaum 2011). Even when wrongdoings deserve sanction, a mob's collective punishment may lack accountability and be disproportionately harsh. Darker scenarios are possible if digital mobs are systematically encouraged by parties with extremist agendas.

Defending Your Good Name

What would you do if you searched for your name online and found that someone had written lies about you—lies with repercussions to your livelihood, family, or standing in the community? Though you may have done nothing wrong and may have no ill will toward any person, anyone can choose to write about you online, and at present there is surprisingly little recourse. Although reputation system designers understand these issues and try to engineer safeguards against misuse, poorly designed reputation systems make it easier to blackball people or organizations.

To guard against unwarranted online reputation attacks, methods have been proposed such as proactively providing accurate information and monitoring one's "namespace" (Fertik and Thompson 2010). How well will such safeguards work in the reputation systems of the future? What might be the effect on our society of reputation records that last for one's entire lifetime, or of the expansion of credit records into "customer desirability scores" that determine when and how warmly one is welcome in a place of business? Reputational harms to individuals might also come from corporate or state actors—perhaps even combined in an intrusive, high-tech "security-industrial complex" (Doctorow 2007). Such asymmetries of power, if not controlled by checks and balances, could pose a threat to the freedoms and liberties of modern societies.

A Look Ahead

Practical steps toward a better world begin with visions of how that world could take shape. The authors in this book highlight a number of dangers associated with online reputation, while giving a sense of what could be a fairer and more livable world: the Reputation Society.

Part I lays a base for what follows by focusing on understanding reputation. Dellarocas looks at the promises and challenges of online reputation mechanism design and considers how to implement the right incentives for good behavior, truthful reporting, and resistance to manipulation. Farmer shares some of the signposts, warnings, and potential solutions he has encountered over two decades of building reputation systems. Clippinger discusses connections between evolutionary biology, finance, and reputation systems, and suggests design principles to make reputation systems more effective.

Part II takes up challenges of regulating societies. Whitfield shows how many aspects of reputation have occurred in the animal world and in the evolution of our own species, and suggests lessons for the future that can be learned from the past. Goldman considers how well-functioning marketplaces depend on the vibrant flow of accurate reputations, and what the challenges and future options are for regulation of reputational information. Strahilevitz discusses how reputation might complement regulation in the context of landlord-tenant relations, antidiscrimination law, and commercial disputes, and proposes that greater access to reputational information could be a twenty-first-century public good.

Part III looks at reputation's role in amplifying signals. Lampe shows that rating and reputation systems can perform socializing functions by making desirable behaviors clear and supporting community norms. Steffen discusses how "attention philanthropy" can help important ideas enter the mainstream by acting as a reputation booster that redistributes attention. Maxson and Kuraishi suggest how reputation information in philanthropy can help determine which worthy-sounding projects achieve real impact.

Part IV explores reputation's functions in supporting science. Nielsen warns of the dangers of overreliance on any single metric of success and suggests a more diverse approach to deciding what risky endeavors to collectively support—a perspective with implications beyond science. Henning, Hoyt, and Reichelt propose moving beyond today's citation metrics to usage-based metrics, which could measure how articles are actually read and used. Willinsky considers the effect that open access has on reputation in academia and research publishing.

Part V considers how reputation can help in improving policies. Picci shows how making government behavior transparent and understandable can enable reputation-based governance, and improve its accountability. Massa discusses design choices and trust metrics that may help balance between the extremes of echo chambers and tyrannies of the majority. Iandoli, Introne, and Klein describe how reputation-enabled "argument maps" can highlight ideas of collective interest and promote more effective and collaborative deliberation.

Part VI brings the book to a close by envisaging scenarios for the Reputation Society. Zimmer and Hoffman address the twin risks of the oversharing of personal information and the spread of online reputation and personal information beyond its intended context. Cascio suggests a taxonomy of reputation systems, distinguishing them by how reputations are generated and whether participation is optional, and then offering an exploration of how each type of reputation system might unfold. Ashby and Doctorow offer a provocative pair of scenarios to illustrate how reputation systems could affect the practice of education.

Several authors have expressed grave reservations about what reputation systems may lead to in the long run: a mob mentality, vigilantism, a pitiless collective memory that never forgets a past misdeed. Daniel Solove framed part of the downside as a balance between the rights of privacy and freedom of speech, asking when we should be free to make claims about others and under what conditions (Solove 2007). Rosen (2004) has suggested that if everyone lived "under the microscope," opportunities for innovation, risk taking, and political and civic discourse could be restricted.

Could the Reputation Society be nothing more than a conformity-enforcing Panopticon—one that could be hijacked by authoritarians as a more effective means of social control? There is no single intervention that will prevent such a dire outcome. However, it is already possible to see measures that can guide the evolution of these systems in a positive direction. These measures lie partly in reputation system design and partly in the development of legal and legislative norms. The way in which we choose to use reputation systems will also play a key role.

We hope that at the end of this book you will be persuaded that reputation tools matter, that they come with real dangers, and that they have great potential for improving social progress and living standards. The time to begin seriously collaborating on understanding, designing, and implementing such tools is now.

References

Bailey, F. G., ed. 1971. *Gifts and poisons: The politics of reputation.* Oxford: Blackwell.

Botsman, R., and R. Rogers. 2010. *What's mine is yours: The rise of collaborative consumption.* New York: HarperBusiness.

Brown, L. R. 2009. *Plan B 4.0: Mobilizing to save civilization.* New York: W. W. Norton & Company.

Craik, K. H. 2009. *Reputation: A network interpretation.* New York: Oxford University Press.

Doctorow, C. 2007. Scroogled. Retrieved from: <http://craphound.com/?p=1902>.

Downey, T. 2010, March 3. China's Cyberposse. *New York Times.* Retrieved from: <http://www.nytimes.com/2010/03/07/magazine/07Human-t.html>.

Farmer, R., and B. Glass. 2010. *Building web reputation systems.* Sebastopol, CA: O'Reilly.

Fertik, M., and D. Thompson. 2010. *Wild west 2.0: How to protect and restore your online reputation on the untamed social frontier.* New York: American Management Association.

Golbeck, J., ed. 2009. *Computing with social trust*. London: Springer.

Goleman, D. 2010. *Ecological intelligence: The hidden impacts of what we buy*. New York: Broadway Books.

Gürkan, A., L. Iandoli, M. Klein, and G. Zollo. 2010. Mediating debate through on-line large-scale argumentation: Evidence from the field. *Information Sciences* 180 (19): 3686–3702.

Jøsang, A., R. Ismail, and C. A. Boyd. 2007. A survey of trust and reputation systems for online service provision. *Decision Support Systems* 43 (2): 618–644.

Klein, D. B., ed. 1997. *Reputation: Studies in the voluntary elicitation of good conduct*. Ann Arbor: University of Michigan Press.

Lathrop, D., and L. Ruma, eds. 2010. *Open government: Collaboration, transparency, and participation in practice*. Cambridge, MA: O'Reilly.

Levmore, S., and M. C. Nussbaum, eds. 2011. *The offensive Internet: Speech, privacy, and reputation*. Cambridge, MA: Harvard University Press.

Masum, H., and Y. C. Zhang. 2004. Manifesto for the Reputation Society. *First Monday* 9 (7).

Noveck, B. S. 2009. *Wiki government: How technology can make government better, democracy stronger, and citizens more powerful*. Washington, DC: Brookings Institution Press.

Picci, L. 2011. *Reputation-based governance*. Stanford: Stanford University Press.

Rosen, J. 2004. *The naked crowd: Reclaiming security and freedom in an anxious age*. New York: Random House.

Shenk, D. 1997. *Data smog: Surviving the information glut*. San Francisco: Harper Edge.

Solove, D. J. 2007. *The future of reputation: Gossip, rumor, and privacy on the Internet*. New Haven: Yale University Press.

Tomz, M. 2007. *Reputation and international cooperation: Sovereign debt across three centuries*. Princeton: Princeton University Press.

Tovey, M., ed. 2008. *Collective intelligence: Creating a prosperous world at peace*. Oakton, VA: EIN Press.

Zhang, Y. C. 2005. Supply and demand law under limited information. *Physica A* 350 (2–4): 500–532.

I UNDERSTANDING REPUTATION

1 Designing Reputation Systems for the Social Web

Chrysanthos Dellarocas

How can online reputation systems be designed to meet the needs of both users and system designers? Chrysanthos Dellarocas looks at the promises and challenges of online reputation mechanism design and how to implement incentives for good behavior, truthful reporting, and resistance to manipulation.

Reputation systems are arguably the unsung heroes of the social web. In some form or another, they are an integral part of most of today's social web applications. Yet they usually play a supporting role and have thus received less attention than some of their higher-profile cousins such as social networks, recommender systems, consumer review sites, and crowdsourcing communities, whose success would often have been unsustainable without the quiet but effective support of reputation systems (Dellarocas 2003). Two examples include eBay, a trading community of virtual strangers, which would have been impossible without the reputation system that builds trust by enabling buyers and sellers to rate each other; as well as Amazon, where product reviews are rendered both more useful and more credible by the presence of a scoring system that allows readers to vote on a review's usefulness. Amazon employs these votes to point customers to the most useful reviews and socially reward the most successful reviewers. Other examples are Yelp.com, a youthful urban review community that similarly uses what is essentially a reputation mechanism to help users better interpret opinions that are inherently subjective, and Xbox Live, a gaming site that makes widespread use of scoreboards to reward skilled gamers, help gamers find opponents of similar skill level, and provide incentives for people of all skill levels to keep playing.

This chapter provides an introduction to what we know about the practical design of these ubiquitous but undervalued systems. It begins by outlining the surprisingly diverse set of business objectives that reputation mechanisms satisfy in today's social web. It then highlights four key decisions related to their design and what we know about each one. It concludes with a brief case study of a real-life reputation system.

What Is a Reputation System?

There are no widely agreed-upon definitions of reputation and reputation systems. Even within this volume, different authors define reputation using slightly different terms. Given the many reasons that websites employ reputation systems, this chapter uses the following correspondingly broad pair of definitions. *Reputation* is a summary of one's relevant past actions within the context of a specific community, presented in a manner that can help other community members make decisions with respect to whether and how to relate to that individual (and/or to the individual's works). Accordingly, a *reputation system* is an information system that mediates and facilitates the process of assessing reputations within the context of a specific community.

Why Do Social Web Applications Use Reputation Systems?

The concept of reputation is most often associated with the notion of trust. Although trust building has historically been an important role of reputation, today's web-based reputation systems serve a much broader set of objectives for users and system designers. These objectives include the following:

• *Trust building* This goal is achieved by encouraging "good" and discouraging "bad" social behaviors within the context of a site. This is perhaps the most obvious and widely discussed role of reputation systems, best exemplified by eBay.
• *Filtering* Most web-based systems are characterized by an abundance of information that can quickly overwhelm their users. In the majority of settings, the quality of contributed content tends to be very uneven. Reputation systems can improve the attractiveness of the systems they support by helping users easily identify the highest-quality contributions.
• *Matching* This objective is important in settings where members vary widely in interests and tastes and where the quality of contributions is characterized by a high degree of subjectivity. In such settings, reputation systems ought to summarize the relevant attributes of a member in a neutral manner so that others can assess the degree to which they can relate to him or her.
• *User lock-in* Because reputation is usually specific to a single community or web system, it constitutes a powerful form of lock-in and can be used strategically by system designers to increase user loyalty and decrease attrition. Once a user has built a reputation on a site, that user will be reluctant to defect to a competitor because he or she would then have to build his or her reputation from scratch. In an increasingly competitive environment, this dimension of reputation mechanisms must not be overlooked. It poses some interesting questions (e.g., who owns a user's reputation?) and may at times pit user interests against system designer interests.

All four objectives are relevant to the design of most reputation systems. Different systems, however, assign different priorities to each of these objectives. For example, building enough trust so that buyers can feel comfortable enough to send their money to sellers they have never met—and, very likely, will never buy from again—is arguably the primary objective of eBay's reputation mechanism. On the other hand, the most important objective of Amazon's reviewer reputation mechanism is to induce members to contribute well thought out, high-quality reviews and to identify (i.e., filter) the highest-quality reviews.

Inducing high-quality contributions is high on Yelp's agenda as well. However, because the majority of Yelp reviews are subjective, it is usually difficult to reliably assess a review's quality. What is more important is to provide tools that can help readers make a personal assessment of a review's credibility and compatibility with their view of the world. Finally, Xbox Live is an example of a system in which user loyalty and retention is the overarching (business) objective of its reputation feature.

What Are the Key Design Decisions of a Reputation System?

According to the definition stated previously, reputation is a summary of relevant past actions. Designing an effective reputation system correspondingly entails four key decisions:

1. What actions are relevant to include in one's reputation profile?
2. How to obtain information about these actions
3. How to aggregate and display reputation information
4. How to deal with manipulation and gaming

Key Decision 1: Which Actions Are Relevant to Include in One's Reputation Profile?

Users typically engage in rich behaviors within the context of a site. Effective reputation systems must carefully choose the aspects of user behavior to track and report on. Making this decision correctly requires a clear understanding and prioritization of the reputation system's business objectives.

There are two questions to be considered in this decision:

• *What actions are most relevant to the reputation system's users?* For example, if the key objective of the system is to help users decide whether a seller is honest, keeping track of the seller's percentage of completed transactions is a very relevant indicator, whereas keeping track of a seller's own purchase history is less relevant. On the other hand, if a system's key objective is to help users determine whether a reviewer has similar tastes to their own, keeping track of a reviewer's purchase history might be a very relevant indicator.

• *What user behaviors are desirable to encourage or discourage?* The mere act of publicly keeping track of someone's actions can encourage or discourage the incidence of those actions (depending on whether the action in question has a good or bad connotation). Therefore, if a site wants to encourage the volume of contributions, its designers might consider keeping track of the number of reviews posted or the number of comments posted on somebody's reputation profile. On the other hand, if a site wants to encourage the quality of contributions, it might want to hide information about contribution volume and to keep track instead of how other people rated a particular contribution.

Key Decision 2: How to Obtain Information about Relevant User Actions
The main choice here is between internally generated (firsthand) information and (secondhand) feedback provided by others. For example, Yelp's counts of the volume of a user's posted reviews or of the size of one's friend network are examples of firsthand information. In contrast, eBay's reliance on asking the buyer and the seller what they thought about a transaction is an example of secondhand feedback.

Firsthand information about user actions is generally preferable, as it is accurate and unbiased. Unfortunately, it is not always available, or its collection might require the development of costly additional infrastructure. For this reason, reputation systems must often rely on secondhand feedback provided by others. Secondhand feedback is subject to two important shortcomings that must be addressed by the designer: untruthful reporting (i.e., lying) and reporting bias. *Untruthful reporting* can often be kept in check by using some form of community policing. "Rate-the-rater" schemes whereby users rate the "usefulness" or "credibility" of feedback postings appear to work well in many settings, even though in theory such schemes are not difficult for determined users to game (Lampe and Resnick 2004). Some researchers have proposed payment mechanisms that induce truthful reporting. Such mechanisms pay reviewers an amount that is based on how well their ratings of an individual can predict future ratings posted by others about the same individual (Miller, Resnick, and Zeckhauser 2005). A schedule of payments that makes it optimal for all reviewers to report the truth can theoretically be devised. However, such mechanisms break down in the presence of collusion and have not been widely used in practical systems.

Reporting bias is a situation in which users are systematically more likely to post feedback when certain types of outcomes occur and to remain silent otherwise. For example, it has been documented that users are generally more likely to post feedback when they have had extreme (either very good or very bad) experiences than when they have had average experiences (Dellarocas and Narayan 2006). Reporting bias can reduce the reliability of the reputational information. For example, reporting bias is largely responsible for the improbably high percentage (approximately 99 percent) of positive feedback that was the norm on eBay until 2009 (when, as I discuss in the next paragraph, eBay made some important changes to its mechanism). It appears that in a lot of middle-of-the-road transactions in which things don't go great but which are still not a disaster, eBay users have preferred to stay silent rather than to post neutral or negative feedback (Dellarocas and Wood 2008).

Preventing reporting bias is tricky, as it is not usually practical or desirable to force members to post feedback. In some cases, one can use domain knowledge and statistical methods to filter out reporting bias when aggregating feedback. In other cases, one might be able to eliminate some of the sources of this bias by redesigning the mechanism. For example, it appears that the fear of retaliatory negative feedback from sellers discourages many buyers from posting neutral or negative feedback when they are unhappy with a transaction. Recognizing this, eBay recently changed its mechanism so that it no longer gives sellers the option to post unfavorable feedback for buyers.

Key Decision 3: How to Aggregate and Display Reputation Information

Reputation mechanisms employ a variety of methods for displaying outputs. These include:

- Simple statistics (e.g., number of reviews posted, number of transactions completed)
- Star ratings (e.g., Amazon reviews)
- Numerical score (e.g., eBay's reputation score, and the technical news site Slashdot's karma score—see chapter 7 in this volume)
- Numbered tiers (e.g., World of Warcraft's player levels)
- Achievement badges (e.g., eBay Power Seller, Yelp Elite Reviewer)
- Leaderboards (lists where users are ranked relative to each other and top users are highlighted, e.g., list of top Amazon reviewers)

The choice of a display method is very important because it can determine: (a) the extent to which the reputation mechanism makes a judgment versus allowing users to make their own judgments, and (b) the extent to which the presence of the reputation system can create competition among users.

Displaying simple statistics of a person's activity within a community is perhaps the most neutral method of summarizing one's reputation. Social network statistics in particular have been rapidly rising in popularity in many contexts. The advantage of using simple statistics is that the reputation system makes minimal judgments and allows users to draw their own conclusions. The disadvantage is that the burden for interpreting these quantities falls on the shoulders of the user, who must be familiar enough with the environment to draw the proper conclusions.

Star ratings and achievement badges solve this problem by immediately communicating to users whether somebody's performance along some dimension is "good" or "bad." This method helps users more easily digest information, but also makes an explicit judgment of quality. It is therefore best applicable in settings in which there is a commonly agreed-upon notion of what "quality" means.

Whereas star ratings and achievement badges highlight individual achievement, numbered tiers and leaderboards go a step further, as they not only confer a judgment but also indicate a user's standing in relation to others. They thus introduce a pecking order among users, which can have a very strong impact on a community's culture and behavior (see chapter 2 in this volume). Supporting direct comparison of users against one another often increases incentives to contribute and enhances the filtering role of a reputation system. On the other hand, such direct comparison instills a culture of competition, which might end up being disruptive in a number of ways. First, obsession with rankings might lead some users to manipulative and counterproductive behavior. Second, users who don't make it to the top ranks might feel resentful and be induced to exit.

The story of Digg.com provides an example of the dangers of introducing too much competition in a community whose culture is otherwise meant to be cooperative. Digg is a system that allows users to recommend news articles that piqued their interest. Other users vote recommended articles up or down. An article's number of votes determines its relative visibility on the site. The site was meant to be a grassroots method of determining what is interesting to read about today.

Digg implemented a reputation mechanism that originally included a leaderboard listing the most "influential" Diggers—members whose recommended articles received the most votes. Some of the leading Digg members became so obsessed with their rankings that they formed a collusion ring for the purpose of ensuring that their recommendations always made it to the top, which ended up eroding the culture and dynamics of the site. Amid controversy, in January 2007 Digg decided to abolish the Digg leaderboard. As of June 2010, Digg's user profiles consisted of various "simple statistics" only.

Key Decision 4: How to Deal with Manipulation and Gaming

The sensitive and personal nature of reputational information makes reputation systems a natural target for manipulation and gaming. Anticipating and minimizing the impact of such behavior ought to be high on every site designer's agenda. Interestingly, making appropriate choices in the preceding three key decisions can often go a long way toward making a reputation system less prone to manipulation.

For example, before deciding to include an item of information on a reputation profile, designers should carefully think through the types of undesirable behaviors that users might engage in to boost their score on that dimension. Also, before asking users for feedback, the designer should carefully consider whether other aspects of the system induce reporting bias or give incentives to lie. Finally, a designer should be careful to not instill an unnecessarily competitive spirit by overemphasizing comparisons across users, which might tempt some users to engage in manipulative behavior.

In addition to these considerations, the following two design dimensions can influence the manipulation resistance of a reputation system:

- *Identity of feedback sources*   The degree to which the true identity of the sources of feedback is known to the system and/or the community is a key variable. Full anonymity and easy creation of virtual identities makes it easy for determined users to flood a reputation system with fake ratings. Mapping virtual identities to real identities (e.g., by asking for credit card numbers during registration) can help keep such behavior in check. At the same time, however, controlling identities has drawbacks of its own. First, it might discourage some users from joining the system. Second, it might discourage users from posting anything but positive feedback, increasing reporting bias and reducing the usefulness and credibility of the system. Sometimes a middle-of-the-road approach whereby a reviewer's identity is fully known to the system but not disclosed to other members can work better than either of the two extremes.
- *Transparency of aggregation rules*   Concealing the details of the algorithms used to aggregate feedback is another way of resisting manipulation and gaming. Amazon and Google.com have gone down that path. The former does not disclose the precise formula they use to rank-order reviewers, and the latter does not disclose all the details of rank-ordering search results. Lack of transparency, however, has a downside, as it can lessen a site's credibility and the users' trust in the reputation system's fairness.

In general, it is impossible to design a totally manipulation-resistant reputation system. No matter what mechanisms one puts in place, creative and determined users are bound to find a way around them. For that reason, community administrators must constantly monitor such systems, organically evolving their designs.

A Case Study: Yelp

Yelp, as mentioned earlier, is an online review community that specializes in reviews of restaurants and entertainment establishments in major urban centers. At the same time, Yelp is a community of mostly young users that relate to each other through similar tastes and interests. Yelp maintains a profile page for each of its members. The profile page is essentially a reputation mechanism.

An important objective of Yelp's profile feature is to help other users decide how to interpret a review by finding out more about a reviewer's personality and tastes. At the same time, the profile allows a member to showcase his or her status and contributions to the system, building site loyalty and providing incentives for continued contributions.

Because Yelp's domain (restaurants, entertainment, and other cultural establishments) is highly dependent on personality and taste, Yelp's profile feature wisely avoids the use of numerical scores and star ratings. Instead, a reviewer's profile primarily consists of a series of simple statistics that summarize salient aspects of the user's activity. In addition to simple statistics, Yelp supports secondhand feedback in the form of "compliments" received from other users. However, these compliments are displayed below the neutral statistics and are thus not highlighted as prominently. There are also several different types of compliments ("good writer," "funny," "you're cool," etc.) underlining the plurality of ways in which a user can make valuable contributions and making it difficult to compare users against each other.

Although Yelp supports a leaderboard, it is interesting that the ranking feature is not easily accessible from the home page and that Yelp offers multiple dimensions across which users can be rank-ordered—once again emphasizing that one can stand out in this community for multiple reasons and making it difficult to compare users against each other.

In summary, Yelp's reputation system design is well suited to its business goals of inducing participation and valuable contributions and facilitating the matching of like users in a domain where the notion of "value" has a highly subjective definition.

Conclusions

Reputation systems are ubiquitous in the social web, and their design principles surprisingly subtle. For a more comprehensive introduction to reputation system design theory, see Dellarocas (2006) and Dellarocas, Dini, and Spagnolo (2007). For a practitioner-oriented perspective, see Dellarocas (2010) and Farmer and Glass (2010).

In closing, it's worth reiterating the following points that the author feels have not received their fair share of attention in previous literature:

• The design choices of a reputation system can profoundly affect a community's culture, making an otherwise collaborative and cordial community into a competitive and even combative space. Users often obsess over rankings and scores even when they do not receive any economic benefit from them. Although such features can increase incentives to contribute, they can also provoke manipulative and antisocial behaviors.
• A reputation system can be an important source of user loyalty and a powerful mechanism for user retention. This aspect of reputation must be factored into any proposed design change.
• Reputation mechanisms serve a variety of objectives apart from trust building. These include filtering content, matching users, and building user loyalty. Understanding and prioritizing a system's business objectives should be a designer's first task.

References

Dellarocas, C. 2003. The digitization of word-of-mouth: Promise and challenges of online reputation systems. *Management Science* 49 (10): 1407–1424.

Dellarocas, C. 2006. Reputation mechanisms. In *Handbook of economics and information systems*, ed. T. Hendershott, 629–660. Amsterdam, The Netherlands: Elsevier Publishing.

Dellarocas, C. 2010. Online reputation systems: How to design one that does what you need. *Sloan Management Review* 51 (3): 33–38.

Dellarocas, C., F. Dini, and G. Spagnolo. 2007. Designing reputation mechanisms. In *Handbook of Procurement*, ed. N. Dimitri, G. Piga, and G. Spagnolo, 446–482. Cambridge: Cambridge University Press.

Dellarocas, C., and R. Narayan. 2006. A statistical measure of a population's propensity to engage in post-purchase online word-of-mouth. *Statistical Science* 21 (2): 277–285.

Dellarocas, C., and C. A. Wood. 2008. The sound of silence in online feedback: Estimating trading risks in the presence of reporting bias. *Management Science* 54 (3): 460–476.

Farmer, R., and B. Glass. 2010. *Building web reputation systems*. Sebastopol, CA: O'Reilly.

Lampe, C., and P. Resnick. 2004. Slash(dot) and burn: Distributed moderation in a large online conversation space. *Proceedings of the SIGCHI Conference on Human Factors in Computing Systems*, Vienna, Austria, 543–550.

Miller, N., P. Resnick, and R. Zeckhauser. 2005. Eliciting honest feedback: The peer prediction model. *Management Science* 51 (9): 1359–1373.

2   Web Reputation Systems and the Real World

Randy Farmer

When anticipating the future of society and technology, it is advisable to look to the past for relevant successes and failures. Randy Farmer shares some of the signposts, warnings, and solutions he has encountered over two decades of building reputation systems.

Digital reputation is rapidly expanding in real-world influence. Bryce Glass and I have studied hundreds of online reputation systems, including dozens that we helped develop. As we noted in the preface to Farmer and Glass (2010a, ix), "Today's Web is the product of over a *billion* hands and minds. Around the clock and around the globe, a world full of people are pumping out contributions small and large: full-length features on Vimeo; video shorts on YouTube; comments on Blogger; discussions on Yahoo! Groups; and tagged-and-titled Del.icio.us bookmarks."

Given the myriad contexts in which reputation is being used, it may be surprising to the reader that there is not yet any consensus on this field's fundamental terminology. We therefore define *reputation* as "information used to make a value judgment about an object or a person." But we acknowledge the special role of the reputation(s) of a person and therefore suggest a special term for this: *karma*. A good example of karma from real life is your credit score.

Reputation System Evolution and Challenges

Preweb Reputation Systems

Modern digital and web reputations are deeply rooted in pre-Internet social systems. In this essay and others in this volume, examples are drawn from real-world models like the credit scoring industry's measures of creditworthiness and its flagship reputation score, FICO, which was created by Fair Isaac Corporation. There are many industries that rate their members and suppliers. Cities get ratings for their bonds. Products have received the Underwriters Laboratories (UL) or the Good Housekeeping seals of approval. *Consumers Digest* published five-star ratings long before anyone had access to computers in the home.

But not all real-world reputation systems have been successful or continued in the same form over time. Looking closely at these systems and how they have evolved may save the developers of digital reputation systems millions of dollars by identifying possible best practices and helping to avoid dead ends.

Web Reputation Systems

As recently as fifteen years ago, it was unlikely that you could gather enough information for a consensus about the quality of some obscure item from your coworkers, friends, and family. Your ability to benefit from reputation was limited by the scope of your social circle.

Now, thousands of strangers are publishing their opinions, which are aggregated into digital reputation. Want to buy an antique chess set? Look for a good seller feedback score on eBay. Want to figure out what movie to rent from Netflix? Five-star ratings and reviews will point you in the right direction. Want to find out what charities your friends are into? Look at their "likes" on Facebook.

On the surface, using digital reputation systems seems better and easier than tapping your social circle. However, there are some interesting—and even troublesome—side effects of reducing reputation to digital scores created from the input of strangers:

• Digital reputation scores are limited in the subtlety of their inputs. Only numbers go in, and those numbers usually come from simple user actions, such as "Marked an Item as Favorite." But these actions don't always accurately represent the sentiment that was intended, such as when marking something as a favorite is used for convenience to tag objectionable or novel items.
• Aggregated numerical scores capture only one dimension of a user's opinions. For example, eBay's seller feedback score was eventually enhanced with detailed seller ratings that reflect features of a transaction with scores called "Item as described," "Communications," "Shipping time," and "Shipping and handling charges."
• Another class of weaknesses in digital reputation is manipulation by stakeholders. A cadre of fraudulent New York electronics vendors reportedly used to invade Yahoo! Shopping every Christmas, building up false good-reputation for sales by cross-rating each other with five stars (Hawk 2005).

In order for digital reputation to come out of its early experimental period, we—that is, the community of web reputation designers and developers—need to acknowledge and address these technical, social, and potentially political issues. We need to work together to mitigate foreseeable risks based on historical lessons and to avoid a high-visibility economic or political event that will thrust these problems into the public domain—with people demanding immediate and perhaps ill-advised action.

Digital Reputation Is Not Classical Reputation

Social networks borrow and redefine the metaphor of connecting to a friend to create an edge in a digital graph of inter-person relationships. Unfortunately, the term "friend" online has lost its real-life subtlety: if you are active on Facebook, you will likely have many "friends" that you are connected to but that you wouldn't think of as close friends in real life. The same kind of oversimplification occurs when we attempt to quantify real-world socially defined reputation.

In designing reputation systems, we generally use numerical scores (ratings) together with small snippets of text (evaluations). But compared to real-world reputation, these computational models are almost too simple to merit even using the same word. Real-life reputation is subtle and dynamic, with personal and cultural elements. Most of the time, it is inherently nonnumerical. On the other hand, a digital reputation's representation of value is typically numerical, globally defined for all, simple to calculate, and often publicly displayed—clumsy, in comparison.

It is the utility provided by digital reputations that makes them so worthwhile. Software uses digital reputations to sort and filter the unmanageably huge morass of content on the web so that a human can make the final selection: where to eat, what to watch, from whom to buy. It is that last interaction—with a choice made by a thinking human being—that imbues the reputation score with its real power.

As reputation systems increase in real-world influence, the importance of who keeps, calculates, and displays the scores will become a greater societal discussion. Online reputation systems have been deployed for more than a decade, and many of the challenges that reputation systems will face are already known. By articulating these weaknesses, systems designers and researchers can address them head on, or at least enter the fray with their eyes wide open.

Karma Is Hard

Though digital reputations for objects are often a poor imitation of the social reputations they attempt to mimic, karma is even more challenging. We have previously detailed a dozen ways in which karma differs from object reputation (Farmer and Glass 2010b).

Incentives are one example. Because karma is reputation for a user, increasing one's karma score is often considered a strong incentive for participation and contributions on a site. This incentive can create trade-offs between the goals of the site and the desire for the rewards granted with high karma. We can see evidence of this desire, for instance, when collusion or fake user accounts are used by individuals to increase their karma. A related design challenge is finding a trade-off between rewards for a high quantity of participation instances versus rewards for providing high quality of contributions.

As a harbinger of possible future karma dilemmas, consider the legal and business debates that have evolved around credit—such as use of FICO and other credit scores—in the hiring process (as discussed later in this chapter and in chapter 6 of this volume). This practice has emerged because the classical job references reputation system has dried up as the result of litigation. When real-life reputation systems falter, it seems likely that more and more uses will be found for digital karma.

If Reputation Has Real-World Value, Then Methods Matter

The power of reputation systems to provide real, actionable information, crowd-sourced from large numbers of people and clever algorithms, will only increase over time. Every top website is using reputation to improve its products and services, even if only internally to mitigate abuse. In short, reputation systems create real-world value. Value often translates to wealth, and where there is wealth, the methods for creating that wealth become optimized—often to the point of exploitation. Ever since people have trusted the written opinions of others, shady contractors have been generating false letters of recommendation to exploit the unwary.

The new wealth of digital reputation is created in large part by software. This software is usually written under extreme time pressure and without much design discipline, which leads to two challenges. First, reputation system bugs become corporate liabilities. Bad reputation model design or even simple coding errors can lead to inaccurate results that may significantly damage the value of an entity or business.

Second, reputation system abuse becomes lucrative. As a score increases in influence, the cost to manipulate that score is less than the value created. Spammers and hackers learned this more than fifteen years ago, and current reputation systems are already under constant attack. SEO (search engine optimization) is already a billion-dollar business created solely to influence search ranking reputation. Likewise, public relations and marketing agencies may create buzz and social networking attention by creating façades of seemingly unbiased individuals.

Potential Solutions

Given the difficulties surrounding digital reputation and the problems of abuse and unreliable code, one wonders who would be brave enough to propose and build a next-generation reputation system. There are lessons from previous systems that can help eliminate—or at least mitigate—the risks.

Limit Reputation by Context (Especially Karma)

The FICO credit score is most appropriately used to represent the context named "creditworthiness" and is built exclusively out of inputs that are directly related to the borrowing and repayment of money. The nature of the input matches the nature of the output. We typically run into trouble when the score is used for noncreditworthiness tests, such as preemployment screening. In fact, according to the National Consumer Law Center, using credit scores for preemployment screening is an unreliable indicator of productivity (H.R. 3149). It is also discriminatory, as certain minority groups statistically have lower FICO scores without necessarily being less productive. Likewise, a corporate executive's excellent eBay buyer feedback has nothing to do with his or her credit score or with the number of experience points for his or her World of Warcraft character. Keep the contexts apart.

Tip: Don't cross the streams. Good digital reputations should always be context-limited—the nature of the inputs should constrain the use of the reputation scores that are output.

Focus on Positive Karma

Numerically scoring a person via karma can have a strong personal and emotional effect (see chapter 1 in this volume). Unlike object reputation, with karma it is a best practice to avoid publicly displayed negative scoring, direct evaluation of the person, and comparison of karma scores on leaderboards. Instead, build karma out of quality-related indirect inputs, such as scores for the person's helpfulness or ratings of objects created by the person. Avoid direct rankings and comparisons, except for competitive contexts. Karma leaderboards can demoralize regular participants and discourage participation by new community members.

Though most object reputation is intended to be displayed publicly, some of the most useful karma scores are either corporate (used internally by the site operator to determine the best and worst users in a context) or private (displayed only to the user). Private karma can still be used as a very strong incentive: just ask any blogger how obsessively they check their blog's visitor analytics.

Tip: Focus on multifaceted positive karma. Avoid direct rankings and comparison of people, except where competition is desired. Reserve negative karma for egregious cases of misconduct; even then, look for alternatives.

Focus on Quality over Quantity

When designing reputation systems for applications and sites, an easy method is often desired to motivate users to take some action. Usually that action is users creating content. The quickest model to build is in broad use across the web today: participation gives users points for taking actions—usually more points for actions that are more desirable. Sometimes the points are redeemable (a virtual currency); other times, they simply accumulate indefinitely. These points are often displayed as a karma score and are sometimes used in competitive forms such as leaderboards.

If these points are a currency or lead to special recognition such as privileged feature access, they often either (1) never catch on because of contextual irrelevance or (2) lead to abuse, as described earlier. Purely participation-based systems often end up in one of these two states, unless they continually evolve to become more relevant and mitigate abuse. A good example of this is when Digg abandoned its leaderboards because all of the top contributors were using bots and friends to manipulate their rank.

When digital karma increases real-world influence or monetary value, abuse will only accelerate. The reputation scores that have the most lasting and trusted real-world value are those based primarily on quality evaluations by other users.

Tip: The best web content karma scores are generated not from participation-based points but from quality evaluations of one's contributions written by other users.

Quality evaluations provide increased protection against simple forms of reputation abuse, as it is more difficult to generate large volumes of fraudulent indirect feedback. eBay protects their seller feedback scores by limiting the scope of user ratings to a single sales transaction, not an overall evaluation of an ongoing history of business with a seller. Yelp is almost the opposite—the business may be evaluated historically, which makes it easier to manipulate. FICO's creditworthiness score is also indirect karma— creditors report only specific transaction facts, not subjective and nonstandardized opinions of the consumer's relationship overall. By tying karma to the quality evaluations of a person's actions instead of rating the person directly, the score is more reliable and easier to interpret.

Mitigate Abuse through Metamoderation

As any reputation score increases in influence—especially if that influence has real-world side effects—the incentives to abuse the reputation model can grow to exceed the costs of manipulating the score, which leads to increased abuse and decreased utility value of the reputation score (and of the corresponding site or sites as a whole). The reputation score can eventually become untrustworthy.

If the community generating the content is sufficiently large—perhaps when moderation costs exceed a certain percentage of the operating budget, such as 5 percent—*metamoderation* reputation systems have been shown to be effective tools in cleaning up the worst content. The technical news site Slashdot uses such a metamoderation scheme to combat indirect input abuse by randomly selecting rated items for a second level of cross-check—in effect, "rating the raters" (as discussed in chapter 7).

In Farmer and Bryce (2010a), we detail a Yahoo! Answers case study in which an internal reputation system allowed automatically determined trustworthy users to instantly remove content from the site. This approach effectively and completely shut down the worst trolls. Response time to remove content that violated terms of service (TOS) fell from eighteen hours (using paid moderation) to thirty seconds (with reputation-based metamoderation) and saved $1 million per year.

Tip: If users are creating and evaluating your mission-critical content, consider using reputation-based moderation and metamoderation techniques to enable your community to cross-check your content, identify the best content, and deal with abuse.

New Solutions, New Problems

Future reputation system designers will hopefully apply narrow context to their data, ensure that publicly displayed karma is generated based on quality of actions and contributions, and mitigate abuse through reputation mechanisms such as metamoderation. But whenever a new technology comes into prominence, techno-optimists emerge who see it as a possible solution to contemporary social ills. So it should come as little surprise that many people have high hopes for the socially transformative power of digital reputation systems.

Though exciting possibilities, these trends require critical evaluation through the filter of experience. Important new problems to address are also likely. Lessons taken from the social evolution of other real-life institutions may apply to digital reputation systems as they increase in real-world influence.

The Naming of Names

This chapter's numerous admonitions to limit reputation to appropriate contexts raise the question: what are these contexts? Certainly reputation contexts within a single website can be narrowly and 100 percent locally defined. eBay seller feedback is a good example: its name describes its inputs and purpose adequately. But outside the web, the most influential reputations aren't built solely out of single-supplier input.

What about cross-site, cross-company, and other globally shared contexts such as creditworthiness? How will data be shared across various boundaries? (See chapters 16 and 17 in this volume.) Who, if anyone, will manage the taxonomy of reputation contexts?

Looking at the credit score industry, we can see a proven model: the reputation system operator (such as Fair Isaac Corporation, which created the FICO scores) creates the context, defines the model, and specifies the data format and API for inputs in exchange for sharing the reputation results. The creditors supply credit history information for their customers in exchange for the right to access the creditworthiness reputation scores of all others, which they use to optimize their business practices.

Is this ad hoc method of identifying reputation contexts sufficient? What are the possible problems? If cross-domain reputation contexts aren't standardized in some fashion, it seems likely that consumer confusion will result. We see some early evidence of this when comparing the five-star ratings of various product and service sites.

For example, why are the reviews on Netflix so different from Yahoo! Movies? It seems likely that the answer is that the context of those who wish to decide what movie to see at the theater for $20–$50 is significantly different from the context of selecting a DVD, delivered in a few days as part of a $9.99 all-you-can-eat watch-at-home subscription. Other factors may include selection bias and known patterns of abuse on movie sites (in which some ad agencies post fake positive reviews of first-run films). Even though the formats of the reviews are virtually identical, merging these two databases while ignoring their contexts would produce confusing results.

Nonetheless, on the week it was released, Facebook's global "Like" system became the most visible cross-site reputation system on the web. We can expect more companies to follow their lead in producing interfaces for integration of reputation systems into applications of all kinds, from websites to social games and mobile phones.

The questions remain: should there be an effort to shape or identify the taxonomy of shared reputation contexts? Should there be a set of suggested practices or even requirements for calculations associated with the important real-world impact of reputation scores—e.g., a set of branded guidelines that build consumer trust in these models? In short, do we need a "Good Housekeeping Seal of Approval" for reputation systems?

Privacy and Regulation

As online reputation's influence in the real world increases, we will face problems of privacy and regulation. These issues have to date generally been deferred with web reputation systems—perhaps because the inputs were single-sourced and under the umbrella legal shield of the site's TOS. Generally, allowing users to completely opt out of a service by deleting their account is seen as sufficient privacy protection, and thus far has limited the potential real-world legal exposure of the host site. In short, the TOS defines the context for inputs and reputation, to which the user agrees, and walking away from the data is the escape clause.

But we are already seeing this perceived corporate protection eroding on sites such as eBay, where some sellers' primary income is threatened by the actions of the hosting company on behalf of certain buyers (Cardingham 2008). Even if the company thinks it is protected by its TOS and "safe-harbor" provisions, most reputation systems depend on the actions of other users to create their scores. These three-party transactions are complicated and confusing, and get worse when users share data.

Once inputs and scores cross domains, information privacy crops up. It's not enough to opt out of a data source—users need to get their data corrected at (or entirely removed from) the data aggregators. Think about a major dispute with a specific credit card company; perhaps a card was stolen and used to rack up a large sum. After the creditors' laborious flagging process, aggregators must be notified of disputed items and must temporarily remove them from creditworthiness scores, but not all aggregators respond at the same rate or have the same policies. On the Internet, reputation spreads rapidly, and traditional simple binary notions of private versus public information can fail us. Existing legal codes do not grant the right to control the dissemination of this increasingly critical data; they need to be updated (Solove 2007).

One way to facilitate thoughtful government regulation of reputation systems is to establish an industry group to define best practices and conventions for managing the privacy and control of data shared in reputation systems. Industry self-policing may be in the best interests of all involved.

The Rise of Online Karma as Offline Power

As more reputation moves online, more karma systems will follow, providing users with incentives to make high-quality contributions to web content, to identify users that don't comply with the rules, and to enhance contributors' personal brand. Craig Newmark, founder of Craigslist.org, in the foreword to this book reflects the thinking of many reputation system optimists: the idea that public karma for users may partially displace other forms of political and economic influence.

This idea—that digital reputation, specifically karma, will increase to enable the intelligentsia to rise from the ashes and take their rightful place among the powerful—is appealing to technical people. The Platonic ideal of the Philosopher King has been with us for more than two millennia. Has its time finally come? Will reputation systems enable us to truly identify the people, products, and ideas that will best solve our problems, or even allow us to govern wisely? Science fiction authors have suggested this for many years (e.g., Card 1985; Stiegler 1999). How far can online reputation take us?

Conversations with proponents of this position suggest that ". . . we then just combine all the relevant reputations into an overall GoodCitizen or SmartPerson karma." As inputs, they then suggest combining factors like credit score, large readership for social media messages and/or blog posts, or strong endorsements on LinkedIn.com.

The largest initial challenge of this model is that good reputation has limited context. Naïvely combining scores from diverse contexts makes the calculation about no context at all. Next, combining scores from multiple sources has the "weakest-link" problem: the security weaknesses or abuses of the least-safe contributor site damage the integrity of the karma as a whole.

Even if one could solve context and weakest-link problems, the basic problem remains that any global SmartPerson karma represents too simple a metric to be used to evaluate a person for a complex role. Such karma may represent traits like popularity or industriousness, but be insufficient to represent one's capacity to lead a large group of fellow citizens. Modern democratic elections could be considered to be reputation systems with a binary result, *isElected*. This binary result is not very fine-grained karma and is highly correlated with the amount of money spent on a campaign.

As noted earlier, paying for higher digital reputation already happens with movie and business reviews. Likewise, individuals, businesses, and political parties try to purchase influence via SEO, advertising, and other methods.

If money can buy digital karma, the idea of karma displacing money as influence in politics is not realistic. What remains are different questions: can online karma (and object reputation) be a productive political force in real life? Can it improve the information we use to select our leaders, and bring more justice to our laws?

When reputation scores are limited to appropriately narrow contexts, they can serve an increased role within those contexts. Being a creator or critical analyst of the web already plays an increasing role in world politics. Recognized web influencers (bloggers, CEOs, etc.) regularly appear before Congress and parliaments worldwide. California's 2010 elections featured two high-tech CEOs nominated for senator and governor, and in 2009 the Pirate party won a seat in the Swedish parliament.

In the near term, especially given its contextual nature, it seems likely that digital karmas will have a political influence similar to that of traditional endorsements by interest groups such as trade associations and charitable foundations. Online, distributed versions of these organizations are already forming. For example, sellers on eBay have formed the Internet Merchants Association, and combined the leverage of their high seller feedback ratings with their aggregated funding to influence the company and related regulatory bodies.

Karma as Currency

What about the idea of converting karma into something you can spend, like money? A romantic notion: reputation given for good acts gets transformed into currency that you can later pay to others to reward their good acts.

Cory Doctorow, in his science fiction novella *Down and Out in the Magic Kingdom* (see chapter 18 in this volume), coined the term "Whuffie" to represent karma as a transferable currency: "Whuffie recaptured the true essence of money: in the old days, if you were broke but respected, you wouldn't starve; contrariwise, if you were rich and hated, no sum could buy you security and peace" (Doctorow 2003, 10). A derivative of this idea has been implemented by the Whuffie Bank, which uses traffic at social media sites such as Twitter to model influence and create a score. Basically, if you get talked about, you gain Whuffie, and you transfer Whuffie when you talk about others. There is a separate mechanism to explicitly grant Whuffie to another user, presumably as a gift or a payment for some product or service rendered.

There are several problems with this model. First, it suffers from the same universal context problem previously defined, only worse: there is no clear way to reliably set an exchangeable numerical value based on user actions across contexts. If one decides to create a different currency for each context—say a science Whuffie and a sports Whuffie and a political Whuffie—then an accounting and exchange nightmare is created. How much science Whuffie trades for a given amount of political Whuffie? Does the market float? It quickly becomes an untenable mess.

Second, this example turns popularity (something that is already reinforced on social networks, leaderboards, and search rankings) into a currency. By extension, the Whuffie Bank could make the pop star of the month the Philosopher King of the Internet. This problem is systemic to any use of karma as currency. It isn't likely to export to real life because popularity and attention often aren't accurate measures of intelligence, trustworthiness, political savvy, technical training, or anything else that might be useful.

Third, it is unclear whether reputation can fulfill the traditional currency function of being a "store of value." As described by Doctorow, any loss of respect would cause a speedy corresponding loss of Whuffie—suggesting a continuous per-person currency revaluation. At Internet speeds, a single scandal could wipe you out in a matter of hours. Karma seems far too fragile to become a significant currency.

In short, Whuffie—global reputation as currency—crashes on the rocks of complexity. The universal context problem suggests that there can be only a few truly global currencies. However, there may be scope for experimenting with reputation as local currency.

Overcoming Challenges Together

Though many reputation contexts will be limited to a single vendor or site, some providers will want to combine scores across all available sources, such as IP address blacklists for email. (Chapter 17 refers to these contexts as *constrained* reputations and *universal* reputations, respectively.)

The taxonomic, privacy, and regulatory challenges facing future digital reputation systems have already been articulated in this volume. How do we minimize the duplicated effort in technology development, policy and taxonomy design, industry standards, reputation modeling, and user interface best practices?

Either we continue reputation system development ad hoc, letting large corporations establish single-vendor-centric de facto standards and practices for cross-context ("universal") reputation, or we use another approach: open standards and open software.

Probably the greatest contributions to the adoption of HTTP and HTML as the backbone data standards for the web were two open source projects: the Mozilla web browser and the Apache web server. These applications provided the stable frameworks required for others to build a new class of Internet software. Though these applications weren't bug-free, they were the focal point of the effort to produce a reliable system.

In an attempt to provide an open, stable, and common infrastructure for reputation systems development, I have started—with the help of many people—the Open Reputation Framework project. Our hope is to make the Open Reputation Framework a home for reputation platform implementations, freely released intellectual property, and resources for modeling reputation systems, including a toolkit based on the reputation grammar described in Farmer and Glass (2010a). Online forums at this site—or others like it—as well as broader societal discussions offline are needed to foster the evolution of best practices for privacy, regulation, reputation taxonomy, and related issues. Open and well-lit places for discussion may be a prerequisite to guiding the development of reputation systems in a positive direction.

References

Card, O. S. 1985. *Ender's game*. New York: Tor Books.

Cardingham, C. 2008, October 24. Man sued for leaving negative feedback on eBay. Retrieved from: <http://www.money.co.uk/article/1001771-man-sued-for-leaving-negative-feedback-on-ebay.htm>.

Doctorow, C. 2003. *Down and out in the Magic Kingdom*. New York: Tor Books.

Farmer, R., and B. Glass. 2010a. *Building web reputation systems*. Sebastopol, CA: O'Reilly.

Farmer, R., and B. Glass. 2010b. On karma: Top-line lessons on user reputation design [web log post.]. *Building reputation systems: The blog*. Retrieved from: <http://buildingreputation.com/writings/2010/02/on_karma.html>.

Hawk, T. 2005, November 29. PriceRitePhoto: Abusive bait and switch camera store [web log post]. *Thomas Hawk's digital connection*. Retrieved from: <http://thomashawk.com/2005/11/priceritephoto-abusive-bait-and-switch-camera-store.html>.

H.R. 3149. 2010. Equal Employment for All Act. 111d Cong. Retrieved from: <http://www.opencongress.org/bill/111-h3149/show>.

Solove, D. J. 2007. *The future of reputation: Gossip, rumor, and privacy on the Internet*. New Haven: Yale University Press.

Stiegler, M. 1999. *Earthweb*. Riverdale, NY: Baen.

3 An Inquiry into Effective Reputation and Rating Systems

John Henry Clippinger

Reputation systems have been implemented in numerous contexts, ranging from massive e-commerce sites to specialist hobby groups. But what are the fundamental principles that make a reputation system effective? John Henry Clippinger discusses connections between evolutionary biology, finance, and reputation systems and suggests design principles to make reputation systems more effective.

Regard your good name as the richest jewel you can possibly be possessed of—for credit is like fire; when once you have kindled it you may easily preserve it, but if you once extinguish it, you will find it an arduous task to rekindle it again. The way to gain a good reputation is to endeavor to be what you desire to appear.

—Socrates

With the success of the web—especially social media—the importance of reputation has been revived to take on a new meaning and relevance. Protecting and promoting "one's good name" as an individual, product, organization, cause, or brand has blossomed into an enormous business. It has also sparked virtual "arms races" of competing reputational interests and strategies.

There is no greater reputation maker than Google. Google's pervasive page ranking algorithm is a trusted global reputation system that uses social or link popularity metrics not only to direct search queries, but also to auction off such queries to promote products and brands. That relatively simple capability has spawned a multibillion-dollar industry of trading, selling, and "optimizing" reputations.

More overt forms of reputation and recommendation systems—such as those used by Yelp, Slashdot, Amazon, eBay, Digg, and others—routinely issue summary judgments, much like a Roman Emperor in the Colosseum who renders thumbs-up or thumbs-down verdicts upon hapless people, movies, software, hotels, and content. Such ratings can have real economic clout. A poor Amazon rating can be a virtual death sentence for a poorly rated product.

If one's good name is tarnished fairly or unfairly on the web, it is very difficult to have the slight removed. For an unwanted Google ranking, there is no easy remedy but to bury an offending picture or paragraph under a slew of more flattering and "popular" hits. Reputation.com (formerly ReputationDefender) and SEO companies provide services to help "manage" the ranking of flattering or not-so-flattering hits on persons, groups, products, topics, and companies. The web is still like an unsocialized teenager who is in the process of exploring identities and acquiring manners and appropriate norms. Yet the web may have reached that point of social awareness at which manners, norms, and one's good name do matter. And as one gains a reputation—what Socrates called that "richest jewel"—its loss, debasement, or appropriation can be highly consequential. Hence, how reputations are won and lost will play an increasingly important role in the social evolution of the web.

An Evolutionary Biological Perspective on Reputation

"Reputation" is a familiar term that is also deceptively subtle. Reputation is not so much a thing as an ongoing contest. From the perspective of evolutionary biology, reputation can be seen as part of the larger struggle of natural selection—in this case, as the competition within and among social species to cooperate, compete, or flee. Building and protecting one's reputation is an unending process for all social species, as there are always those who can benefit from a false reputation (e.g., deception), and there are similar benefits to be reaped from investing in a stellar reputation. There is value in seeing these "reputational arms races" as part of a broader evolutionary process. It grounds the discussion in the well-developed science of evolutionary and computational biology, and can draw upon Nature's billion years of experimentation. (See chapter 4 in this volume for another perspective on these ideas.)

Having a "good name" is fundamental to biological survival and replication. In sexual competition, the attainment of a "good name" is rivalrous—a zero-sum game, the right to mate and promote one's own genes. Not only do males have to compete among themselves, but they also have to convince the female that they are worthy mates that will produce healthy offspring to promote her genes as well. For the female, the challenge is to determine how "honest" the signals of the male are. Is he really fit? Will his offspring survive? Will he defend her and her offspring against predators? Can he be relied upon as a provider? In each and every case, there has to be a decision made about whether to assume a particular kind of risk. In short, what markers—reputation signals—can she rely upon?

Given the nature of the risks involved in mate selection, there are strong selective pressures for honest signals: those that can be easily understood and not readily faked. Take the case of the peacock's tail, in which all the extra energy needed to produce a huge, colorful and extravagant tail is a clear, unfakeable signal of the health of the male (Zahavi 1997). In the case of elk and moose, the imposing antlers are not only a signal of health, but also signals of dominance and actual instruments of male competition.

Honest *social* signals, on the other hand, are much harder to achieve. It is often not difficult to fake a signal that is not biologically based and within your control. The reason the peacock's tail is such a reliable signal is that it is beyond the peacock's capacity to control. Yet all social signals are, in effect, social constructs. They can be made to appear to be something other than they are. (See chapters 7 and 9 in this volume for more on social signals.)

For instance, the social equivalent of health or reproductive worthiness might be found in an expensive car, a magisterial home, or a name in the social register—all seemingly reliable manifestations of social "health." Social institutions are attempts by societies to create costs for social signals such as wealth, status, and competence that make them more difficult to fake. Such costs can include resources to acquire symbols of status and competence, as well as sanctions for falsely asserting trusted social signals. As executive fraud, credit rating fiascos, infomercials, and one's own junk email box so eloquently testify, many signals of social and financial "health" are easily and profitably spoofed. The prescript of Socrates—"The way to gain a good reputation is to endeavor to be what you desire to appear"—seems to be more honored in the breach than in the observance.

Bubbles and Runaway Signals

In evolutionary biology, it is a given that all social life forms, from the simplest to the most complex, are engaged in an endless cycle of deception and detection. The invisible hand of natural selection manifests itself in this contest, favoring and punishing by continuously testing the authenticity of a *reputation holder* and the thoroughness of the entity that relies on the reputation information (the *reputation relier*).

Although competition can certainly improve the fitness of a group, there are times when unbridled competition can destroy the group through what is called the "Red Queen Effect" (Ridley 2003). The notion of the Red Queen Effect was taken from Lewis Carroll's *Through the Looking-glass*, in which the feared and mad Red Queen ran faster and faster in place without getting anywhere (Carroll 1986). The Red Queen Effect alludes to the huge resources that can be expended among competitors in deception-detection schemes. A biological example of an arms race gone awry is the Irish elk, which grew ridiculously large antlers. The Irish elk's antlers wastefully consumed energy and made it impossible to navigate forests, contributing to its eventual extinction.

An equivalent in human interaction is competition around social status, a pivotal reputational marker that governs the allocation of collective resources and reproductive rights. In preindustrial societies, potlatches—gatherings in which people with high status compete to acquire and give away their wealth—can have distributional benefits, but they can also degrade into wasteful, socially destructive competitions.

Likewise, the competitive consumption of status goods from clothes to jewels to boats to homes to planes can have a similarly deleterious effect. Such competition drains public resources and capital from more generative uses and needed basic social goods, thereby exacerbating social inequities and encouraging environmentally destructive patterns of consumption. Such bubbles of consumption can be seen as the result of a collusion of incentives to overvalue positive reputational scores and undervalue negative scores. Because there is no penalty for a false positive score—only a penalty for a negative score—the bubble grows until someone eventually bears the cost.

Some economists would argue that price signals and markets could eventually correct for such "runaway excesses" by having short sellers (those who bet on the asset value declining) come into the market and discipline the excessive long sellers. However, short sellers need to "time" the market and long sellers do not, as we saw in the financial crisis of 2007–2008. It is hard to know what a "short seller" would look like for status markets—other than some kind of "social register" or "blue book" that tries to distinguish false social claims from legitimate ones. Indeed in some status-exclusive groups, notably adolescent groups, alpha females and males set and impose signals of membership to enforce exclusivity and limit reputational inflation, that is, the devaluation of their own reputational currency (Pronk and Zimmer-Gembeck 2010). The media has short and long sellers for whom there are financial and reputational incentives to inflate and deflate the reputations of celebrities, entrepreneurs, experts, and companies.

There are also situations in which short sellers—those benefiting from a collapse of a reputation—can materially change a reputation by creating a self-reinforcing negative reputation trend. Some observers attributed the collapse of Lehman Brothers in part to short sellers using rumor to drive down share prices, which in turn caused real reputational damage that resulted in having creditors demand repayment and refuse further credit. In both cases, corrective feedback loops were weak because there was a lack of corrective signal that could dampen the effects of runaway positive and negative signals. Outside of markets, one can see reputational social bubbles through fads, gossip, mobs, riots, movements, and other forms of collective action that seem to take on a life of their own until they run their course.

Blind Referee: Honest Reputation Signals for Fairness

All successful social species use social roles and signals to facilitate cooperation and mitigate excessively competitive behaviors. Dominant males and females intervene to resolve destabilizing behaviors, as do coalitions of peers.

Among highly social species, there appears to be a kind of "metacooperative" game, supraordinate to the competitive games (De Waal 1989). These metagames are "games about games" that encourage cooperative outcomes by providing special rule sets that enable a third party to prevent pyrrhic outcomes. Such metagames select for the role of an impartial referee who has sufficient reputational powers to oversee and modulate destructive competition. For example, among some primates such as chimpanzees and bonobos, a powerful member of a group (or coalition of members) can act to curtail the unbridled aggression of one dominant member against another. This kind of reputational power is of a different order than healthy males challenging one another or impressing a prospective mate. It not only must signal a credible capacity to enforce a sanction, but also must be seen by the competitors as being fair (Clarkson and Van Alstyne 2009).

A reputation for fairness depends upon the actions of the referee being accepted as impartial by all competing parties. In the case of chimpanzee groups, it is the duty of the leader to remind the overly contentious to subordinate their rivalries to the long-term cooperative interests of their group (De Waal 1989). In the case of humans, the referees rule on the fairness or the legitimacy of behaviors (as in a sports game) and enforce their "ruling" by their capacity to punish or throw offending players out of the game. In this analogy, the metagame defines the rules of play, and all parties benefit from the game being both competitive and fair.

With this background, we are now in a position to venture a preliminary definition of reputation and the ancillary mechanisms that make reputations effective.

A Definition of Reputation

A reputation is a social signal that one party conveys to a relying party to mitigate the risk of the relying party in accepting that signal.

Let us apply this definition to some of our examples thus far. In the example of the peacock, the relying party is the peahen and the tail is the reputation signal. In the example of the Irish elk, the large antlers are not only reputational signals to the female, but reputational signals of strength to competing males—a second relying party. By assessing the strength of the signals (the size of the antlers), competing males can assess the relative strength of a competitor and avoid a costly and potentially fatal challenge. Such competitions can be somewhat self-regulating because competing males defer to the signals and avoid ruinous competition.

In continuous forms of competition in which new entrants can come and go and disguise their real identities, such as an eBay seller faking an identity, there is the need to authenticate the identity of a reputation holder. In this case, it is not so much a matter of a deceptive reputation signal as of masking the true identity of the party holding the reputation. For if the underlying identity of a reputation holder is not knowable, it is possible for a third party to manipulate a reputational signal to build trust and then to "defect" with no penalty. This is a common scam and a problem with some early eBay sellers, who would build up large scores of successful ratings for small transactions—and then, with a major transaction, abscond with the proceeds. Were the full provenance of the seller disclosed and independently authenticated, then the full risk would have been apparent to the buyer and the process could have been self-regulating. Reputation is tied to identity, and in order for a reputation score to be trusted, it must be transparent and tied to an underlying, authenticated and persistent identifier of the actual physical person.

Similar points apply to search-based reputation scores. Although Google doesn't sell higher rankings directly, it does sell keyword search phrases to companies that want to reach customers who use those searches. The individual company relies upon the validity of Google's reputation scoring to reach potential customers. These customers in turn rely upon another Google score—in this case, page rankings—to find relevant websites. Those using Google to search want to find sites that genuinely match their search interests, and therefore rely upon the integrity of the ranking scores. Advertisers seek to increase their ranking scores by means both overt and subtle. The interests of the searchers and the advertisers are not necessarily aligned, especially if the advertiser is promoting websites and products that do not match the searches.

Yet can a search engine like Google really be an independent and disinterested referee of reputation? Its revenue comes from auctioning off high-volume and "high-quality" keywords and search terms to the highest bidder. But who determines the measures of volume and quality? Is there any independent audit? Search engines are not paid for the quality of their search results by the end user, but rather for the popularity of their search results by advertisers. Popularity is a proxy measure for quality or relevance, but it is a very imperfect and gameable metric—yet it is what sets the price for search terms.

In short, there is an absence of transparency on a number of counts. Only Google knows how the reputation scores are calculated, and only they conduct auctions. Google thereby controls both the supply of product *and* the measures of its value. All the incentives seem to point in the direction of generating inflated scores without any corrective. If the quality of the search experience becomes poor, however, and end users stop using it, then that might act as a check on Google's behavior. But by owning a major portion of the search market, Google reaps the benefits of scale, requiring any competitor to have a vastly superior service to be viable.

Rating Risks

If one ever doubted how readily and credulously we rely upon compromised, opaque, and gamed reputation scores, one need look no further than the role of credit rating agencies in the financial crisis of 2007–2008. The entire financial system depends upon such rating agencies, yet they are by and large paid for by the companies they rate. They failed catastrophically in the financial meltdown, yet they continue to be relied upon.

How can that be? There is no real penalty for their being wrong. They are typically not rewarded for their ability to accurately predict risk, but for their ability to help their clients sell securities, because a high rating can make a security more appealing to potential buyers. It has been suggested that they and their clients are not really parties to the risks they rate, but rather that these risks are off-loaded to buyers of the securities (Roubini and Mihm 2010).

The fact that many financial service companies and banks that were given AAA (extremely strong) ratings failed catastrophically is indicative of a structural failure in the rating system (Lewis 2010). As a financial bubble bursts and threatens to undermine the entire system, the metagame referee (government) steps in to absorb risk for the collective good. Unless transparency, feedback, accountability, and correction mechanisms are improved, the rating system may simply go on generating bigger and bigger bubbles.

Although there is a grassroots movement to use Web 2.0 technology to create more transparency in finance, so far this has not proven effective. One example is the Freerisk.org project, whose goal was to make financial data more open and available through open standards. Freerisk aimed to crowdsource the rating of companies and securities and in effect to make a competitive market for the rating methods that have the best predictive value. However, it appears that these efforts have not yet taken hold.

Although open crowdsourcing is a possible starting point, at some point it will become important to link reputation scores to authenticated identities. With an identity system in place, it is possible to monitor activity for signs of collusion. By having many diverse and seasoned eyes looking at the data and the different rating algorithms, a kind of "third eye" of the market can come into play that acts to keep the invisible hand, buyers, and sellers honest by keeping all transactions and incentives transparent and open. The third eye could be made up of actors who do not have a vested interest in an outcome and who can act as checks upon one another. As in the case of open source software, the third eye would provide the requisite independence and legitimacy to securities ratings to help restore trust to the markets. (See chapter 5 in this volume for a related invisible hand concept.)

Data alone does not create transparency. Analysis and even visualization are required to make sense of relationships that make the data actionable. As part of its effort to encourage greater transparency in government, the software company Palantir is making its analytic tools available through the AnalyzeThe.US project to enable ordinary citizens to analyze the government's key data sets conceptually. When tools like this are applied in the open, then the reputation and risk metrics they develop are not only more credible and robust—they themselves can also be questioned, challenged and improved.

Building a Robust Reputation System

To what extent can one rely upon a signal from another party to be valid and authentic? A widely used and valuable reputation system is like a currency; it has enormous stored value. But like a paper currency, it has no inherent value—only a redemption value. As soon as the "good name" becomes compromised, it becomes very costly to restore. Like currencies, reputation systems are social constructs that derive their value and liquidity through networks of reciprocal trust. Reputation systems are the social equivalent of the vault doors for banks: they are not only a security barrier, but also a social signal of trustworthiness.

But perhaps reputation systems can be designed to be more secure than banks. In the digital world, there is an enormous opportunity to design reputation, identity, transparency, and anticollusion mechanisms that are simply impossible in the physical world. Here are a few mechanisms that, if put into place, could significantly enhance the effectiveness and trustworthiness of a reputation system:

1. *Secure, open, and multiple-identity system*   If someone can act with full anonymity, then there is no basis for transparency or accountability. Verifiable identity is absolutely essential to building a reputation system. The downside is that a persistent identity can also be used for surveillance and control by third parties and bad guys. So it is important to have *authenticated* anonymity, which simply means that you can have your identity authenticated without having to reveal personal identifying information. It is important to recognize that identity is contextual and multiple, and that reputations are hence also contextual and multiple. One's reputation as a father or husband may be very different than that as an athlete or financier. Fortunately, considerable work has already been undertaken by academia, the open source community, and corporations to deploy an open, interoperable identity "metasystem" to give people control over information about themselves. (See <http://www.eclipse.org/higgins>, as well as <http://informationcard.net>.)

2. *Membership in a network with identity and governance rules*   There must be membership boundaries in order for there to be viable, enforceable, and evolvable reputation systems. Unlike most social networking sites (whose membership rules are defined by their Terms of Service Agreements, which may be primarily drafted to preserve the commercial interests of the site owners), membership networks are designed around governance principles for the members themselves. Typically, the reputation score is what gives a member standing in a particular network, and a poor reputation score can be grounds for expulsion.

3. *Metadata about members' behaviors and artifacts*   Full transparency and accountability require collecting and analyzing metadata about members in a network. Such data can itself be used to generate reputation scores based on the behaviors and contributions of the members. Given that the identifiers used are not personally identifying,

it is possible to have such monitoring capabilities without necessarily compromising privacy. Such data can be used to generate social graphs that are highly identifying and predictive of behavior (Pentland 2009).

4. *Independently authenticated member attributes* Members make claims as to their gender, age, education, financial status, employment history, and so forth. These claims must be independently authenticated in order for them to be a valid basis for building a trustworthy reputation. Some of the independent methods for authenticating reputation attributes (such as education or financial standing) can be done through third-party services such as independent credit bureaus. But as more and more data becomes available on people and organizations within and outside of member networks, peer-to-peer methods will be used to vet, bond, and authenticate members.

5. *The blind referee: transparent, testable, and independent reputation metrics* The more powerful and important a reputation metric is, the greater the forces will be to capture and subvert it. Information asymmetries create competitive advantages and can stimulate genuine innovation, but such asymmetries should not be allowed at the meta level—the processes by which reputation metrics are selected and tested should themselves be open and subject to scrutiny and inspection. One of the reasons that open source software is highly trusted is that it is hard to hide "back doors" and proprietary hooks when a piece of code is completely transparent. This transparency, however, is not easily achieved, which brings us to the next topic.

The Power of Digital: Breaking the Cycle of *Quis Custodiet Ipsos Custodes*

Quis custodiet ipsos custodes? ("Who will guard the guards themselves?") This issue has been the Achilles' heel of human institutions since time immemorial. The inevitable entropy of human frailty weakens the independence of any oversight function, and this oversight inevitably becomes captive to those very forces it was intended to oversee. This problem will not be solved here. That said, there is reason for some optimism. In situations in which both activities and their associated reputation systems become fully digital, they can in principle be made fully transparent and auditable. Hence the activities of interested parties to subvert or game policies or reputation metrics can themselves be monitored, flagged, and defended against. Ideally, this identification and defense can happen early in the process.

But the question at hand is still "protected by whom"—*quis custodiet ipsos custodes?* In the physical world, there can be genuine coercion and intimidation because it is possible to identify the "guard" and either physically threaten or bribe that person. In the digital world, that is not necessarily the case. Moreover, with an appropriate degree of transparency, the ability of parties to collude to alter a policy, skew a metric, or obfuscate an audit path can be greatly reduced. In order for a party to exercise an oversight (or *referee*) function, they need access to certain kinds of information, metrics, logs, and privileges. These access privileges can be designed to require that all referees have "keys" for access to enter the "room" to exercise their oversight functions. Rules can be programmed that require all referees to have independent keys for entry into the oversight room, that certain referee functions require simultaneous collaboration by multiple referees, and—this is the important point—that referees are randomly selected from a very large and unbiased pool of qualified members whose identities are authenticated for the desired expertise. Their access privileges could be dynamically assigned and revoked based upon time, role, and suspicious behavioral data.

This approach is not immune from being breached: a third party could physically and forcibly compromise or destroy the system. At the same time, given normal operating conditions for the majority of organizations, information leakage, patronage, collusion, and self-interest would be significantly checked if a high-value, robust, and independent reputation system were available.

Conclusion

Reputation is continually shaping how identities, relationships, norms, rules, values, and social institutions evolve. The assertion that reputation creates selection pressures is intended not metaphorically, but literally. The foregoing examples and arguments show that research into social signaling theory, biological regulation, and evolutionary game theory is of considerable relevance to the design of effective member networks and new kinds of digital institutions.

Increasingly, as social networks and online engagement are relied upon, the trustworthiness and evolution of reputation systems will prove to be of institutional importance. If current trends continue, users will soon demand from their vendors and governments greater transparency and more targeted and reliable reputation metrics. If the science and technology are available to deliver robust reputation systems, then new models will arise to harness the reputation arms race toward positive ends and to thereby spur unprecedented social and institutional innovation.

References

Carroll, L. 1986. *Through the looking-glass*. New York: Ariel Books/Knopf.

Clarkson, G., and M. W. Van Alstyne. 2009, November 26. *The social efficiency of fairness*. Boston University School of Management Research Paper No. 2009–11. Gruter Institute Squaw Valley Conference—Innovation and Economic Growth, 2010. Retrieved from <http://ssrn.com/abstract=1514137>.

De Waal, F. 1989. *Peacemaking among primates*. Cambridge, MA: Harvard University Press.

Lewis, M. 2010. *The big short: Inside the doomsday machine*. New York: W. W. Norton.

Pentland, A. 2009. Reality mining of mobile communications: Toward a new deal on the global information technology report. In *The global information technology report 2008–2009*, ed. S. Dutta and I. Mia, 75–80. Geneva: World Economic Forum.

Pronk, R. E., and M. J. Zimmer-Gembeck. 2010. It's "mean," but what does it mean to adolescents? Relational aggression described by victims, aggressors, and their peers. *Journal of Adolescent Research* 25 (2): 175–204.

Ridley, M. 2003. *The red queen: Sex and the evolution of human nature*. New York: Harper Perennial.

Roubini, N., and S. Mihm. 2010. *Crisis economics: A crash course in the future of finance*. New York: Penguin Press.

Zahavi, A. 1997. *The handicap principle: A missing piece of Darwin's puzzle*. Oxford: Oxford University Press.

II REGULATING SOCIETIES

4 The Biology of Reputation

John Whitfield

Online reputation rests on our instinctive traits, which have evolved over millions of years. John Whitfield shows how aspects of reputation show up in the animal world and how these traits regulate and sustain our societies, suggesting lessons for the future that can be learned from the past.

We all understand intuitively that reputation is a fundamental force of social life. But only in the past decade or so have researchers working at the interface of biology, economics, and psychology truly begun to grasp how powerful that force is and how much of human behavior our concern for our reputations can explain.

Another recent development is the discovery that reputation is a force in not just human behavior. Animal behavior researchers have found that many other species use two basic forms of reputation to make their decisions: social learning and eavesdropping. In the first of these, social learning, animals learn where to feed or nest or how to avoid predators by watching what their neighbors do, rather than sampling the environment directly—a process with obvious similarities to the way that humans choose what to buy, where to vacation, and so on. In the second, eavesdropping, animals observe or listen in on encounters between two other animals and use this information to plan their own behavior. If a female black-capped chickadee, for example, hears her mate defeated in a song duel, she becomes significantly more likely to bear chicks by another male (Mennill 2002). And, as with humans, the presence of an audience changes the performers' behavior: the cleaner wrasse, a small coral reef fish, decides whether to cooperate with its clients by removing parasites and dead tissue or to cheat them by biting mucus and scales (which are more nutritious) partly on the basis of whether other potential clients are watching (Bshary and Grutter 2006). These studies and others are complicating biologists' view of animal communication and decision making by forcing them to consider the influence of the wider social environment on interactions such as fights and mate choice that have until recently been considered as only two-party interactions (McGregor 2005).

Where humans stand out, of course, is in the extent to which we have developed the cognitive and social technology of reputation. We are uniquely interested in what other people have been doing in our absence and uniquely concerned about what others know and think about us. Humans are highly—and apparently unconsciously—sensitive to being watched, as shown by a series of experiments in laboratory and natural settings showing that people become more honest and generous under the gaze of a stylized picture of eyes (Bateson, Nettle, and Roberts 2006; Burnham and Hare 2007; Haley and Fessler 2005; Rigdon et al. 2009). These results suggest that a website designer hoping to encourage fair and honest behavior might put a banner image of some staring eyes in a prominent position, although the effect of such stimuli varies: where two players interact directly, this interaction seems to override the effects of eye cues (Fehr and Schneider 2010).

The physical manifestations of emotions such as shame and pride signal to those watching when we have done something socially damaging or rewarding, and influence observers to repair the damage or enhance the reward (Tracy, Robins, and Tangney 2007). Most human conversation takes the form of gossip about what people who are not present have been doing (Wert and Salovey 2004). Many of our most notable abilities, such as language and the ability to think about what others are thinking, seem likely to have evolved in significant measure to keep track of what other humans have been doing and to influence their view of our own behavior.

Not coincidentally, humans are also more willing to be cooperative and altruistic toward other, unrelated members of their species than any other animal. People will cooperate with strangers that they are unlikely to ever encounter again. This behavior poses a puzzle for evolutionary theory because any animal displaying such traits opens itself up to cheats and free riders—a process that unchecked would drive cooperative behavior out of the population.

Reputation is one of the key means through which humans defend cooperation. It allows us to incentivize and reward altruism and to deter and punish antisocial behavior. Anthropological studies suggest that concerns for reputation underpin many cooperative behaviors in hunter-gatherer societies, such as meat sharing (Hawkes and Bliege Bird 2002). In many such societies, the most severe punishment is ostracism, in which those whose reputation sinks to the lowest depths find that their society withdraws its cooperation en masse. Even as societies became larger and more complex, reputation remained an important means of enforcing cooperation and punishing norm breaking. Greif (1989), for example, has shown that international trade in the Mediterranean during the Middle Ages relied heavily on reputation mechanisms to create trust between merchants and their geographically and culturally distant agents. As Adam Smith said in his 1766 *Lecture on the Influence of Commerce on Manners*: "A dealer is afraid of losing his character, and is scrupulous in observing every engagement. When a person makes perhaps 20 contracts in a day, he cannot gain so much by endeavouring to impose on his neighbours, as the very appearance of a cheat would make him lose" (quoted in Klein 1997, 17).

The general problem of how natural selection for self-interested behaviors could lead to altruism began to receive attention only in the second half of the twentieth century, when the idea that animals would make sacrifices, such as limiting their fecundity or aggression, "for the good of the group" fell from favor; mathematical modeling suggested that altruistic groups are highly vulnerable to invasion by selfish individuals. The application by biologists of such ideas to human behavior came later still, with the rise of sociobiology and evolutionary psychology in the 1970s and 1980s.

The theoretical problems with group selection led most evolutionary biologists to a view of evolution that focused on natural selection operating on individuals and genes—as reflected, for example, in Richard Dawkins's *The Selfish Gene*. From this viewpoint, natural selection favors altruism and cooperation only if it yields a net benefit to the cooperative individual. Hamilton's (1964) theory of kin selection showed that one option is to invest in family members, who share one's own evolutionary interests by virtue of sharing genes. This concept seems to lie at the root of most nonhuman examples of cooperation, such as the insect societies of ants, wasps, bees, and termites (although the theory is still debated). Trivers's (1971) theory of reciprocal altruism, which gave the Prisoner's Dilemma—a game in which the choice is whether to help or cheat another person—a central place in evolutionary theory, showed that sharing a history can also promote cooperation. Where animals can recognize one another, and where there is a high probability of long-term interaction, animals can cooperate today and—if their favors are not returned—retaliate tomorrow.

There is a wealth of evidence that kin selection and reciprocal altruism are important elements of human social behavior. But neither concept seems to explain the high level of one-shot cooperation that binds human societies together, because such one-shot interactions give their participants no chance to return favors or punish cheating. The first biologist to explore the idea that reputation can underpin the broad cooperation characteristic of human societies was Alexander (1987). He coined the term *indirect reciprocity* to describe the process whereby altruistic acts are repaid not by their recipients, but by third parties. In this scenario, person A decides to cooperate with person B because A knows that B has previously cooperated with person C, and A hopes to gain C's cooperation in the future. Indirect reciprocity, Alexander argued, can enforce cooperation and maintain solidarity.

For a decade, however, biologists' attention remained largely focused on explaining human cooperation through direct reciprocity and kin selection. One exception was a model by Boyd and Richerson (1989) that treated indirect reciprocity as the passage of altruistic acts through a circuit, so that A helps B, who helps C, who helps A. This pattern of helping, they concluded, can be sustained only in small groups—otherwise, the cognitive powers needed to monitor, remember, disseminate, and act upon the behavior of third parties seemed prohibitive, and the possibilities for escaping one's reputation through concealment and mobility seemed too great.

It was not until Nowak and Sigmund's (1998) model that Alexander's verbal argument was translated into a theory that supported indirect reciprocity as a force in human cooperation. In their simulation, individuals meet in pairwise interactions. One party is randomly chosen as a potential donor, and the other as a potential recipient. The cost of helping is less than the benefit of being helped, so the returns of mutual cooperation outweigh those of asociality, providing that cheaters can be prevented from invading the population. Nowak and Sigmund achieved this using a simple form of reputation based on what they called *image scoring*. If the donor pays the cost of helping the recipient, his or her image score increases by one. If the donor declines, it decreases by one. Donors decide whether to cooperate based on past behavior, as reflected in the potential recipient's image score. The simulation showed that cooperative behavior could arise and persist if donors discriminated in favor of recipients with positive image scores. In human populations, Nowak and Sigmund suggested that the equivalent of a person's image score would be constructed and transmitted via gossip.

Nowak and Sigmund's study triggered a boom in theoretical and experimental studies of indirect reciprocity that shows no sign of ending, and it has placed reputation front and center in our understanding of human cooperation. Experimental support for their model was provided by Wedekind and Milinski (2000), who showed that donors in an experimental setting were more generous toward recipients with a positive image score. Olson and Spelke (2008) obtained similar results in an experiment in which three-year-old children were asked to distribute resources between dolls based on stories of their past behavior toward one another.

Other theoreticians, however, have challenged image scoring as a basis for indirect reciprocity. In Nowak and Sigmund's model, a donor that withholds help from a recipient with a low image score pays a cost because its image score drops a point, making other members of the population less likely to assist it. Leimar and Hammerstein (2001) showed that a population of image scorers can be invaded by a strategy that avoids the cost of refusing to cooperate by ignoring others' image score and instead cooperating indiscriminately just enough to maintain its own image score.

Leimar and Hammerstein also showed that a strategy of indirect reciprocity based on *relative standing*, an idea pioneered in economics by Sugden (2004), was more robust to invasion by alternative strategies. In a population basing its decision on standing, a donor who denies help to a recipient with a poor reputation suffers no reputational damage. Tournaments pitting different strategies against one another have found that those that use standing—that it's good to be bad toward another with a bad reputation—can resist invasion by other strategies (Ohtsuki and Iwasa 2006; Pacheco, Santos, and Chalub 2006), although such strategies are less good at invading populations without cooperation (Panchanathan 2011). Some experimental evidence, however, seems to suggest that humans use image scoring, not standing, as the basis for deciding whether to help or not (Milinski et al. 2001), perhaps because standing requires too much information about the motives of all parties involved and is vulnerable to mistakes and missing data. It may well be, of course, that humans use both standing and image scoring, depending on the information available.

Online social interaction takes place in an "unbiological" environment in which the cues that let humans know that their reputation is at stake, such as gaze, are absent. Reputation systems are an attempt to overcome the corrosive effect that such solitude and anonymity have on altruism and cooperation. Feedback on eBay, for example, has similarities to Nowak and Sigmund's image-scoring model. When a buyer and a seller do business on eBay, it may well be a one-shot interaction. But each can change the other's image score by leaving feedback (it even takes the +1 or −1 form used by Nowak and Sigmund) and thereby influence how other members of the community treat them in the future. One way in which eBay users differ from the simple image scorers in Nowak and Sigmund's model is that they tend to give negative ratings far more weight than positive ratings—a strategy that theory suggests may help to maintain coopera- tion (Rankin and Eggimann 2009). Indirect reciprocity also manifests itself in online communities in less formal ways: Bravo (2010), for example, found that many contrib- utors to an Italian TeX users group did so because they had received help in the past.

Reputation, then, can promote cooperation in pairwise interactions that resemble the Prisoner's Dilemma. Here, cheating is the main threat to cooperation. But rep- utation can also help maintain cooperation in group endeavors that more closely resemble the public goods game, in which the choice is between contributing to a common resource—such as building and maintaining an irrigation system, exploiting a fishery sustainably, or keeping a common area clean—or free riding. In such groups, the presence of a few free riders can cause initially cooperative members to withdraw their labor, which in turn can cause further withdrawals of labor, ultimately leading to the collapse of cooperation and a tragedy of the commons. Maintaining a common resource requires collective effort.

One way to bring free riders into line is to punish them, even if it is costly to do so (Fehr and Gachter 2002). Human punishment behavior also becomes more pro- nounced when an audience is present. When players' past decisions in the ultimatum game are made public, they become less tolerant of low offers than they are in anony- mous situations (Fehr and Fischbacher 2003). Experimental subjects also invest more in third-party punishment, in which they themselves have not been treated unjustly, when they can make their decisions public (Kurzban, DeScioli, and O'Brien 2007). Both types of punishment are costly, in that those who punish do not maximize their short-term returns. But the long-term benefits of making it known that you drive a hard bargain, or that you are willing to enforce cooperative norms, may justify an increased investment in punishment in the short term. If punishers earn a reputation that makes them more likely to receive help in the future, this can sustain such behav- ior (Santos, Rankin, and Wedekind 2010).

Reputation, however, can also reduce the need for punishment in problems of collective action. In the conduct of our social business, we move between large and small groups. Experiment (Milinski, Semmann, and Krambeck 2002a) and theory (Panchanathan and Boyd 2004) have shown that when public goods games are alternated with two-person games, players that contribute to the common good build a reputation that others reward through indirect reciprocity—both in monetary terms, and with political support (Milinski, Semmann, and Krambeck 2002b). The desire to reap the rewards of a good reputation in private interactions encourages players to behave cooperatively in a group, a result that has led some biologists to turn their attention to how reputation might help address our most challenging collective-action problem: climate change (Milinski et al. 2006; Rand and Nowak 2009). Reputation is powerful among a group with shared values and dense social connections along which information, favors, and punishment can travel. But when these connections are lacking—as, for most of human history, they have been between nations—reputation has no force, and cooperation is much harder to promote and sustain.

The benefits to an individual's reputation might also promote collective action in online societies. The work of open source software coders, for example, might be rewarded in improved employment prospects. Such rewards can also be formalized: Amazon's "Vine" program gives top reviewers access to prerelease products. This decision has provoked criticism, with some online commentators fearing that such rewards could bias and corrupt reviewers—a hint that the link between public contribution and private rewards may not always have positive consequences for society.

Neither indirect reciprocity nor private rewards for public behavior, however, seem able to explain much cooperative behavior, both offline and online. Many public resources are maintained by a small group of altruists and used by a large group of free riders. Only 5 percent of the population, for example, gives blood, but most will need a transfusion at some point in their lives (Lyle, Smith, and Sullivan 2009). People give money to disaster relief efforts in far off countries that will never be repaid in kind. Online, it is likely that more people download files from peer-to-peer networks than upload files to them (Lyle and Sullivan 2007), and many more people read Wikipedia than work to build and maintain it.

What motivates altruists in such apparently thankless surroundings? One important consideration in online societies is that virtual public goods are not depleted by being consumed and shared, so the balance of costs and benefits may set the threshold for cooperation much lower—one might upload a file for the benefit of a handful of friends, only for it to also be downloaded by thousands of strangers. Another possible answer is that altruists in such situations are building a different kind of reputation to the one created by indirect reciprocity and displaying to their audience not their trustworthiness, but their wealth, be it physical, financial, or intellectual.

The study of this form of reputation has its roots in the evolutionary theory of costly signaling. Costly signals used by animals such as roaring, croaking, and gaudy plumage are difficult to fake, and are therefore an accurate guide to their sender's quality (see chapter 3 in this volume). Likewise, altruistic behavior might be a signal not of how good the altruist is, but how great—so rich in resources that they can be given away, as occurred in Native American potlatch ceremonies. Competitive altruism and indirect reciprocity operate together—by donating to charity, you show not only what a good person you are, but also how wealthy. But as a promoter of altruism, costly signaling has the added advantage that free riders are irrelevant, because costly signals are advertisements, not trades.

Costly signaling has been invoked to explain both meat sharing in hunting societies (Smith, Bird, and Bird 2003) and illegal file sharing in peer-to-peer networks (Lyle and Sullivan 2007). Many online reputation systems use status perks to encourage their users to make costly contributions to public resources. Reaching a high position on Amazon's table of top reviewers, for example, requires time and effort, but displays the reviewer as well-read, insightful, and public-spirited—all traits likely to be valuable to potential friends, employers, allies, and mates.

Cooperative and altruistic behavior isn't normally motivated by a cold calculation of self-interest. Rather, people are driven by the pleasure of being helpful or by the enjoyment of writing code, reviewing books, and so on. Surveys suggest that contributors to review sites or open-source software feel themselves to be acting out of disinterested altruism, rather than a conscious desire to boost their reputations (Baytiyeh and Pfaffman 2010; Utz 2009). But such explanations do not contradict the evolutionary view. People are not driven to eat ice cream or have sex by calculations of evolutionary fitness, but by the anticipation of pleasure. However, the evolutionary advantages of eating and copulation—and consequently of an appetite for food and sex—are obvious. Similarly, morality is an appetite for certain kinds of behavior, in ourselves and others, that helps us make decisions that are personally beneficial.

Social conditions that encourage altruism and discourage cheating include: transparency, so that people's behavior is known to one another; accountability, so that people have the power to reward and punish one another; and interconnectedness, which provides the social links along which reputation travels. Although online societies make connecting easy, the bandwidth of electronic communication is tiny compared to the wealth of nuance that we absorb in face-to-face interaction, which may limit the capacity to build trust, cooperation, and collective action in a purely online context. The anonymity and fluidity of online society, in which multiple or fake identities are easy to create and difficult to detect, also poses a barrier to cooperation. It's difficult, for example, to know whether to trust an online reviewer without knowing anything about his or her tastes, motivations, and possible conflicts of interest. Social networking sites help to overcome this problem, at the cost of some of the users' privacy, and this trade-off is present in all social contexts—to be trusted, we must also be known, and to an extent exposed. Secrecy, impunity, and isolation breed antisocial behavior.

Reputation also has a dark side. As well as displaying that they can be trusted, humans sometimes try to show one another that they are to be feared. Here, the benefits of an intimidating reputation can make people harm one another more than they otherwise would in the absence of an audience. Theoretical analyses show that fighting will be more intense in front of an audience, as the benefit of deterring future aggression makes belligerence more valuable, even in defeat (Johnstone and Bshary 2004), and studies of human aggression offer some support for this idea (Felson 1982).

An intimidating reputation seems particularly valuable in environments where collective punishment, either informally from the community or centrally from the state, is weak, so individuals are forced to rely on self-defense and deterrence. Nisbett and Cohen (1996) argue that the culture of honor in the southern United States, in which seemingly small slights sometimes provoke extreme violence, has its roots in the herding backgrounds and continuing herding economy of the Scots and Irish who settled the region. In herding cultures, populations are thinly spread and animal wealth is highly vulnerable to theft. An intimidating reputation may be the best defense in such a situation. Similar environments are also seen in criminal economies, in which—for obvious reasons—disputes cannot be settled through the courts (Bourgois 2003). This aspect of reputation may be detectable in some of the darker corners of cybercrime, in cyberbullying on social networks, and possibly in the actions of "griefers," who take pleasure from antisocial behavior in virtual worlds and online games.

The challenge to those who design our societies—both online and in the real world—is to enhance those features of the environment that encourage people to use reputation to sustain cooperation and to minimize those features that drive people to use reputation as a destructive force. Most people's first impulse is to be decent and helpful, but this is more an opening gambit than a cast-iron rule—unless such impulses are returned and rewarded, people quickly switch to other behavioral strategies. Neuroscience studies show that a concern for reputation activates the same brain regions as are involved in other forms of self-control, when we resist the urge to take a quick gain in anticipation of a greater future payoff (Knoch et al. 2009). But even the best of us are open to temptation if the benefits are great and the cost and likelihood of exposure small. The job of reputation systems is to reward cooperation and reduce temptation.

Online societies are places in which the ideas of evolutionary biologists can be tested and in which they might be applied. And evolutionary biology is reminding us that reputation comes in many forms—and that it is probably the most powerful peaceful means that humans have of controlling one another's behavior.

References

Alexander, R. D. 1987. *The biology of moral systems*. Piscataway, NJ: Transaction Publishers.

Bateson, M., D. Nettle, and G. Roberts. 2006. Cues of being watched enhance cooperation in a real-world setting. *Biology Letters* 2:412–414.

Baytiyeh, H., and J. Pfaffman. 2010. Open source software: a community of altruists. *Computers in Human Behavior* 6:1345–1354.

Bourgois, P. I. 2003. *In search of respect: Selling crack in El Barrio*. New York: Cambridge University Press.

Boyd, R., and P. J. Richerson. 1989. The evolution of indirect reciprocity. *Social Networks* 11: 213–236.

Bravo, G. 2010. Voluntary contribution to public goods in mutual-help forums: reciprocity or group attachment? *Socio-economic Review* 8 (4): 709–733.

Bshary, R., and A. S. Grutter. 2006. Image scoring and cooperation in a cleaner fish mutualism. *Nature* 441:975–978.

Burnham, T. C., and B. Hare. 2007. Engineering human cooperation. *Human Nature* 18:88–108.

Dawkins, R. 1976. *The selfish gene*. Oxford: Oxford University Press.

Fehr, E., and U. Fischbacher. 2003. The nature of human altruism. *Nature* 425:785–791.

Fehr, E., and S. Gachter. 2002. Altruistic punishment in humans. *Nature* 415:137–140.

Fehr, E., and F. Schneider. 2010. Eyes are on us, but nobody cares: are eye cues relevant for strong reciprocity? *Proceedings of the Royal Society B: Biological Sciences* 277:1315–1323.

Felson, R. B. 1982. Impression management and the escalation of aggression and violence. *Social Psychology Quarterly* 45:245–254.

Greif, A. 1989. Reputation and coalitions in medieval trade: Evidence on the Maghribi traders. *Journal of Economic History* 49:857–882.

Haley, K., and D. Fessler. 2005. Nobody's watching? Subtle cues affect generosity in an anonymous economic game. *Evolution and Human Behavior* 26:245–256.

Hamilton, W. D. 1964. The genetical evolution of social behaviour, I. *Journal of Theoretical Biology* 7:1–16.

Hawkes, K., and R. Bliege Bird. 2002. Showing off, handicap signaling, and the evolution of men's work. *Evolutionary Anthropology: Issues, News and Reviews*. 11:58–67.

Johnstone, R. A., and R. Bshary. 2004. Evolution of spite through indirect reciprocity. *Proceedings of the Royal Society B: Biological Sciences* 271:1917–1922.

Klein, D. B., ed. 1997. *Reputation: Studies in the voluntary elicitation of good conduct*. Ann Arbor: University of Michigan Press.

Knoch, D., F. Schneider, D. Schunk, M. Hohmann, and E. Fehr. 2009. Disrupting the prefrontal cortex diminishes the human ability to build a good reputation. *Proceedings of the National Academy of Sciences of the United States of America* 106:20895–20899.

Kurzban, R., P. DeScioli, and E. O'Brien. 2007. Audience effects on moralistic punishment. *Evolution and Human Behavior* 28:75–84.

Leimar, O., and P. Hammerstein. 2001. Evolution of cooperation through indirect reciprocity. *Proceedings of the Royal Society B: Biological Sciences* 268:745–753.

Lyle, H. F., E. A. Smith, and R. J. Sullivan. 2009. Blood donations as costly signals of donor quality. *Journal of Evolutionary Psychology* 7:263–286.

Lyle, H. F., and R. J. Sullivan. 2007. Competitive status signaling in peer-to-peer file-sharing networks. *Evolutionary Psychology* 5:363–382.

McGregor, P. K., ed. 2005. *Animal communication networks*. Cambridge: Cambridge University Press.

Mennill, D. J. 2002. Female eavesdropping on male song contests in songbirds. *Science* 296:873.

Milinski, M., D. Semmann, T. C. Bakker, and H. J. Krambeck. 2001. Cooperation through indirect reciprocity: Image scoring or standing strategy? *Proceedings of the Royal Society B: Biological Sciences* 268:2495–2501.

Milinski, M., D. Semmann, and H. Krambeck. 2002a. Reputation helps solve the "tragedy of the commons." *Nature* 415:424–426.

Milinski, M., D. Semmann, and H. Krambeck. 2002b. Donors to charity gain in both indirect reciprocity and political reputation. *Proceedings of the Royal Society B: Biological Sciences* 269:881–883.

Milinski, M., D. Semmann, H. Krambeck, and J. Marotzke. 2006. Stabilizing the Earth's climate is not a losing game: Supporting evidence from public goods experiments. *Proceedings of the National Academy of Sciences of the United States of America* 103:3994–3998.

Nisbett, R. E., and D. Cohen. 1996. *Culture of honor: The psychology of violence in the south*. Boulder: Westview Press.

Nowak, M. A., and K. Sigmund. 1998. Evolution of indirect reciprocity by image scoring. *Nature* 393:573–577.

Ohtsuki, H., and Y. Iwasa. 2006. The leading eight: Social norms that can maintain cooperation by indirect reciprocity. *Journal of Theoretical Biology* 239:435–444.

Olson, K. R., and E. S. Spelke. 2008. Foundations of cooperation in young children. *Cognition* 108:222–231.

Pacheco, J. M., F. C. Santos, and F. A. C. C. Chalub. 2006. Stern-judging: A simple, successful norm which promotes cooperation under indirect reciprocity. *Public Library of Science: Computational Biology* 2:e178.

Panchanathan, K. 2011. Two wrongs don't make a right: The initial viability of different assessment rules in the evolution of indirect reciprocity. *Journal of Theoretical Biology* 277:48–54.

Panchanathan, K., and R. Boyd. 2004. Indirect reciprocity can stabilize cooperation without the second-order free rider problem. *Nature* 432:499–502.

Rand, D., and M. Nowak. 2009. Name and shame. *New Scientist* 204 (2734): 28–29.

Rankin, D. J., and F. Eggimann. 2009. The evolution of judgment bias in indirect reciprocity. *Proceedings of the Royal Society B: Biological Sciences* 276:1339–1345.

Rigdon, M., K. Ishii, M. Watabe, and S. Kitayama. 2009. Minimal social cues in the dictator game. *Journal of Economic Psychology* 30:358–367.

Santos, M. D., D. J. Rankin, and C. Wedekind. 2010. The evolution of punishment through reputation. *Proceedings of the Royal Society B: Biological Sciences*.

Smith, E. A., R. B. Bird, and D. W. Bird. 2003. The benefits of costly signaling: Meriam turtle hunters. *Behavioral Ecology.* 14:116–126.

Sugden, R. 2004. *The economics of rights, co-operation and welfare.* 2nd ed. London: Palgrave Macmillan.

Tracy, J. L., R. W. Robins, and J. P. Tangney, eds. 2007. *The self-conscious emotions: theory and research.* New York: Guilford Press.

Trivers, R. L. 1971. The evolution of reciprocal altruism. *Quarterly Review of Biology* 46:35–57.

Utz, S. 2009. "Egoboo" vs. altruism: The role of reputation in online consumer communities. *New Media and Society* 3:357–374.

Wedekind, C., and M. Milinski. 2000. Cooperation through image scoring in humans. *Science* 288:850–852.

Wert, S. R., and P. Salovey. 2004. A social comparison account of gossip. *Review of General Psychology* 8:122–137.

5 Regulating Reputation

Eric Goldman

When should reputation systems be regulated? Eric Goldman explores challenges and regulatory options, and extends Adam Smith's famous metaphor by pointing out the role played by secondary and tertiary invisible hands.

This chapter considers the role of reputational information in our marketplace and society. It explains how well-functioning marketplaces depend on the vibrant flow of accurate reputational information and how misdirected regulation of reputational information could harm marketplace mechanisms. The chapter then explores some challenges created by the existing regulation of reputational information and identifies some regulatory options for the future.

Reputational Information Defined

Typical definitions of "reputation" focus on third-party cognitive perceptions of a person. As one commentator explained:

Through one's actions, one relates to others and makes impressions on them. These impressions, taken as a whole, constitute an individual's reputation—that is, what other people think of you, to the extent that their thoughts arise from what they know about you, or think they know about you. (De Armond 2007, 1065)

Other legal sources generally follow this theme. For example, *Black's Law Dictionary* defines reputation as the "esteem in which a person is held by others." (Garner 2004). Bryan Garner's *A Dictionary of Modern Legal Usage* defines reputation as "what one is thought by others to be" (Garner 1990, 148). The Federal Rules of Evidence also reflect this perception-centric view of "reputation." (Fed. R. Evid. 803(19), 803(21)).

These definitions might reflect lay perceptions about the meaning of "reputation," but this chapter emphasizes how information affects prospective decision making. Accordingly, this chapter defines "reputational information" as:

information about an actor's past performance that helps predict the actor's future ability to perform or to satisfy the decision-maker's preferences.

This definition assumes that actors create a pool of data (both subjective and objective) through their conduct. This pool of data—the reputational information—can provide insights into the actors' likely future behavior.

Reputation Systems

Reputation systems aggregate and disseminate reputational information to consumers of that information. Reputation systems can be unmediated or mediated. In unmediated reputation systems, the producers and consumers of reputational information communicate directly. Examples of unmediated reputation systems include word of mouth, letters of recommendation, and job references. In mediated reputation systems, a third party gathers, organizes, and publishes reputational information. Examples of mediated reputation systems include the Better Business Bureau's ratings, credit reports and scores, investment ratings such as Morningstar mutual fund ratings and Moody bond ratings, and consumer review sites.

The Internet has led to a proliferation of mediated reputation systems and, in particular, consumer review sites. Consumers can review just about anything online. Examples include:

- Yelp, which enables shoppers to review local businesses
- TripAdvisor, where travelers can review hotels and other travel attractions
- eBay's feedback forum, which allows eBay's buyers and sellers to rate each other
- Amazon's product reviews, which encourages the public to rate and review millions of marketplace products
- RealSelf.com, which lets patients review cosmetic surgery procedures
- Avvo.com, where clients can rate and review attorneys
- Glassdoor.com, which permits employees to share salary information and critique the working conditions at their employers
- Honestly.com, which lets coworkers review each other
- RateMyProfessors, where students can publicly rate and review their professors.
- DontDateHimGirl.com, which allows women to create and "find profiles of men who are alleged cheaters."
- TheEroticReview.com, a site allowing clients to rank prostitutes (see Richtel 2008). PunterNet.com is a similar site for reviews of British sex workers (see Omizek 2009).

Why Reputational Information Matters

In theory, the marketplace works through an "invisible hand": consumers and producers make individual and autonomous decisions that—without any centralized coordination—collectively determine the price and quantity of goods and services. When it works properly, the invisible hand maximizes social welfare by allocating goods and services to those consumers who value them the most.

A properly functioning invisible hand also should reward good producers and punish poor ones. Consumers allocating their scarce dollars in a competitive market transact with producers who provide the best cost or quality options. Over time, uncompetitive producers should be drummed out of the industry by the aggregate but uncoordinated choices of rational and informed consumers.

However, in the presence of transaction costs, the invisible hand can be subject to distortions. In particular, if information about producers is costly to obtain or use, consumers may lack crucial information to make accurate decisions. In such cases, consumers may not be able to easily compare producers or their price or quality offerings and therefore good producers may not be rewarded and bad producers may not be punished.

When information about producers and vendors is costly, reputational information can improve the operation of the invisible hand by helping consumers make better decisions. In this case, reputational information acts like an invisible hand of the invisible hand (an effect I call the *secondary invisible hand*) because reputational information can guide consumers to make marketplace choices that in aggregate enable the invisible hand. Thus, in an information economy with transaction costs, reputational information can play an essential role in rewarding good producers and punishing poor ones.

Given this crucial role in marketplace mechanisms, any distortions in reputational information may effectively distort the marketplace itself. In effect, it may cause the secondary invisible hand to push the invisible hand in the wrong direction, allowing bad producers to escape punishment and failing to reward good producers. To avoid this unwanted consequence, any regulation of reputational information needs to be considered carefully to ensure that it is improving—not harming—marketplace mechanisms.

Note that the secondary invisible hand is itself subject to transaction costs. It is costly for consumers to find reputational information and to assess its credibility. Therefore, reputation systems themselves typically seek to establish their own reputation. I describe the reputation of reputation systems as a *tertiary invisible hand*—it is the invisible hand that guides reputational information (the secondary invisible hand) to guide the invisible hand of individual uncoordinated decisions by marketplace actors (the primary invisible hand). Thus, the tertiary invisible hand allows the reputation system to earn consumer trust as a credible source (such as the *Wall Street Journal*, the *New York Times*, or *Consumer Reports*) or to be drummed out of the market for lack of credibility, such as the exit of JuicyCampus.com (Ivester 2009). (See chapter 3 in this volume for a related invisible hand analogy.)

Regulatory Heterogeneity

We now turn to some ways in which the regulatory system interacts with reputation systems and some issues caused by those interactions. Regulators have taken divergent approaches to reputation systems. For example, consider the three different U.S. regulatory schemes governing job references, credit reporting databases, and consumer review websites:

• Job references are subject to a mix of statutory (primarily state law) and common law tort regulation.
• Credit reporting databases are statutorily micromanaged through the voluminous and detailed Fair Credit Reporting Act, codified at 15 U.S.C. § 1681–81x.
• Consumer review websites are virtually unregulated, and many potential regulations of consumer review websites (such as defamation) are statutorily preempted.

These different regulatory structures raise some related questions. Are there meaningful distinctions between reputation systems that suggest the desirability of heterogeneous regulation? And are there "best practices" we can observe from these heterogeneous regulatory approaches that we can use to improve other regulatory systems?

These questions are important because regulatory schemes can significantly affect the efficacy of reputation systems. As an example, consider the differences between the job reference and online consumer review markets. A former employer giving a job reference can face significant liability, regardless of whether the reference is positive or negative: "Employers are finding that they are being sued no matter what course they take; whether they give a bad reference, a good reference or stay entirely silent" (Baldas 2008, 1). Giving unfavorable references of former employees can lead to defamation or related claims (Employment Screening 2008), and there may be liability for a former employer giving an incomplete positive reference (*Randi W. v. Muroc Joint Unified Sch. Dist.*, 14 Cal. 4th 1066 [1997]).

Employers may be statutorily required to provide certain objective information about former employees. These laws are called *service letter statutes* (Employment Screening 2008). Otherwise, given the potential no-win liability regime for communicating job references, most knowledgeable employers refuse to provide any subjective recommendations of former employees, positive or negative (Baldas 2008).

To curb employers' tendency toward silence, many states enacted statutory immunities to protect employers from lawsuits over job references. The immunizations protect employer statements (Employment Screening 2008). However, the immunities have not changed employer reticence because courts have interpreted them narrowly, leaving employers still exposed to unavoidable liability. The continuing liability despite the statutory immunities has contributed to a virtual collapse of the job reference market (Finkin and Dau-Schmidt 2009). As a result—and due to miscalibrated regulation—the job reference market fails to provide reliable reputational information.

In contrast to the job reference market, the online consumer review system is one of the most robust reputation systems ever. Millions of consumers freely share their subjective opinions about marketplace goods and services, and online consumer review websites keep proliferating.

There are several reasons why online reputation systems like consumer review websites might succeed where offline reputation systems might fail. One possible explanation is 47 U.S.C. §230, passed in 1996—at the height of Internet exceptionalism—to protect online publishers from liability for third-party content. §230 lets websites generate and organize individual consumer reviews without worrying about crippling legal liability for those reviews. As a result, mediating websites can motivate consumers to share their opinions and then publish those opinions driven by marketplace mechanisms (i.e., the tertiary invisible hand) and not concerns about legal liability.

The success of online consumer review websites is especially noteworthy given that individual reviewers face the same legal risks that former employers face when providing job references, such as the risk of personal liability for publishing negative reputational information. Indeed, numerous individuals have been sued for posting negative online reviews (see, e.g., Davis 2009), and many consumers do not understand the legal risks of speaking out publicly (Savage 2010). As a result, rational actors should find it imprudent to submit negative reviews, and over time, consumers' increased awareness of these risks could substantially limit their willingness to share their views.

Yet despite the risks, millions of such reviews have been published online. In part this is because mediating websites, privileged by their own liability immunity, find innovative ways to get consumers over their fears of legal liability. Their review-eliciting techniques include paying reviewers, directly or through sweepstakes or other virtual currency, to publish their thoughts (e.g., Epinions); helping reviewers gain commercially valuable recognition for their expertise; making it fun for reviewers; and in some cases, simply asking for consumer opinions when no one has ever asked for them before.

What lessons can we draw from this comparison between job references and online consumer reviews? One possible lesson is that reputation systems are too important to be left to the market. In other words, the tertiary invisible hand may not ensure accurate and useful information, or the social costs of inaccurate information (such as denying a job to a qualified candidate) may be too excessive. If so, extensive regulatory intervention may be necessary to protect the marketplace.

Given the online consumer review successes, another possible conclusion is that the tertiary invisible hand can produce better results than regulatory intervention when it is coupled with liability protections for mediating publishers such as the §230 immunity. As a result, it may be worth exploring possible mechanisms to provide similar liability immunities for other mediating publishers.

System Configurations

The existing regulatory heterogeneity raises a theoretical inquiry: is there an "ideal" regulatory configuration for reputation systems, especially given the tertiary invisible hand and its salutary effect on mediating publishers' behavior? Two brief examples illustrate the choices available to regulators, including the option of letting the marketplace operate unimpeded.

Antigaming

A vendor may have financial incentives to distort the flow of reputational information about it. This reputational gaming can take many forms, including disseminating false positive reports about the vendor, disseminating false negative reports about the vendor's competitors, or manipulating an intermediary's sorting or weighting algorithm to get more credit for positive reports or reduce credit for negative reports.

Another type of gaming can occur when users intentionally flood a reputation system with inaccurate negative reports as a form of protest. For example, consumers protesting the digital rights management (DRM) in EA's Spore game flooded Amazon's review site with one-star reviews, even though many of them actually enjoyed the game (Modine 2008). A similar protest hit Intuit's TurboTax 2008 over its increased prices (Musil 2008).

Do regulators need to curb such gaming behavior, or will other forces be adequate? There are several marketplace pressures that curb gaming, including competitors policing each other just as they do in false advertising cases (BeVier 1992). In addition, the tertiary invisible hand may encourage reputation systems to provide adequate "policing" against gaming. However, when the tertiary invisible hand is weak—such as with fake blog posts for which search engines provide the only level of mediation—government intervention may be worth considering to fill the vacuum left by the absence of a strong intermediary.

Right of Reply

A vendor may wish to publicly respond to reputational information published about it in an immediately adjacent fashion. Many consumer review websites allow vendors to comment or otherwise reply to user-supplied reviews, but not all do. For example, Yelp initially drew significant criticism from business owners who could not effectively reply to negative Yelp reviews because of Yelp's architecture, but Yelp eventually relented and voluntarily changed its policy (Miller 2009a, 2009b). As another example, Google permitted quoted sources to reply to news articles appearing in Google News as a way to "correct the record." (Meredith and Golding 2007).

Regulators could require consumer review websites and other reputation systems to permit an adjacent response from the vendor (Pasquale 2006, 2008). We already provide an analogous process for consumer credit reports by giving consumers a statutory process to append information to their record in some cases (see 15 U.S.C. § 1681i(b) and (c)). At the same time, the tertiary invisible hand can prompt reputation systems to voluntarily provide a reply option (as Yelp and Google did) when they think the additional information helps consumers. Furthermore, mandatory rights of reply raise constitutional questions in the United States (Miami Herald Publishing Co. v. Tornillo 1974).

It remains an open question whether the tertiary invisible hand is powerful enough to pressure reputation systems to voluntarily give vendors reply rights or other tools to correct errors in marketplace information. If it is, mandating a right of reply may be unnecessary.

Undersupply of Reputational Information

Inadequate Production Incentives

Much reputational information starts out as nonpublic (i.e., "private") information in the form of a customer's subjective mental impressions about his or her interactions with a vendor. To the extent that this information remains private, it does not help other consumers make marketplace decisions. These collective mental impressions represent a vital but potentially underutilized social resource.

The fact that private information remains locked in consumers' heads could represent a marketplace failure. If the social benefit from making reputational information public exceeds the private benefit, public reputational information will be undersupplied. If so, the government may need to correct this failure by encouraging the production of "public" reputational information. But government intervention is not clearly warranted. Marketplace mechanisms have contributed to the proliferation of online review websites that elicit large amounts of formerly private reputational information.

Further, relatively small amounts of publicly disclosed reputational information might be enough to properly steer the invisible hand. For example, the first consumer review of a product in a reputation system creates a lot of value for subsequent consumers, but the thousandth consumer review of the same product may add very little incremental value. So even if most consumer impressions never become public, perhaps mass-market products and vendors still have enough reputational information produced about them to keep them honest.

At the same time, vendors and products in the "long tail" (Anderson 2004) may have inadequate nonpublic impressions put into the public discourse, creating a valuable opportunity for comprehensive reputation systems to fix the omission. However, reputation systems tackle these obscure marketplace options only when they can keep their costs low (given that consumer interest and traffic will, by definition, be low). Liability immunities can encourage reputation systems to increase their coverage of long-tail offerings by reducing the system's costs—both the legal liability costs as well as the costs of addressing takedown demands from unhappy vendors.

Vendor Suppression of Reputational Information

Vendors are not shy about trying to suppress unwanted consumer reviews after they are made (see Goldman [2008] discussing lopsided databases in which all negative reviews are removed, leaving only positive reviews), but vendors might try to preemptively suppress such reviews. For example, one café owner grew so tired of negative Yelp reviews that he put a "No Yelpers" sign in his windows (Olsen 2007).

That sign probably had no legal effect, but MedicalJustice.com in the United States offers an ex ante system to help doctors use preemptive contracts to suppress reviews by their patients. Medical Justice provides doctors with a form agreement that has patients waive their rights to post online reviews of the doctor (Tanner 2009). Further, to bypass 47 U.S.C. § 230's protective immunity for online reputation systems that might republish such patient reviews (§ 230 does not immunize against copyright infringement), the Medical Justice form prospectively takes copyright ownership of any patient-authored reviews (Carbine 2009). This approach effectively allows doctors—or Medical Justice, as their designee—to get reputation systems to remove any unwanted patient reviews simply by sending a DMCA takedown notice (17 U.S.C. § 512(c)(3)).

Ex ante customer gag orders may be illegal. In the early 2000s, the New York attorney general challenged software manufacturer Network Associates' end user license agreement, which stated that the "customer will not publish reviews of this product without prior consent from Network Associates, Inc." (New York Office of the Attorney General 2002). In response, the New York Supreme Court enjoined Network Associates from restricting user reviews in its end user license agreement (People v. Network Associates, Inc 2003). Medical Justice's scheme may be equally legally problematic.

From a policy standpoint, ex ante customer gag orders pose serious threats to the invisible hand. If they work as intended, they starve reputation systems of the public information necessary to facilitate the marketplace. Therefore, regulatory efforts might be required to prevent ex ante customer gag orders from wreaking havoc on marketplace mechanisms.

Distorted Decision Making from Reputational Information

Reputational information generally improves decision making, but not always. Most obviously, reputational information relies on the accuracy of past information in predicting future behavior, but this predictive power is not perfect.

First, marketplace actors are constantly changing and evolving, so past behavior may not predict future performance. For example, a person with historically bad credit may obtain a well-paying job that puts him or her on good financial footing. Or, in the corporate world, a business may sell to a new owner with different management practices. In these situations, the predictive accuracy of past information is reduced. See for example *Badwill* (Harvard Law Review Association 2003), describing how companies can mask a track record of bad performance through corporate renaming.

Second, some past behavior may be so distracting that users of information might overlook other information that has more accurate predictive power. For example, a past crime or bankruptcy can overwhelm the predictive information in an otherwise unblemished track record of good performance.

Ultimately, a user of information must make smart choices about what information to consult and how much predictive weight to assign to that information. Perhaps regulation can improve the marketplace and society's operation by shaping the information that people consider. For example, if some information is so highly prejudicial that it is likely to distort decision making, the marketplace might work better if we suppress that information from the decision maker (see Fed. R. Evid. 403, which says "although relevant, evidence may be excluded if its probative value is substantially outweighed by the danger of unfair prejudice, confusion of the issues, or misleading the jury"). One common example involves minors, who may suffer a lifetime of adverse consequences from their youthful indiscretions. This has led a number of people to advocate for "reputational bankruptcy," which would allow individuals to wipe their reputation slate clean (Zittrain 2008, ch. 9; Reid 2010). European regulators are, in fact, considering ways to implement this concept (DGS 2010). (For another perspective on these issues, see chapter 6 in this volume.)

At the same time, taking useful information out of the marketplace could create its own adverse distortions of the invisible hands. It would allow marketplace actors to escape their bad reputation, even when such choices would be highly salient to decision makers. We already have a difficult enough time keeping fraudsters out of the marketplace; reputational bankruptcy would unquestionably foster additional fraud by letting offenders repeat their bad actions with no reputational history. Therefore, we should tread cautiously in suppressing certain categories of information.

Conclusion

It is crucial that we avoid mistakes when regulating reputation systems. Those mistakes can ripple through the information economy, degrading the efficiency of our marketplace. At the same time, the marketplace benefits from improvements in the flow of reputational information, so regulations that help the reputational ecosystem can improve society. Sorting between helpful and harmful regulations is a tricky art.

As this chapter indicates, the marketplace has self-correcting mechanisms—the tertiary invisible hand encourages reputation systems to do a better job of providing reputational information. Because of this, regulatory intervention makes the most sense only when the tertiary invisible hand is likely to fail.

References

15 U.S.C. (United States Code) § 1681–81x.

15 U.S.C. (United States Code) § 1681i(b) and (c).

17 U.S.C. (United States Code) § 512(c)(3).

47 U.S.C. (United States Code) § 230.

Anderson, C. 2004, October. The long tail. *Wired*. Retrieved from: <http://www.wired.com/wired/archive/12.10/tail.html>.

Baldas, T. 2008. A rash of problems over job references. *National Law Journal* (March 12): 1.

BeVier, L. R. 1992. A puzzle in the law of deception. *Virginia Law Review* 78:1–48.

Carbine, M. E. 2009, March 30. Physicians use copyright infringement threat to block patient ratings on the web. *AIS's Health Business Daily*.

Davis, W. 2009, January 21. Yelp reviews spawn at least five lawsuits. MediaPost Online Media Daily. Retrieved from: <http://www.mediapost.com/publications/?fa=Articles.showArticle&art_aid=98778>.

De Armond, E. D. 2007. Frothy chaos: Modern data warehousing and old-fashioned defamation. *Valparaiso University Law Review* 41(3): 1061–1142.

DGS. 2010, August 23. New law to stop companies from checking Facebook pages in Germany. Spiegel Online. Retrieved from: <http://www.spiegel.de/international/germany/0,1518,713240,00.html>.

Employment Screening 1–2 § 2.05 (Matthew Bender and Co. 2008).

Fed. R. Evid. 403.

Fed. R. Evid. 803(19), 803(21).

Finkin, M. W., and K. G. Dau-Schmidt. 2009. Solving the employee reference problem. *American Journal of Comparative Law* 57:387.

Garner, Bryan. A. 1990. *A Dictionary of Modern Legal Usage*. New York: Oxford University Press.

Garner, Bryan A. 2004. *Black's Law Dictionary*. 8th edition. St. Paul, MN: Thomson/West.

Goldman, E. 2008. Online word of mouth and its implications for trademark law. In *Trademark law and theory: A handbook of contemporary research,* ed. G. B. Dinwoodie and M. D. Janis. Cheltenham, UK: Edward Elgar Press, 404–429.

Harvard Law Review Association. 2003. Badwill. *Harvard Law Review* 116 (6): 1845–1867.

Ivester, M. 2009, February 4. A juicy shutdown [web log comment]. Retrieved from: <http://juicycampus.blogspot.com/2009/02/juicy-shutdown.html>.

Meredith, D., and A. Golding. 2007, August 7. Perspectives about the news from people in the news [web log comment]. *Google News Blog*. Retrieved from: <http://googlenewsblog.blogspot .com/2007/08/perspectives-about-news-from-people-in.html>.

Miami Herald Publishing Co. v. Tornillo, 418 U.S. 241 (1974).

Miller, C. C. 2009a, March 3. The review site Yelp draws some outcries of its own. *New York Times*, p. B1.

Miller, C. C. 2009b, April 10. Yelp will let businesses respond to web reviews. *New York Times*, p. B8.

Modine, A. 2008, September 10. Amazon flash mob mauls Spore DRM. *The Register*. Retrieved from: <http://www.theregister.co.uk/2008/09/10/spore_drm_amazon_effect>.

Musil, S. 2008, December 7. Amazon reviewers slam TurboTax fee changes. CNET News. Retrieved from: <http://news.cnet.com/8301-1001_3-10117323-92.html>.

New York Office of the Attorney General. 2002, February 7. Spitzer sues software developer to protect consumers' free speech rights. Press release. Retrieved from: <http://www.ag.ny.gov/me-dia_center/2002/feb/feb07a_02.html>.

Olsen, S. 2007, August 14. No dogs, Yelpers allowed. CNET News. Retrieved from: <http://news .cnet.com/8301-10784_3-9759933-7.html>.

Omizek, J. 2009, October 5. PunterNet thanks Harriet for massive upswing. *The Register*. Retrieved from: <http://www.theregister.co.uk/2009/10/05/punternet_harman>.

Pasquale, F. A. 2006. Rankings, reductionism, and responsibility. *Cleveland State Law Review* 54:115.

Pasquale, F. A. 2008. Asterisk revisited: Debating a right of reply on search results. *Journal of Business and Technology Law* 3 (61–85).

People v. Network Associates, Inc., 758 N.Y.S.2d 466 (N.Y. Sup. Ct. 2003).

Randi W. v. Muroc Joint Unified Sch. Dist., 14 Cal. 4th 1066 (1997).

Reid, D. 2010, January 8. France ponders right-to-forget law. *BBC Click*. Retrieved from: <http:// news.bbc.co.uk/2/hi/programmes/click_online/8447742.stm>.

Richtel, M. 2008, June 17. Sex trade monitors a key figure's woes. *New York Times*, p. A12.

Savage, D. G. 2010, August 23. Online rants can turn costly. *L.A. Times*, p. 1.

Tanner, L. 2009, March 3. Doctors seek gag orders to stop patients' online reviews. Associated Press. Retrieved from: <http://www.usatoday.com/news/health/2009-03-05-doctor-reviews_N .htm>.

Zittrain, J. 2008. *The future of the Internet and how to stop it*. New Haven: Yale University Press.

6 Less Regulation, More Reputation

Lior Jacob Strahilevitz

Can reputation complement regulation? Lior Jacob Strahilevitz addresses this question in the context of landlord-tenant relations, antidiscrimination law, and commercial disputes and proposes that greater access to reputational information could be a twenty-first-century public good.

Displacing Statistical Discrimination with Reputation Tracking

Can people get all the benefits of small-town life while living in the big city? For much of human history, such a question was irrelevant because big cities did not exist. Following the rise of urbanization, such a question was fantastical because big cities required interactions with many strangers. Villages offered the security of knowing almost everyone around you, as well as everyone else's business. Those who moved from villages to the city traded the security blanket of familiarity for opportunities to attain wealth, education, culture, and excitement. During the twentieth century and the early part of the twenty-first century, mass media and the rise of the Internet distributed educational and cultural opportunities to small-town denizens a bit more broadly, but cities and suburbs continued to pull people from more rural areas, as many of the children of those who grew up in small towns continued to view local lifestyles as stifling and unrewarding.

Having moved to the cities and suburbs, people found that they missed the richness of interactions in small towns. Voluntary associations provided some substitute for the missing sense of community, as did educational and religious institutions. Still, day-to-day life was likely to bring people into contact with countless strangers—at the mall, on the freeways, at sporting events, at workplaces, in the park—and these interactions were sometimes fraught with danger. The vendor you didn't know might cheat you. The driver you didn't know could crash his car into yours. The person walking down the poorly lit urban street might mean you harm.

To deal with stresses associated with urban and suburban anonymity, people adopted a variety of coping strategies. They tried to do business with the same shops repeatedly so that the merchants would have financial incentives to behave honestly. They bought large vehicles to provide a greater sense of security on the road. And they purchased homes in gated communities, took self-defense classes, or agitated for concealed-carry gun laws to protect themselves against would-be muggers and burglars.

Most relevant for our purposes, they often used mental shortcuts to navigate everyday interactions with strangers. Does the shoe salesman seem honest or shifty? Competent or feckless? Is that driver in the oncoming vehicle a reckless teenager or a conscientious soccer mom? What are the race, age, affect, and gender of the person walking toward me on a deserted street? In each of these examples, people are engaged in statistical discrimination. The honest-seeming shoe salesman might nevertheless sell us sneakers that do not fit well or wear out quickly. The soccer mom might distractedly plow into our vehicle, whereas the teenager may drive with great caution. A pedestrian dressed like a hoodlum might be just as afraid of us as we are of him. But these rules of thumb, with which we look to demographic characteristics to try to gauge whether someone is friend or foe, probably work better than relying on pure chance. Because there is often some truth to stereotypes, statistical discrimination of this sort is often a rational strategy for individuals to pursue.

It would be folly to criminalize crossing the street to avoid a scary-looking oncoming pedestrian, even if the pedestrian turns out to be harmless. But in many contexts in which statistical discrimination arises, these shortcuts are unlawful. One cannot rely on statistical discrimination as the basis for a refusal to rent to a qualified tenant or hire a qualified candidate for a job.

This chapter argues that an important potential upside of new reputation tracking technologies is their potential to displace statistical discrimination on the basis of race, gender, age, appearance, and other easily observable characteristics. Reputation tracking tools such as feedback scores on eBay, profiles on Facebook, credit scores, and criminal background histories provide detailed information about individuals, thereby reducing the temptation for decision makers to rely on group-based stereotypes (Strahilevitz 2006, 2008a, 2008b, 2011). Governments should take advantage of this relationship and reduce the prevalence of statistical discrimination by making reputation information more transparent.

We begin with a recent historical example showing how reputation information can change the prevalence of statistical discrimination in the marketplace and then explore the promise of new technologies to displace law in other sectors. Though examples are drawn from the United States, similar dynamics apply in many other jurisdictions. Formal law is costly and inefficient, whether it operates through tort remedies, criminal or administrative enforcement, or other avenues. In small towns, formal law does rather little work, and informal social norms keep people from behaving badly (Ellickson 1991). Recent advances in reputation tracking hold out the possibility that social norms can displace formal law in cities and suburbs too.

Landlord-Tenant Relations

During the 1970s and 1980s, it was not unusual for landlords in New York City to re-fuse to rent apartments to lawyers. At first blush, this seems like an odd trend. Lawyers may be loathed by the public, but they typically bring home a nice paycheck. A New York City landlord who refused to rent to lawyers would be depriving him- or herself of many prospective, well-heeled tenants. Still, as one landlord explained to a New York court, his refusal to rent an apartment to a qualified attorney applicant was based on his preference for "a person who was likely to be less informed and more passive" rather than someone "attuned to her legal rights" (*Kramarsky v. Stahl Mgmt.* 1977). That court noted that lawyers were not a protected class under fair housing laws and thus ruled in the landlord's favor. After nine years, New York eventually prohibited discrimination in the housing market on the basis of profession, at the urging of law-yers who had troubles finding rental units in the city.

The 1986 enactment of New York's profession-based fair housing protections did not prompt the city's landlords to stop screening tenants. Landlords still wanted to screen out tenants who seemed likely to invoke their rights under New York's landlord-tenant laws. Some landlords quietly tried to circumvent the law, offering pretexts for their continued refusals to rent to lawyers. But other landlords instead began relying on involvement in prior litigation as a proxy for litigiousness. Information brokers began data-mining state and municipal court records, hoping to identify tenants who had been involved in landlord-tenant litigation of any sort. Those landlords essentially blacklisted tenants who had been parties to such litigation. In such a world, even ten-ants who had won suits against their landlords faced a difficult time obtaining hous-ing. As the founder of a tenant screening company told the *New York Times*, "It is the policy of 99 percent of our customers in New York to flat-out reject anybody with a landlord-tenant record, no matter what the reason is and no matter what the outcome is, because if their dispute has escalated to going to court, an owner will view them as a pain" (Rogers 2006).

From one perspective, tenant screening services are popular in New York precisely because landlord-tenant regulations in that city slant so heavily in the direction of tenants. Faced with high eviction and litigation costs, landlords devote more resources to trying to screen out prospective tenants who pose heightened risks of future legal entanglements. This screening means that the reputational consequences of involve-ment in litigation are so severe that a rational tenant should often elect not to seek enforcement of the substantive entitlements provided by landlord-tenant law. Pro-tenant regulations, in short, might not make tenants better off, though they do seem to improve the lot of tenant screening firms.

This dynamic explains why some of the landlord-tenant reforms of the 1960s and 1970s, which were supported by well-meaning tenants' rights advocates, may have ultimately backfired. One such reform is the prohibition on "self-help evictions" by landlords. In such evictions, landlords were able to remove the belongings of tenants who had violated the terms of their lease and change the locks unilaterally, provided that they did not use excessive or unreasonable force (Dukeminier et al. 2006; Schissler 2000). Beginning in the 1960s, tenants began legal reform efforts, arguing that legal process should be the exclusive means of ousting a tenant in possession. This largely successful reform movement was premised on the view that self-help evictions tend to spark violence between the landlord and tenant, and that unless checked by the courts, some landlords would evict tenants who had a legal right to remain on the premises (*Berg v. Wiley* 1978).

The prohibition of self-help evictions by landlords sparked fears that landlords would pass the high costs of judicially evicting deadbeat tenants onto the tenants who paid their bills on time. Some passing on of these costs undoubtedly occurs, but we can now identify a deeper criticism of the prohibitions on landlord self-help. Eviction via self-help typically creates no public records. Courts are not involved in a self-help eviction, and a landlord has no economic incentive to report such a dispossession to a credit bureau or any other information broker. Evictions via summary legal proceedings, on the other hand, necessarily generate public records, and it is those public records that will prove so damaging to tenants the next time they try to rent an apartment.

Tenants' rights advocates who appreciate the ways in which earlier reforms have produced unintended consequences are not powerless to address this situation. If society believes that second chances are important in the landlord-tenant context, then it might require that information about involvement in landlord-tenant litigation be purged from consumers' credit reports after a relatively brief period of time. Currently, the Fair Credit Reporting Act requires that information about someone's involvement in landlord-tenant litigation be removed from his or her credit report after seven years (Fair Credit Reporting Act 2006). But a seven-year cloud on one's suitability as a tenant still imposes substantial harms on tenants who become involved in litigation. During the 1990s, California tried to address this broader concern legislatively, prohibiting credit reporting agencies from including information about a tenant's involvement in landlord-tenant litigation where the tenant was the prevailing party. This legislation was invalidated by the courts on First Amendment grounds (*U.D. Registry, Inc. v. State of California* 1995). In short, legislators cannot easily prevent landlords from receiving information about tenants' prior involvement in litigation. They can try to ban landlords from acting on that information, but the enforcement of such prohibitions will be spotty, expensive, and prone to false positives.

There are two sides to every reputational coin. Just as a substantial market has developed for tenant screening services, a market has also arisen for clearinghouses of information about landlords' reputations. In a prior era, these were confined mainly to university housing offices, where students could swap stories about the good, bad, and ugly landlords. Today, in markets in which prospective tenants often hire brokers to assist in their searches, brokers who depend on repeat business and positive word of mouth have an incentive to learn which landlords behave inappropriately.

Not surprisingly, the Internet has given rise to far more sophisticated resources for tenants. One of the best developed among them is ApartmentRatings.com, a website that contains tens of thousands of landlord ratings written by current and former tenants. This website and similar sites provide a wealth of information that would not easily be discerned in their absence, and their existence gives tenants some recourse in dealing with recalcitrant or bullying landlords. To the extent that websites like these are used by prospective tenants, landlords should fear developing a reputation for unfair or overly aggressive behavior. The best check on landlord misbehavior may become not the threat of a lawsuit by the tenant, but the threat of a series of complaints by aggrieved and eloquent tenants.

Antidiscrimination Law in the Job Market

There are two basic forms of discrimination: animus-based discrimination and statistical discrimination. *Animus-based discrimination* occurs when an individual treats members of a group differently because of (conscious or unconscious) antipathy toward that group. *Statistical discrimination* occurs when an individual treats members of a group differently because he or she believes that group membership correlates with some attribute that is both relevant and more difficult to observe than group membership. Someone engaged in statistical discrimination would not harbor any ill will toward members of the group against which he or she is discriminating, beyond the belief that membership in that group correlates with some undesirable characteristic. A landlord who refuses to rent to lawyers because he or she fears litigious tenants and thinks lawyers are more likely to be litigious is engaging in statistical discrimination. A landlord who will not rent to lawyers because he or she hates lawyers is an animus-based discriminator.

To illustrate how statistical discrimination plays out in contemporary society, suppose that a person charged with hiring a sales clerk wants to avoid employing someone with a criminal background. Assuming that the decision maker lacks reliable access to information about applicants' criminal records, her decision-making process may impose an obnoxious form of collective punishment on those who have had no run-ins with the law, penalizing them for crimes that others have committed. She might, for example, choose to hire a Caucasian female over an equally qualified African American male based on the relatively high percentage of African American males and the relatively low percentage of Caucasian females who are involved in the criminal justice system. Because many decision makers may exercise the same decision-making criteria, a law-abiding African American male may face repeated rejection and economic marginalization. For these reasons, antidiscrimination law prohibits the use of race or gender proxies, even where race or gender might correlate with some relevant qualification.

Policing statistical discrimination through traditional antidiscrimination measures has proven difficult: many victims of statistical discrimination never bring suit, many nonvictims bring unmeritorious suits that prompt defendants to settle so as to avoid the costs of litigation, and enforcement of the laws has been sporadic. Concerned about the courts being flooded with frivolous claims, judges have imposed substantial burdens on plaintiffs seeking to enforce antidiscrimination laws, such as interpreting statutes of limitations aggressively.

Holzer, Raphael, and Stoll (2006) have illustrated the prevalence of statistical discrimination and the failure of traditional antidiscrimination laws to curtail it. The authors began by noting that 28 percent of African American males, 16 percent of Hispanic males, and 4 percent of white males would be incarcerated at some point in their lives, and that the median prison sentence was less than two years. As a result, a sizable minority of the male labor pool in the United States consists of people with criminal records.

Their study then surveyed employers about their most recent hire for a position that did not require a college degree. They found that statistical discrimination against African American males is widespread and that employers were using race as a proxy for involvement in the criminal justice system. Surveying their results, the study authors concluded that "the adverse consequence of employer-initiated background checks on the likelihood of hiring African Americans is more than offset by the positive effect of eliminating statistical discrimination" (Holzer, Raphael, and Stoll 2006, 473). The results of this study suggest that curtailing access to criminal history records may actually harm more people than it helps and aggravate racial differences in labor market outcomes.

The implications of this and similar studies on the employment market (Autor & Scarborough 2008; Bushway 2004; Finlay 2008) are chilling, but they should not be surprising. Employers in a variety of sectors admit their heavy reliance on proxies, especially in sorting "good" and "bad" workers from marginalized groups. Employers who expend resources on criminal background checks will be able to sort effectively among those who have had run-ins with law enforcement and those who have not, but other employers will rely on race or other observables as a proxy for criminality, imposing a distasteful sanction on many law-abiding citizens.

Given the deleterious consequences of this predictable behavior, it is worth examining the possible avenues for the state to prevent statistical discrimination. One way to protect disadvantaged groups would be to make them appear indistinguishable from the majority. Indeed, some efforts to reform antidiscrimination law have suggested that statistical discrimination can be mitigated if the relevant decision makers are deprived of information about a candidate's race, religion, or gender (Post 2000). Of course, depriving employers and job seekers of the opportunity to communicate face to face before a job offer is extended and accepted is problematic.

We should therefore consider approaching the statistical discrimination problem from the opposite direction: using the government to help provide decision makers with something that approximates complete information about each applicant. Thus, readily discernable facts like race or gender will not be overemphasized, and more obscure but relevant facts like past job performance or social capital will loom larger. For instance, the state could make available information about all individuals' involvement (or lack thereof) in the criminal justice or bankruptcy systems, publish military records that document individuals' performance and conduct while in the service, or verify and vouch for applicants' educational credentials.

On this theory, a major factor driving unlawful discrimination on the basis of race, ethnic status, gender, or religion is a lack of verifiable information about the individual seeking a job, home, or service. By making the media liable for publishing individuals' criminal histories (*Briscoe v. Reader's Digest Ass'n* 1971) or making it expensive for reporters to obtain aggregated criminal history information that is already in the government's hands (*U.S. Dep't of Justice v. Reporters Comm. for Freedom of the Press* 1989), information privacy protections can run counter to antidiscrimination interests. This behavior makes privacy law and institutional arrangements that obscure information about individuals' reputations far more problematic than courts and theorists presently suppose.

Commercial Disputes and Consumer-Oriented Ratings

Imagine a mundane dispute between a consumer and a service provider: a bank customer orders foreign currency to be delivered to his bank branch and the bank promises to deliver the currency before the customer's departure date, but the currency does not arrive on time due to a bank error. As a result, the customer must pay an additional $100 in higher currency exchange fees abroad. The customer could demand a refund of the extra fees from his bank, but if the bank refuses to pay up, the customer's remedies are not particularly attractive.

The customer could sue the bank for breach of contract, perhaps in small claims court or via an alternative dispute resolution mechanism that the customer may have consented to unwittingly at the time he opened the account. But the opportunity cost of filing suit or pursuing arbitration will easily exceed any potential recovery. The customer could search for similarly situated individuals in the hopes of assembling a class action, but even a successful lawsuit is likely to leave the plaintiffs' lawyers as the primary beneficiaries. Or perhaps the customer could complain to the Federal Reserve, which regulates the bank. An isolated complaint is likely to lead nowhere, but a flurry of similar complaints to the Fed could prompt it to take action. None of these avenues seem particularly promising methods of dealing with a garden-variety dispute.

Enter Epinions, the Better Business Bureau, Yelp, and similar clearinghouses for information about the behavior of companies. The disgruntled customer can post a review of the bank's services on Epinions, a website that might include 145 other reviews of the bank's service—some favorable and some unfavorable. Adding a 146th review would contribute incrementally to a public good. Most Americans have multiple banking options, and consumers who are trying to decide which bank to choose will now have the benefit of a richer range of views. Such a posting might have salutary effects on the bank's future behavior as well, as it tries to improve its service so as to avoid further negative reviews that will scare away potential customers.

We now encounter a puzzle. The state subsidizes the courts to a very significant degree. If the customer chooses to pursue this case in small claims court, state court, or any other similar tribunal, the state will pay the salary of the judges, law clerks, and administrative personnel who help resolve the matter. If, on the other hand, the customer chooses the more sensible route in this case of posting a bad review on Epinions, the state subsidy disappears. On the margins, then, the state is shifting individuals from what will sometimes be the more efficient dispute resolution forum toward a far less efficient dispute resolution forum. (Similar observations have been made about other forms of alternative dispute resolution, as in Pearlstein [2007]).

There is an argument, of course, that whenever litigation occurs, a public good is created. That is, litigation creates precedents, and precedents guide third parties in their efforts to understand what the law requires of them. But litigation is not the only mechanism for achieving such benefits. Consider our bank complaint. In articulating a grievance about his bank, a customer has both encouraged that corporation to respond to the substance of his complaints and made the interested public aware of one data point that reflects on the company's customer service. This is not as valuable as a legal precedent—because it lacks a resolution of the contested issues by a neutral third party, it is more akin to the benefits that would arise if all legal briefs were made public.

Another potential benefit resulting from litigation is the potential for the judgment to defuse a controversy that might otherwise escalate. When the courts resolve an issue, it reduces the probability that the parties will use violence to settle a dispute and that violence could harm both the parties themselves and innocent third parties who get caught in the crossfire. Here again, though, it is by no means clear that court adjudication or administrative action is superior to negative feedback as a mechanism for defusing heated disputes. There is a large psychological literature suggesting that aggrieved individuals feel much better after posting a complaint about another's misconduct, even if the source of the complaint takes no subsequent remedial action (Jones, McCleary, and Lepisto 2002; Mattila and Wirtz 2004; Nyer 2000; Pennebaker 2000). Written venting, simply put, has great psychological value. It provides a release for the frustrated consumer. The process of recalling, describing, and making sense of a negative experience seems to make it easier for consumers to forget those negative experiences and the accompanying angst. It enables a consumer to warn other customers about a merchant's misbehavior. It also raises the likelihood that the merchant will take measures to try to improve the consumer's experience. Customers who have their problems addressed successfully are not quite as happy as customers who never have any problems to begin with, but they are significantly happier than customers whose complaints went unheard (Zeithaml, Berry, and Parasuraman 1996).

Imagine if every plumber, manufactured product, cell phone provider, home builder, professor, hair stylist, accountant, attorney, golf pro, and taxi driver were rated in the same way, with both the detailed written reviews and summary statistics similar to those that Netflix.com provides for movies. In such a world, there would be a diminished need for regulatory oversight and legal remedies because consumers would police misconduct themselves. In such a world, fewer disputes would wind up in court because unscrupulous or inept merchants or service providers would have a harder time finding customers.

The technology for these resources already exists. In some cases, Web sites have already been launched—Avvo for lawyers, RateMyProfessors for college instructors, or AngiesList.com for service companies. That said, these websites lack the large data sets characteristic of Netflix and eBay. Though Netflix customers are quite willing to write reviews of movies, customers of plumbers are a bit more reluctant. Problems arise when that reluctance manifests as a dearth of reviews; if there are only a few evaluations of each plumber, readers may ascribe undue weight to a bogus review written by the plumber's friend or enemy. And although RateMyProfessors sports a handful of student reviews of professors, universities do not allow the export of their own much richer and more reliable data collected from official end-of-the-semester evaluations into those databases. When there is a dearth of reviews and reliability at these websites, there is insufficient incentive for consumers to consult the sites before hiring a service provider or enrolling in a class.

These problems suggest the appeal of subsidizing consumer-oriented ratings websites and other low-cost mechanisms for dispute resolution and avoidance. There is much that government can do in kind to help these resources along as well. In many instances, the government has information about a merchant or service provider's performance that members of the public might lack. For example, only the government and the inspected restaurateur know the contents of public health inspections in many jurisdictions. But there is no reason why this information should not be posted to restaurant rating websites like Yelp and Zagat.com as soon as it becomes available. In a heartening development, New York City's health department created a widget to permit precisely such information dissemination, and Zagat contemplated linking to it (Cardwell 2010).

Similarly, the government may have information about criminal proceedings brought against accountants, state bar disciplinary proceedings brought against attorneys, or public commentary generated by license renewal requests for radio frequency broadcasters. Again, it would be a relatively simple task to aggregate the information that is already in the government's hands and use it to supplement existing privately run rating resources. Yet in many circumstances such as disciplinary actions taken against lawyers, the information is actually suppressed by the government (Levin 2007). Such policies are penny-wise and pound-foolish.

Conclusion

Reputation tracking cannot and will not solve all our problems. But neither can courts, police officers, or regulatory agencies. These various tools of maintaining social order work in concert, and they offer different competencies in varied contexts.

Of this much we can be sure: government strategies designed to increase the transparency of information—especially information that consumers and decision makers will value—are an underutilized arrow in the government's policy quiver. The salary of a single bureaucrat or prosecutor can be redeployed to pay for the aggregation and publication of a great deal of information. If the state is strategic about the sorts of information it gathers and disseminates, then it will have at its disposal an additional, indispensable tool for combating discrimination, fraud, professional incompetence, and various other social ills.

References

Autor, D. H., and D. Scarborough. 2008. Does job testing harm minority workers? Evidence from retail establishments. *Quarterly Journal of Economics* 123 (1): 219–277.

Berg v. Wiley, 264 N.W.2d 145, 149–50 (Minn. 1978).

Briscoe v. Reader's Digest Ass'n, 483 P.2d 34 (Cal. 1971).

Bushway, S. D. 2004. Labor market effects of permitting employer access to criminal history records. *Journal of Contemporary Criminal Justice* 20 (1): 276–291.

Cardwell, D. 2010, August 3. Restaurants complain health dept. web site misleads the public. *New York Times*, p. A17.

Dukeminier, J., et al. 2006. *Property*. 6th ed. New York: Aspen Publishers.

Ellickson, R. C. 1991. *Order without law: How neighbors settle disputes*. Cambridge, MA: Harvard University Press.

Fair Credit Reporting Act, 15 U.S.C. §§ 1681c(a)(2)–(5) (2006).

Finlay, K. 2008, April. Effect of employer access to criminal history data on the labor market outcomes of ex-offenders and non-offenders. National Bureau of Economic Research. *Working Paper Series*, w13936. Retrieved from: <http://ssrn.com/abstract=1121727>.

Holzer, H. J., S. Raphael, and M. Stoll. 2006. Perceived criminality, criminal background checks, and the racial hiring practices of employers. *Journal of Law and Economics* 49 (2): 451–479.

Jones, D. L., K. W. McCleary, and L. R. Lepisto. 2002. Consumer complaint behavior manifestations for table service restaurants: identifying sociodemographic characteristics, personality, and behavioral factors. *Journal of Hospitality and Tourism Research* 26 (2): 105–123.

Kramarsky v. Stahl Mgmt., 401 N.Y.S.2d 943, 944–45 (N.Y. Sup. Ct. 1977).

Levin, L. C. The case for less secrecy in lawyer discipline. *Georgetown Journal of Legal Ethics* 20(1): 1–50.

Mattila, A. S., and J. Wirtz. 2004. Consumer complaining to firms: The determinants of channel choice. *Journal of Services Marketing* 18 (2):147–155.

Nyer, P. U. 2000. An investigation into whether complaining can cause increased consumer satisfaction. *Journal of Consumer Marketing* 17:15–16.

Pearlstein, A. B. 2007. The justice bazaar: Dispute resolution through emergent private ordering as a superior alternative to authoritarian court bureaucracy. *Ohio State Journal on Dispute Resolution* 22:783–788.

Pennebaker, J. W. 2000. Telling stories: The health benefits of narrative. *Literature and Medicine* 19 (1): 3–18.

Post, R. 2000. Prejudicial appearances: The logic of American antidiscrimination law. *California Law Review* 88:14–16.

Rogers, T. K. 2006, November 26. Only the strongest survive. *New York Times*, p. 1.

Schissler, K. B. 2000. Come and knock on our door: The fair debt collection practices act's intrusion into New York's summary proceedings law (note). *Cardozo Law Review* 22:328–329.

Strahilevitz, L. J. 2006. "How's My Driving?" for everyone (and everything?). *New York University Law Review* 81:1699–1765.

Strahilevitz, L. J. 2008a. Lior Jacob Strahilevitz, Reputation nation: Law in an era of ubiquitous personal information. *Northwestern University Law Review* 102:1667–1738.

Strahilevitz, L. J. 2008b. Privacy versus antidiscrimination. *University of Chicago Law Review. University of Chicago. Law School* 75:363–381.

Strahilevitz, L. J. 2011, (forthcoming). *Information and exclusion*. New Haven: Yale University Press.

U.D. Registry, Inc. v. State of California, 40 Cal. Rptr. 2d 228, 233 (Cal. Ct. App. 1995), reaff'd, U.D. Registry, Inc. v. State of California, 50 Cal. Rptr. 3d 647, 667 (Cal. Ct. App. 2006).

U.S. Dep't of Justice v. Reporters Comm. for Freedom of the Press, 489 U.S. 749 (1989).

Zeithaml, V. A., L. L. Berry, and A. Parasuraman. 1996, April. The behavioral consequences of service quality. *Journal of Marketing* 60 (2): 31–35.

III AMPLIFYING SIGNALS

7   The Role of Reputation Systems in Managing Online Communities

Cliff Lampe

Rating and reputation systems typically provide decision support to their users. However, as Cliff Lampe shows, they can also perform more subtle socializing functions—making desirable behaviors clear, supporting community norms, and mitigating the harm from asocial actions.

The first and most familiar use of ratings and implicit feedback is to guide people: to help them choose which items are worth their attention and which people are trustworthy. Systems that guide people about content are often referred to as *recommender systems* (Resnick and Varian 1997; Terveen and Hill 2002) and those that guide people about other people are often referred to as *reputation systems* (Resnick et al. 2000; Dellarocas 2003). For both systems, user ratings and traces of user behavior are made available to help in individual decision making—thus providing *decision-support functions*.

However, in addition to their primary use in decision making, recommender and reputation systems have a valuable secondary use as tools for organizing online interactions. Reputation and assessment are natural parts of online systems and are increasingly being reified in technical systems to help in tasks such as socializing new members and sanctioning normative behavior. Resnick (2001) considers technologies like reputation systems to be important in the construction of "sociotechnical capital," which is the trust and common ground developed in a network through persistent interactions. This trust and common ground helps facilitate collaborative activities between members by reducing the cost of creating shared understanding about goals and tasks. By providing feedback about behavior, penalizing negative actions, signaling desired outcomes, and rewarding users, reputation and recommender systems are providing *socializing functions* and becoming valuable tools for organizing online environments.

Rating Systems for Decision Making versus Community Management

Often, the primary purpose of reputation and other rating systems is to provide decision support. In recommender systems, feedback about products is intended to help potential consumers in cases when options are so numerous or difficult to judge that making a choice between them bears a high cost. Similarly, reputation systems are used with the assumption that "the past is predictive of the future" (Resnick et al. 2000)—that is, with stable pseudonyms or the use of real names, feedback based on evaluation by other users or the accumulation of prosocial behaviors within a system can accurately predict that a user will act in a certain way in the future. Although it is difficult to evaluate each person in an online community individually, reputation systems leverage the collective work of other users to reduce the costs of evaluation. Consequently, reputation information gives an individual user a sense of whom he or she might effectively engage with in a commercial transaction, which person's comments are worth his or her time, or how much administrative privilege a user should have in a content generation system.

However, there are also socializing functions of reputation and rating systems in sociotechnical systems. Receiving explicit feedback from other users is a way for people to learn the effect they've had, which can be essential for learning and enforcing social norms within these spaces, and for socializing new users as they enter the system for the first time. Reputation helps with decisions and also provides important "signals" about users that are essential for the overall governance and maintenance of complex sociotechnical systems.

Examples of Socializing Functions of Rating Systems

Several online services have used reputation systems (either intentionally or otherwise) to shape user behavior.

Slashdot

The technology news and discussion site Slashdot was founded in 1997 and is one of the first examples of complex rating and reputation systems used to assist in site governance. Although the past few years have seen the rise of many competitors, including Digg and Reddit.com, Slashdot continues to be popular, with several hundred thousand users daily accessing the site to read news and user comments.

Slashdot started by having only site administrators rate content, but as the site grew beyond the capacity of this small group to moderate, they identified users whom they could also trust to rate content. Site administrators chose this group of users based on the users' history of posting (an implicit form of feedback) and the tenor of their comments. As the site grew further, site administrators evolved a system by which all users were eligible to participate in moderating content; reputation scores were used to identify which users qualified for the task.

Comments on Slashdot, of which there are several thousand daily, all receive ratings with aggregate scores ranging from −1 to +5. This scoring range is achieved through two processes. First, every comment starts with an initial score based on the reputation of the user posting it, with a range of −1 (for a user with bad reputation), 0 (for an anonymous user), 1 (for a registered user with neutral reputation), or 2 (for a user with good reputation). To provide further discrimination between comments, ratings are assigned by registered users of the site, who are occasionally given "moderator points" that they can use to add to or subtract from the score of a comment. Each user receives only five moderator points at a time, and those points expire in three days. Each moderator can rate a comment only once and may not rate comments in a thread in which they've posted. Additionally, Slashdot has a system of "metamoderation" whereby each rating as described above is reviewed by five users of the site and labeled as "fair" or "unfair."

Users can choose to view only those comments whose score is above a threshold of their choice, that is, only those comments that have been highly rated by the community at large. Users can also gain reputation in the system, which is referred to as "karma." Slashdot karma scores are based on reading behavior, the ratings of comments users have made, the overall number of comments they have made, the number of ratings users have made, and the assessment of users' ratings through the metamoderation system. In addition, some posting behavior may affect the generation of karma disproportionately. Users who had a comment that was initially voted to +5 but who have subsequently been found to be gaming the system may have the comment reduced to −1. However, users typically receive a far stronger reduction in their karma points than the difference between those scores would indicate. Several mechanisms, most of which are closely guarded secrets held by the Slashdot administrators, are designed to punish gaming behavior within the system. Users with poor karma have their comments automatically posted below the viewing threshold, whereas users with high karma have their contributions automatically assigned a higher rating and receive moderation privileges more often. Reputation on this site is being used to enforce norms of contribution by rewarding those users with more privileges within the system.

Previous research has found that the kinds of reputation just described are compelling for people in shaping how they interact on Slashdot (Lampe 2006; Lampe and Resnick 2004). Lampe, Johnston, and Resnick (2005) studied new users on Slashdot, looking at how the ratings on first comments posted to the site predicted future behavior. They found that both positive and negative ratings of a first comment predicted future posting activity, but that not receiving a rating (effectively being ignored by other users) was strongly correlated with departure from the site. Another finding was that users who spent more time reading content before posting had more positive ratings on their first comments. One interpretation of this was that the feedback provided by the rating system allowed users to see what type of content was valued on the site before posting themselves. In a separate study that surveyed registered Slashdot users, Lampe (2006) found that 79 percent of respondents felt that the rating system on the site was important in shaping good discussions, and 84 percent felt that the rating system was important in identifying good comments. In other words, registered users largely agreed that feedback provided by ratings was important in shaping Slashdot's overall social interaction.

Everything2

Everything2.com is a user-generated online encyclopedia started by the founders of Slashdot in 1999, making it older than Wikipedia. Due to a combination of factors including time of launch (before the first dot-com bust) and editorial issues, Everything2 never matched the popularity of Wikipedia. However, it is still a compelling example of sociotechnical interactions. Users submit articles, which are then rated on a +/- scale by other users of the site. Users have reputation scores called "experience" and—at a certain strata of scores (and number of submissions)—gain "levels." The designers of the site had a history of playing fantasy role-playing games both on- and offline, and this structure mimics those game patterns. In a sample of several months in 2010, Everything2 received approximately 1.85 million unique visits per month, of which 85 percent were new visits, largely driven by Google search referrals. There are just under one million articles on the site, which is run by volunteer administrators who self-organize from the user community. As registered users gain levels on the system, they are given more privileges, which include the abilities to vote on others' content, tag items as "cool," use communication tools, and post profile pictures. Each level is associated with more system privileges, creating a direct link between reputation and governance.

Although Everything2 is not as large as many other online communities, it was one of the first to intentionally use reputation and rating systems as a means of governing user behavior. Recent research has shown that even users who are very new to the site and have not bothered to create their own accounts still notice the rating systems on Everything2 and use those rating systems to guide their use of the site (Lampe, Wash, Velasquez, and Ozkaya 2010).

Social Science Theory and Explicit versus Implicit Reputation

Online environments have been accused of fostering miscommunication and bad online behavior due to the effects of *deindividuation*, or the loss of personal identity cues caused by fewer information channels like tone of voice and facial cues (Sproull and Kiesler 1991). According to this research, when we lose the ability to judge information about others that is often supplied through visual and auditory cues, we are both more likely to engage in antisocial behavior (flaming and trolling) and to misinterpret the meaning of the people with whom we're interacting—often assigning malicious motives that may not exist.

However, other researchers have shown that mediated environments can not only foster communication, but in some cases may also have technological characteristics that create new types of interaction. Walther's (1992) theory of Social Information Processing predicts that in mediated environments, people collect cues over time that help them form stable impressions of people they interact with. In particular, he points out that third-party cues "warrant" information about a user and allow for trust between users. These stable cues allow people to form the shared understanding necessary for sustained social interaction.

In a similar vein, Donath (2007) uses research from biology to distinguish between *conventional* signals in mediated systems versus *assessment* signals. Conventional signals are those that are easy to fake; assessment signals are not. Consider the difference between a user who makes a claim (a conventional signal) to be an active participant in a particular forum and a user who is shown to be active through the calculation and display of the number of messages he or she has posted (an assessment signal). In a study of conventional versus assessment signals in Facebook, Lampe, Ellison, and Steinfield (2007) found that assessment signals were better predictors of number of friends on Facebook. In unpublished interviews that we conducted with Facebook users to pretest study assumptions, we found that people looking at new profiles attended to assessment signals like pictures, offline contact information, and wall posts more than conventional signals.

Consequently, by providing information about users, rating systems can act as "cues" or "signals" in online communities, allowing users to reach common ground about each other and facilitating social interaction. The types of ratings that can lead to these socializing functions (i.e., functions that support social interaction) can be user-generated or system-generated.

User-Generated (or Explicit) Reputation

In many cases, reputation is provided directly by users who have interacted with the person being rated. For example, eBay allows members who have bought something from a user to rate that user on multiple dimensions of the sale, such as communication and shipping time, and these ratings are aggregated to make up the reputation of the seller. CouchSurfing.com, a social network site devoted to travel, uses direct reputation feedback both to warrant the person within the system and to provide the information necessary for a traveler to decide if he or she wants to stay in the home of that person. "Endorsements" on LinkedIn provide feedback about a user from someone who has interacted with that person in the past.

Often these explicit ratings are tied to a transaction of some sort. In eBay, it's a commercial transaction, but in Slashdot the transaction is between a poster and reader. Amazon reviewers similarly receive reputation scores based on other users' assessment of their contributions. In Everything2, users receive reputation based in part on user evaluations of their contributions. In the cases described earlier, user reputation is designed to reduce the cost of choosing interaction participants, which is a decision support function of the reputation system. However, in some cases this explicit feedback can also be used to help determine an individual's system privileges.

System-Generated (or Implicit) Reputation

Reputation can also be linked to user behavior that is independent of evaluations by other users. Numbers of posts, accepted stories, replies to others, number of ratings made, and similar metrics are not gathered through explicit ratings, but are still valuable signals. For example, in eBay, the number of times a seller has retracted a bid is made available to buyers thinking of purchasing from that seller. On Digg, one may go to a registered user's profile and see their latest posts and also view aggregates of activity that include number of votes a user has made, stories the user has submitted, comments he or she has written, and the number of views of the user's profile.

In the popular online game World of Warcraft, users advance in levels and gain new items and powers. Elite players gain elite items, which are viewable to all players and act as assessment signals about the skill of the player. If a certain item is available only to dedicated, skilled players, possession of that item acts as a type of reputation cue. On Slashdot, an important signal of reputation was the number associated with each user's name. Slashdot assigns user numbers sequentially, so the lower the number of the user, the longer he or she has been a member of the site. In user interactions, these numbers are often mentioned as a form of reputation at Slashdot. In other systems, "User since [date]" information plays a similar role, analogous to businesses that advertise their date of establishment. Where available and applicable, system-generated reputation may be seen as less gameable by the user population.

Community Mechanisms Enabled by Socializing Functions of Ratings

Both explicit and implicit feedback can help maintain online communities. Helping new users learn about social norms, assisting in the enforcement of those norms, and alerting site administrators to instances in which intervention may be necessary are all mechanisms enabled by socializing functions of ratings.

Enforcing Norms

When ratings and implicit feedback are used to guide other users' choices, they create a system of rewards and sanctions. In the case of eBay, only in the extreme instance of a user with a net feedback score of −5 or lower does the company itself exclude the member. The visibility of feedback profiles to others, however, creates its own rewards and punishments. A good reputation in eBay has commercial value. Resnick et al. (2000) concluded from a field experiment that a good reputation was worth about 8 percent more in revenues as compared to selling under a new identity. Khopkar, Li, and

Resnick (2005) concluded that eBay buyers give more negative feedback to sellers who have recently received other negative feedback, so the natural sanctions associated with any single negative evaluation are amplified by the propensity to get additional negative feedback. Similarly, on conversational sites, simply having one's posts more likely to get noticed creates a reward for posting messages that conform to the conversational norms. Luckily, these types of "information cascades" are brittle and can be disrupted. Rewarding users for supporting minority viewpoints, having editors review homogeneous series of ratings, or metareviewing ratings can all disrupt feedback loops.

The power of reputation systems to establish and enforce social norms in online communities can be a mixed blessing. Social norms are often difficult to detect, are constantly evolving, and are rarely established through design. In rare cases, site creators have designed the reputation system to take advantage of these socializing functions. However, reputation systems can enforce norms that are not intended by the site designer or can lead to antisocial norms in the same way they do prosocial norms.

On Everything2.com, described previously, there is a complex reputation system that is based on both number of articles submitted by a user and the rated value of those articles by other members. Previously, the system was set up to improve a user's reputation primarily by the total number of articles posted by that individual. Consequently, there was a strong incentive to write many short, poor-quality articles, which created the community term "noding for numbers" to indicate the practice. Because the community designers and owners wanted articles that were long and of higher quality, they revised the reputation system to deemphasize the number of articles in favor of user ratings of the articles.

Groups of users may have norms that are contrary to other groups on the site or to the owners of the site. On Slashdot, a small group of users purposely engage in an activity called *trolling*—a term originating in Usenet interaction, which derives from the fishing practice in which a baited line is dragged through an area to attract whatever it can. In online communities, it has come to mean posting purposely incendiary material in order to evoke responses from other users. The same indicators that contribute to user reputation, such as number of votes on and replies to a comment, can also mark successful trolls. Previously on Slashdot, a user account called TrollTalk would track successful trolls based on the reputation of the users responding, the number of moderator points used to respond, and number of replies to the troll comment. In this case, the reputation system is an external marker of successful antisocial behavior that a maladaptive community of users is employing to reward their own norms, which are orthogonal to the norms desired by the administrators of the site.

Socializing New Users

The socializing functions of ratings can help new members to learn norms. For example, at Slashdot, new members can see each message's score and how it was labeled (insightful, funny, troll, etc.) and make inferences about what kinds of messages are valued. A survey of members with new accounts on Slashdot indicated that new users evaluated the ratings of comments before posting their own messages (Lampe and Johnston 2005). Empirically, there is also a positive relationship between the length of time a new user waits before posting his or her first comment and the score of the user's first comment.

Implicit feedback can also be useful. On Wikipedia, edits that violate the norms for content creation on the site (unsupported, nonneutral, controversial, incorrect) are "reverted," which is in effect a deletion. This action constitutes strong feedback to the posting user about the type of content that's appropriate for the site. Without direct communication ever being sent to the user—which is often impossible, given the anonymity of some edits—the implicit feedback of reversion teaches new users about content that should be posted to the site. At Everything2.com, each article is automatically linked to several others based on which articles readers visit directly after viewing the article. Cognizant of the feedback effect that these traversal links will provide, readers sometimes deliberately visit concepts with titles such as "Suggestions for making your contributions better" in order to cause a link to that topic to be inserted into an article. Sometimes the links are more pointed, with links pointing to facetious articles like "Learn how to spell, moran [sic]" or "Cut and paste write ups will die." These links provide quick feedback to the poster about how their contributions are being received by the community already in place on the site, although the links weren't originally designed to be feedback mechanisms.

Informing Administrators

In many online communities, the population of users is too large—and interactions too frequent—for administrators to govern them individually. However, the same systems that provide information to users about each other can provide feedback to administrators about when the appropriate moment for direct intervention has come.

On Slashdot, administrators use a combination of tools to identify problems with user behavior as early as possible. As described previously, metamoderation helps identify problematic moderators by having ratings themselves be rated for fairness by other users. Many other types of ratings-related information are tracked, including sudden changes in a user's reputation, an unusual number of moderator points being spent in a single thread, suspicious correlations between the ratings of two users, and sudden changes in the scores of comments. These are all patterns that can indicate moments when direct intervention is necessary. The information provided by the process of rating reduces the cost to the administrators of finding antisocial users or maladaptive interactions to which they should respond.

On Wikipedia, administrators play essential roles that include setting site policy, locking controversial content, identifying content to post on the front page, and adjudicating articles where there is conflict. These administrators are elected from the pool of editors in a complex process, but to become eligible for election, they must first have submitted many edits of good quality, where quality is defined as surviving the edits of subsequent users. In this case, the implicit feedback from *not* having content deleted and from overall posting behavior is a necessary prerequisite before gaining higher-level administrator functions.

On Facebook, information about relationships between people is important in selecting the content that appears in an individuals' News Feed. The News Feed is a main point of interaction between users on the site. Appearing in a picture together, sending direct messages, or posting on each others' Wall are all indicators that there is a meaningful relationship between users, which Facebook uses to help decide which News Feed content about specific "friends" is seen by users. In this case, interaction between users provides implicit feedback to the system itself about the importance of the relationship.

Future Directions and Implications

One significant change that occurred in online communities approximately between 2005 and 2010 was the reduction in the use of pseudonyms in favor of real names, such as in Facebook and LinkedIn. Previous research has shown that the majority of social network site connections are made in face-to-face encounters. The signals from those physical interactions may compete with—or possibly complement—sociotechnical reputation in online systems. How will reputation play out in social network sites, online dating sites, or online collaboration sites when there are signals available from multiple sources?

For researchers, the interplay between human behavior and technical systems (in this case, ratings) offers opportunities to understand how online environments affect social interaction. Traditional research methods such as surveys, interviews, and experiments need to be combined—where appropriate—with newer methods such as server log analysis and "screen scraping." Disciplines ranging from computer science and communication to economics, sociology, and psychology can add depth to the understanding of reputation-mediated interaction.

There are two clear points to take from this research. First, reputation and recommender systems can provide the feedback necessary to assist in the governance of online communities. Second, feedback provided both directly by users and from site information about a user's behavior is useful in governing online communities.

For the designers and managers of online communities, considering reputation as a feedback system leads to two principles. First, there needs to be an awareness that reputation systems created for decision support will also have a socializing function: whether intended or not, rating systems will have social implications that should be considered as they are being implemented. Second, site designers and managers interested in socializing users should implement feedback systems, even when there are no decision outcomes. It could be that we are missing opportunities to use feedback systems for socialization by not considering socialization as a goal in its own right.

There are great opportunities in the social media landscape for people to participate in novel activities through online discussions, social networking, content generation, and sharing and collaboration with other people. Tools like rating systems can help realize the individual and societal benefits inherent in online community participation. Reputation systems provide useful cues in constrained information channels and give feedback to users that might be difficult to detect in other ways. This information allows people to learn about each other more efficiently. Costs are also reduced for online community managers, which allows quick identification of antisocial behavior.

Most reputation systems research to date has focused on better algorithms for recommendation and on the individual effects of reputation. A stronger group focus—from dyads to massive communities—will allow us to more effectively design online systems that support positive interactions.

References

Dellarocas, C. 2003. The digitization of word of mouth: Promise and challenges of online feedback mechanisms. *Management Science* 49 (10): 1407–1424.

Donath, J. S. 2007. Signals in social supernets. *Journal of Computer-Mediated Communication* 13 (1): 12.

Khopkar, T., X. Li, and P. Resnick. 2005. *Self-selection, slipping, salvaging, slacking, and stoning: The impacts of negative feedback at eBay.* Paper presented at the ACM EC05 Conference on Electronic Commerce, Vancouver, Canada.

Lampe, C. 2006. *Ratings use in an online discussion system: The Slashdot case.* Unpublished doctoral thesis. University of Michigan, Ann Arbor.

Lampe, C., N. Ellison, and C. Steinfield. 2007. *Profile elements as signals in an online social network.* Paper presented at the ACM Conference on Human Factors in Computing Systems (CHI '07), San Jose, CA.

Lampe, C., and E. Johnston. 2005. *Follow the (Slash)dot: Effects of feedback on new members of an online community.* Paper presented at the International Conference on Supporting Group Work (GROUP'05), Sanibel Island, FL.

Lampe, C., E. Johnston, and P. Resnick. 2007. *Follow the reader: Filtering comments on Slashdot.* Paper presented at the ACM Conference on Human Factors in Computing Systems (CHI '07), San Jose, CA.

Lampe, C., and P. Resnick. 2004. *Slash(dot) and burn: Distributed moderation in a large online conversation space*. Paper presented at the Conference on Human Factors in Computing Systems (CHI), Vienna, Austria.

Lampe, C., R. Wash, A. Velasquez, and E. Ozkaya. 2010. *Motivations to participate in online communities*. Paper presented at the ACM Conference on Human Factors in Computing Systems (CHI'10), Atlanta, GA.

Resnick, P. 2001. Beyond bowling together: Sociotechnical capital. In *HCI in the New Millenium*, ed. J. Carroll, 647–672. New York: Addison-Wesley.

Resnick, P., and H. Varian. 1997. Special issue on recommender systems. *Communications of the ACM* 40 (3):56–58.

Resnick, P., Zeckhauser, R., Friedman, E., and Kuwabara, K. 2000. Reputation systems. *Communications of the ACM* 43 (12):45–48.

Sproull, L., and S. Kiesler. 1991. *Connections: New ways of working in the networked organization.* Cambridge, MA: MIT Press.

Terveen, L., and W. Hill. 2002. Beyond recommender systems: Helping people help each other. In *HCI in the New Millennium*, ed. J. M. Carroll, 487–509. New York: Addison-Wesley.

Walther, J. B. 1992. Interpersonal effects in computer-mediated communication: A relational perspective. *Communication Research* 19:52–90.

8   Attention Philanthropy: Giving Reputation a Boost

Alex Steffen

Sometimes there are ideas that should have a stronger reputation, but don't. Without greater recognition, their potential utility is lost to society. Alex Steffen discusses how "attention philanthropy" can amplify these faint signals, helping important ideas enter the mainstream and acting as a reputation booster that redistributes attention.

What Is Attention Philanthropy?

Attention philanthropy is a gift of notice. In a noisy world, deluged in advertising, overrun with PR flacks, and crowded with the superficial, one of the biggest barriers to success for a good idea or noble enterprise can simply be getting noticed in the first place (Shenk 1997).

Even when their intentions are good, the gatekeepers of attention in the media, political, and philanthropic spheres are inefficient in recognizing certain kinds of value. Attention philanthropy is all about shining a light on work that's worth supporting, yet falls outside the notice of the usual sources of funding or acclaim. It is grant making that deals in access, rather than cash; that helps gatekeepers and grant-givers find new investments; and that gives good initiatives their first leg up. Such philanthropy funds innovation that would otherwise not emerge and supports action where none would otherwise be taken.

It is nearly a truism that innovation comes from the fringe of any field, out where strikingly new thinking is taking place. As Thomas Kuhn put it, ideas must be "sufficiently unprecedented to attract an enduring group of adherents away from competing modes" of thought (Kuhn 1996). The problem is that unprecedented ideas tend to fall outside of funding guidelines or journalistic beats, which creates difficulties for philanthropists who wish to support worthwhile innovation. Because the frontier of knowledge is advancing so quickly in sustainability and social change, most people who give away money are increasingly forced to rely upon the judgment of others when making their decisions: no one but the most intensely focused can keep abreast of changes in every field relevant to their work. But relying on individual experts for advice—especially if those experts are long established in their field—can prove problematic if (like many) they have a tendency to resist new ideas—and work, however unintentionally, to aid their own protégées and colleagues, even to the detriment of more meritorious outsiders.

So one challenge is whether we can find truly innovative thinkers without going through the established experts. Can we create a mechanism by which the conflicts of interest experts have can be filtered out, or where enough experts are brought into the conversation that the biases of any one participant will not overly skew the outcomes?

Stewart Brand, in his obscurely famous 1971 "Destination-Crisis" paper for the POINT Board of Directors (Brand 1974), proposed that the answer to the question, "What is most worth doing now?" is probably something that can be discovered only by individuals who move between disciplines and across fields, and among various factions and tribes—people who we might call *circuit riders*.

I suspect that there's something to this idea. If we want to learn what's on the fringes that might be worth bringing to the core, we need to go spend time out on the fringe. Better yet, we need colleagues who live there, who share the strange obsessions, hothouse fads, and passionate convictions of those who spend all their time thinking about what's next and how to make it cooler. In the case of attention philanthropy, the judgment of circuit riders, holistically minded experts, and mavericks can combine to shine a light on future winners.

We're seeing this already on the web. Independent and entrepreneurial nonprofit and public benefit sites like Worldchanging, RealClimate, GOOD, SciDev, Global Voices, and NextBillion have been the epicenters of action in the sustainability and social innovation movements, especially among energetic, youthful, and engaged audiences. Yet the budgets for any of these sites would be—to borrow a phrase I heard from the coordinator of the first Earth Day, Denis Hayes—"a rounding error for most large nonprofits."

These sorts of projects can be cultivated and fed. On the web, the start-up and scale-up costs are low. Social media, in turn, allows multiplier effects previously unseen, meaning that once good work reaches a critical mass of public awareness, it can spread like wildfire. With the right combination of funding and vision, winning formulas can be replicated with new projects and participants—but only if those people and projects can attain a critical mass to begin with. That's why attention philanthropy is so needed.

Of course, this doesn't mean that we shouldn't continue to invest in tried and true solutions, such as refugee relief, hospitals, universities, and large-scale environmental initiatives. But innovation also requires ongoing investment into venture or catalytic philanthropy (Kramer 2009). Each risky bet on a game-changing initiative may or may not pay off; those that do pay off become the received wisdom of tomorrow. The same experts and systems that can be good at implementing existing philanthropy may not be suited to supporting worthwhile innovative philanthropy—and that's where attention philanthropy and circuit riders come in.

Does Attention Philanthropy Work?

How do we know when attention philanthropy succeeds? Perhaps most obviously, we know it works when it leads to larger follow-on funding, growing a promising seed idea to scale. In this sense, it can be seen as complementary to initiatives like the X PRIZE Foundation and the Grand Challenges Explorations grants, which have created competitions at the edge of the possible in which the best performers tend to receive subsequent larger investments (Morgan 2008). In cases in which attention philanthropy leads directly to next-stage funding, it has clearly "worked."

Success can also be measured by coverage in larger media, by increased opportunities to present ideas at conferences, and by explicit citations in documents like government policy papers and design briefs. By clarifying and connecting ideas, attention philanthropy can encapsulate the case for new opportunities in a credible and compelling way.

More intangibly, innovative doers may benefit from finding a larger network of sympathetic doers and supporters—the early adopters and codesigners who can bring their own brilliance to bear on improving and spreading a good idea. In this age of networked action, growing a larger and smarter network can itself be both a sign of a project's success and a necessary stage for its further growth. Such network nurturance is almost inherent in attention philanthropy.

Attention philanthropy has significant potential and could be taken up more widely. It is surprising how little energy goes into sharing, evaluating, and cross-pollinating new ideas and into making the uptake and implementation of new methods more effective. One gets the sense that twentieth-century institutions are struggling against twenty-first-century possibilities.

Meritocracy sits at the very core of the idea of modern democracy. It is a cornerstone of modern societies that the public benefit is maximized when all have equal opportunity to contribute, subject to effort, talent, and interest. However, in the case of today's toughest problems, that meritocracy has broken down. The need for bold, holistic innovation has outstripped the ability of many traditional avenues of meritocracy to respond. Academia, the media, foundations, and investors all have legacy practices and social filters that may serve to exclude needed new ideas—or at the very least to delay their recognition for years. We don't have the luxury of this inefficiency any more.

How Could Reputation Enable More Effective Attention Philanthropy?

There have been modest attempts to make money and attention available based on ratings by "the attention of crowds." Kickstarter.com is an example. It's a website where people post pitches and solicit support for projects that they'd like to work on—for example, "I need $3,000 to complete this documentary film." If they raise enough, everybody pays—if not, nobody pays.

However, such systems run the risk of devolving into zero-sum popularity contests in which a sophisticated microenterprise system for slum-dwellers, say, may lose to a cutely named feel-good initiative to provide homes for wayward puppies. Simply aggregating votes may result in seeing only which option sounds best to large groups, few members of which may have insight about which approaches are truly effective, novel, or scalable. Although initiatives that win such popularity contests can be worthwhile, they tend to be insufficiently innovative as far as unusual solutions are demanded. Sometimes, of course, they lack substance altogether: popularity is no guarantee of effectiveness.

That's why *curated participation* is critical. Experience suggests that attention philanthropy works best when preference is given to ideas and ratings by people who understand the deeper issues at play and the reasons why an idea has long-term potential—especially if such people have themselves been innovators.

The challenge is that smart, experienced people tend to also be busy people. How can we harvest quick insights from people who have a lot to say? How can attention philanthropy systems adjust the roles of participants based on demonstrated competence?

To suggest some answers to these questions, we imagine a reputation-enabled future incarnation of the Worldchanging attention philanthropy project, and ask what kind of functions it might or should support.

First, the curation of participants could be made easier and more systematic. In the past, Worldchanging simply asked people we thought very highly of what projects and people they would recommend—acting as a sort of reputation boost by passing around a megaphone, as it were. There is a certain degree of network effect to this, so one option for the future is to see whether "friends of friends" or other reputational mechanisms can be used to find people from outside the usual networks or from geographic regions that are usually not heard from. What if we could easily bring in the most insightful voices from Uganda or Afghanistan, for instance, when evaluating policy or philanthropic initiatives?

Second, there is a natural opportunity to draw from the moderation and metamoderation used in systems like Slashdot (see chapter 7). If begun with a core of participants who themselves represent the kind of circuit riders, holistically minded experts, and mavericks whose insight we seek to tap, standards of excellence and innovative thought could become part of the culture of the attention philanthropy effort from the start. Moderation and metamoderation could help an attention philanthropy site make more effective use of an expanding set of evaluators and trend spotters. This change would help identify new participants (perhaps initially unknown to the others) who are good at finding new and worthwhile initiatives.

Third, new participants might be organically brought on board by a combination of having existing participants rate or refer new users and demonstrating competence by gradually increasing contributions. Imagine an online semiautomated seminar course that would evaluate people while getting them up to speed in a field of interest. Imagine a series of tasks both fun to do and useful to the attention philanthropy system whose successive completion increased the reputation of new contributors. Those who successfully completed such tasks would demonstrate competence, drive, and an ability to contribute.

Fourth, core participants and a much larger occasional user base could become mutually supportive through the use of reputation and filtering systems. The larger user base could become fans of core participants whose work they especially value, making those participants proxies for larger groups of people. Being able to follow and show support for brilliant people would be a natural system function. Suppose that there is a group of ten or a hundred high achievers whom the user trusts or finds inspiring. Imagine that each item liked by such an evaluator gets a little credibility boost in the users' personalized experience of the site—or of the web as a whole. Wouldn't the collective set of ideas that this group reads and likes be worthwhile to the user? Why not use such a group as a collective filter on ideas and opportunities?

Fifth, with such personalized user site experiences, the impact of crowdfunding could be leveraged. Already, crowdfunding sites like Kickstarter or Kiva.org serve to connect users with opportunities to give to causes that inspire them as individuals. (See chapter 9 in this volume.) Attention philanthropy systems could make sure that users see causes that are more likely to connect with their expressed values and interests, increasing the likelihood that they'll give to and promote those causes. It could also lead to communities of crowdfunders who coalesce around high-reputation core participants.

A linked tactic might be to collect revenue (from foundation gifts, major donations, membership dues, or user fees) and distribute some fraction of this revenue to the initiatives with the best reputation—or even to ask high-reputation people within the system to themselves redistribute some of the money raised. When a foundation or rich individual wants to give away a large amount of money, might it not be worthwhile to allocate some fraction of it to a range of people with outstanding reputations and achievements, to themselves give to less obvious seed opportunities? This might act as a "high-risk, high-return" part of a giving portfolio—a sort of distributed MacArthur grant program.

Finally, a more subtle and long-term tactic is suggested by the fact that the cutting edge of innovation is advancing more rapidly than the diffusion of such innovation (Rogers 2003). In other words, development of good solutions is moving more rapidly than diffusion of those good solutions into the mainstream. This problem is compounded when tackling complex interlinked problems such as climate change, poverty, and security. Isolated solutions do not work as well as holistic solutions, and these problems should therefore be viewed as parts of one big problem, with useful advances coming from the frontiers of many disciplines.

Telling stories about these kinds of problems is difficult and has been a major spur to the rise of solutions-based journalism (which examines complex problems through the lens of innovative solutions). To coalesce ideas about complex problems and solutions requires planetary thinking and transdisciplinary insight and a new breed of "renaissance journalists." Being able to incorporate reputation systems into attention philanthropy will provide a positive feedback loop for information and help solutions-based journalists find more innovative solutions to cover. Conversely, good solutions-based reporting will help improve attention philanthropy. Indeed, in a time when money for doing good journalism has become increasingly scarce, investing in solutions-based reporting offers another potentially exciting application for the crowdfunding function of an attention philanthropy system.

Attention Philanthropy Challenges

Attention philanthropy does face significant challenges. The most obvious have to do with the difficulty of getting such systems built and operational in the first place. This is a challenge that can probably only be met by risk-taking philanthropists and hard-working participants, who together establish effective practices and an innovation-friendly organizational culture. Another hurdle to building a reputation-enabled attention philanthropy system is making the case for its importance and feasibility, and then assembling a core team to overcome technical, cultural, and financial barriers.

Then, too, there is the difficulty that although attention philanthropy is designed to extend meritocratic selection to a more entrepreneurial and innovative group of people and projects, it ironically probably can't work without strong filters on participation in the attention philanthropy process itself. Users need to reach common understanding and shared assumptions about complex topics to allow meaningful deliberation and debate. They need to grasp the scope, scale, and speed of the problems being addressed and to understand the degree to which large, interconnected systems are at work in these problems. This is a bigger challenge than many people realize; it's all too easy to assume simple answers—compact fluorescent bulbs or local food—are the solution, when we barely understand the problem.

Gatekeepers and funders may themselves offer a cultural barrier to implementation of attention philanthropy systems. They are not always interested in creating an impartial record of their impact, giving up power to allocate resources, or losing control over the spotlight—especially if having that control returns social benefits in their lives, like getting invited to exclusive conferences and dinner parties. Not everyone supposedly working for social change is doing it entirely for altruistic reasons, and some career-minded funders and gatekeepers may consider attention philanthropy to be a threat to their advancement. It would be naïve to expect that any redistribution of the power to select and fund (even if ultimately beneficial to all parties' expressed goals) will not encounter some resistance.

On the technical side, systems such as Slashdot have demonstrated metamoderation for news (see chapter 7 in this volume). However, no similar system yet exists to evaluate complex innovations, and to evaluate the evaluators of such innovations.

Conclusion

On a planet hurtling with great speed toward an interconnected series of crises, we desperately need better ideas, applied more quickly, by a wider group of people. We need more spotlights searching the gloom for innovative projects and ideas.

Much of the operation of democracy has been a function of selection by elites. It would be easy to make the case that a relatively small number of people still control most media, political levers of power, and pools of investment. In the past, it was often presumed that by strictly controlling access to the institutions of power, the most able people were put in positions to make decisions for the public good (while often also benefiting themselves).

Now, however, we see an unprecedented surplus of the capacity to do innovative good, yet a dearth of access to the resources and attention needed to do it. The rise of attention philanthropy is an answer to this contradiction. The goal is not to create a new closed elite, but rather to make the allocation of resources and attention more insightful and effective—to speed the process of recognizing good opportunities and good opportunity evaluators.

Attention philanthropy does not need to operate at a huge scale to succeed at offering huge impacts. The goal doesn't need to be changing how every dollar is given or how every story is assigned: simply increasing the flow of world-changing projects and people into the system will result in echo effects throughout the system, more strongly connecting the mainstream to the leading waves of innovation and speeding the uptake of good ideas throughout society. Attention philanthropy, done right, is a scale multiplier. And that is precisely what we'll need to meet the challenges of the chaotic and fast-changing century ahead of us.

References

Brand, Stewart. 1974. Destination-crisis. In *The seven laws of money*, M. Phillips. New York: Random House.

Kramer, M. R. 2009. Catalytic philanthropy. *Stanford Social Innovation Review* Fall:30–35.

Kuhn, Thomas S. 1996. *The structure of scientific revolutions.* 3rd ed. Chicago, IL: University of Chicago Press.

Morgan, J. G. 2008. Inducing innovation through prizes. *Innovations* 3 (4):105–117.

Rogers, Everett M. 2003. *Diffusion of innovations.* 5th ed. New York: Free Press.

Shenk, David. 1997. *Data smog: Surviving the information glut.* San Francisco: Harper Edge.

9 Making Use of Reputation Systems in Philanthropy

Marc Maxson and Mari Kuraishi

"Peer-to-peer philanthropy" leverages online systems to connect donors directly with charitable causes, but it can still be difficult to determine which worthy-sounding projects achieve real impact. Marc Maxson and Mari Kuraishi suggest how reputation information in philanthropy can overcome this gap, drawing lessons from their GlobalGiving platform.

Lack of Reputation Information in International Philanthropy

There are millions of registered nongovernmental organizations (NGOs) around the world and very limited resources to support them. There is a need for a functional reputation system in international philanthropy, because donors, organizations, and clients rarely interact with each other in person. Without open communication between the stakeholders in international development, there is little trust. And without a trust network to validate members, a reputation system cannot develop.

The principal actors in the not-for-profit or social sector are donors (who can be foundations or individuals), staff at NGOs (who carry out the work), and the "clients" (who benefit from the work). One would hope that the good reputation of an NGO would be primarily determined by doing good work for clients, but this is only one part of their overall reputation-building strategy. Some NGOs maintain a good reputation through direct marketing, by engaging media, and by enlisting leaders who will protect their reputation. Others sustain support by personally courting donors who base their funding decisions on impressions gathered from personal relationships.

Donors and clients also have reputations from the organization's point of view. Clients may be reliable sources of information about the work being done in the community. Donors may be known as reliable funders, when there is evidence that the work outputs are desirable.

We consider a reputation system for philanthropy to be a set of tools that guide donors in making funding decisions. The ideal reputation system enhances both the flow (quantity) of money as well as the impact (quality) of the money spent by providing donors with the means to identify the most deserving organizations. Existing formal systems have used several factors to determine reputation, including ratings based on accounting and overhead (Charity Navigator, BBB Wise Giving), feedback from those with whom the nonprofit has interacted (GreatNonprofits), and fund-raising effectiveness and responsiveness to donors (GlobalGiving).

The most widely-recognized barrier in philanthropy is distrust of NGOs by potential donors, since NGOs have sometimes failed to allocate resources as promised. NGO mistrust of other NGOs also prevents collaboration, such as when there is a reputation risk to an organization of being associated with fraud (Brown and Moore 2001). More recently, target populations have become increasingly suspicious of noncommunity-based NGOs. These NGOs are forced to make additional efforts to gain the cooperation of the people they serve (Muttart Foundation 2006; Brown and Moore 2001). All three parties would benefit from a global reputation system.

There are four kinds of relationships in which greater trust would be particularly helpful:

1. Relationships between donors and organizations
2. Relationships between organizations and other organizations
3. Relationships between clients and organizations
4. Relationships between donors and clients

The limited interactions between donors and clients cause a *principal-agent problem* in international philanthropy: donors allocate funding to organizations with imperfect information on beneficiary (client) needs. Lack of information can cause donor backlash against NGOs that fail to allocate resources as promised. This backlash has severe and broad-scale consequences on philanthropy in general, as donors appear to treat misuse of their donations as a breach of trust that is "nearly impossible to repair" (Arumi et al. 2004). Reinhardt argues that "as [NGOs] strive to be more efficient in operating and maintaining donor relationships, they can lose effectiveness in serving their target populations" (Reinhardt 2009: 284).

The difficulty in building trust is that the reputations of most NGOs are based on cursory experience and limited engagement. Many donors spend more time reading articles about NGO mismanagement in the news than they will spend reading a funding appeal sent to them in the mail. The average donor spends about 30 seconds reading an NGO fund-raising letter before deciding to act or discard (Vogele 1992; Dixon 2008). If a reputation system (one that genuinely helped to overcome these trust issues) were widely adopted in philanthropy, we believe more support could be mobilized for nonprofit organizations and more aid provided to client populations.

Factors of a Reputation System: Indices and Signals

An organization's reputation is determined by *indices* (immutable attributes) and *signals* (flexible attributes) (Reinhardt 2009). The age of an organization is one example of an index. Organizations that have been around longer are more reputable, and it is hard for them to falsify this attribute. Perceived level of professionalism and the size of an organization's donor base are both signals. The organization can improve its reputation or attract broader support by improving these kinds of signals.

Which signals most affect the behavior of individual donors is a matter of debate. Recent research indicates that about 30 percent of affluent donors have sought out information about the NGOs they give money to (Hope Consulting 2010). Research has been largely focused on which signals foundations react to. (Reinhardt 2009). However, it is also worth considering the signals that individual donors value. If a system conveys clear and honest signals to donors and does so efficiently, the most effective organizations should attract the greatest support.

Just as successfully completing projects is a sign of credibility to potential donors for future projects, failure in the eyes of one institution can spell doom for that organization with other donors. In the words of the leader of one NGO, "I can't get IDB [Inter-American Development Bank] money if I drop the ball with the World Bank" (Reinhardt 2009). In an unregulated marketplace, where reputations are not systematically maintained, mere allegations of misconduct can "blackball" an organization.

A Reputation System for International NGOs

GlobalGiving.org is a nonprofit online marketplace that connects people who have community- and world-changing ideas with people who can support them. It provides reputation information primarily to donors about hundreds of NGOs in more than a hundred countries. Individuals seek this reputation information because they are considering giving money to an NGO. Some charitable foundations also use the platform to verify that an organization is reputable prior to grant making.

GlobalGiving began as a website for connecting people with money to people with ideas. To offer donors the best ideas and organizations, GlobalGiving had to provide each organization with the means to establish its reputation. Interpersonal relationships—specifically, endorsements by trusted friends and colleagues who ask others to give—ultimately dictate fund-raising success for most organizations, and fund-raising success is the final measure of reputation in philanthropy. Therefore, GlobalGiving monitors signals from the members of each organization's social network.

We started by working with organizations that had been vouched for by umbrella organizations such as Tech Museum, World Bank Development Marketplace, and Ashoka. These umbrella organizations use a variety of methods for recognizing good ideas. Tech Museum awards a recognition prize to organizations, which we accepted as sufficiently credible to allow prize-winning organizations to post projects. Ashoka vets individual social entrepreneurs and provides them with money to pursue their innovative solutions. If an Ashoka fellow chose to form an NGO, then that NGO was invited to post projects. This approach served to expand our network rapidly at first, but the trusted partner approach was ultimately limited by our capacity to coordinate closely with a large number of intermediaries.

In all cases, we were still required to double-check financial documentation, so by 2007 we started vetting organizations from scratch. We began by determining whether an organization was equivalent to a U.S. 501(c)3 organization, as required by U.S. tax law. We found that many organizations doing good work were ineligible because they were not registered in their host countries, lacked oversight by community members or a board, or had simply not existed long enough to have any budget information. A document-based approach for vetting new members was defensible and minimized legal risk, but was not scalable and was limited by the quality of the documentation. There was no guarantee that it would select for high-impact organizations.

In 2009, we started adding two crucial elements to our vetting process. These were designed to verify that a community knows about and supports the organization. We examined the organization's social media footprint on the Internet and also required new organizations to raise fifty donations in the first month, thereby demonstrating that people support them. Those that failed to attract at least fifty donations were given additional training and invited to try again. In 2010, we began experimenting with another approach: asking people in communities across Kenya to share a story about a "community effort" they had witnessed. This process gathered nearly 3,000 stories in 3 months, reflecting local knowledge of 242 organizations. We are now using this data to identify and invite new organizations with demonstrated community endorsement.

Donor Experience and Trust Signals

Our reputation system is different from many others because the principal unit is a specific activity of an organization, not the organization itself or one of its staff. One organization can have several activities posted on the site. Donations received are restricted to specific activities and cannot be redirected to overhead or to another project without the consent of the donor.

Our user testing confirms that several signals on the project description page first draw prospective donors' attention. The first item is the project title, which is usually a call to action ("Send a child in India to school for a year, #1877") or a description of the intended outcome ("A retired cheetah teaches poor South African youth, #2540"). After reading the title of the project, users typically look at the project photos. We advise organizations to present images of ongoing project activities and beneficiaries. Organizations whose beneficiaries are willing to appear on the site find their own reputations enhanced. Research has found that people respond more generously to images that create empathy, particularly close-cropped photos of one face with eyes locked in a gaze with the donor.

The next point of attention on the project page is the list of *value outcomes*, which are specific deliverables that the individual can expect a donation of a certain size to achieve. For example, the project "Send a child in India to school for a year, #1877" publishes the value outcome: "$40: Provides 1 child with quality education for 1 year." Another value outcome is: "$50: Provides stationery/books to 1 centre for 6 months." These outcomes communicate the core activities of the project to donors. This format also reinforces our message to project administrators that donations to the project are intended solely for these types of value outcomes (called *restricted funding* in the non-profit world).

The value of the outcome relative to its cost sends a signal to donors about the effectiveness of the organization in carrying out the work. If a particular project promises to carry out a significant activity at a modest cost, this signals to prospective donors that the organization doing the project probably has low overhead. Overhead costs in philanthropy have spawned a vigorous debate recently (Pallotta 2008; Schimmelpfennig 2009; Handy and Katz 1999), and donor reluctance to support NGOs with high overheads reflects an inherent distrust. Our approach to building trust is to encourage all organizations to break down broad goals into specific projects and itemize value outcomes into specific donation options, as this sets clear expectations for both donors and project leaders.

The next signal that donors focus on is previous financial support for the project. On every project description page, we publish the number of past donations, the total amount raised, and the fund-raising goal of the organization for that project. For example, project #1877 had 2,355 donations for a total of $92,531 at the time this article was written. Also published was the amount remaining of $7,468 in order to reach the $100,000 goal for this project. If 100 percent of donors chose the school fees rather than the school supplies donation option, we would predict that the organization would be writing to inform donors that 2,500 children had received a full stipend to attend public school that year at the completion of the project's funding. In reality, the actual number will vary due to inexact cost estimates, but the proximity of the actual number of children served versus the expected number is yet another signal that the project is well managed. More broadly, positive online signals generate offline "buzz" through word-of-mouth referrals to friends and family of donors and spread through other online social networks—ultimately increasing a project's success.

Project Updates

The reason individual donors receive frequent information from project leaders about the ongoing progress of the project that they chose to support is because we require every project leader to email a quarterly update to all donors. Those that fail to comply lose the right to accept donations until an update is posted. Donors who receive regular messages trust the organization more. Updates with honest, engaging content also build a personal relationship between the donor and the organization. The total number of updates posted by an organization for the project may also serve as an index measure for the project's reputation, analogous to how the age of an organization affects its overall reputation among donors (Reiner and Wolpert 1981). We rank the order in which projects appear in search results based on a project's track record of informing donors (40 percent) and their relative fund-raising performance (donations, dollars raised, and proximity to their funding target: 60 percent).

Along with an organization's historical track record, project updates have the greatest potential to affect the project's reputation and that of the implementing organization. The required quarterly self-reports force organizations to manage their reputations by building a history of activities and ongoing statistics about the immediate impact of donations. We invite donors to comment, asking them, "Was this update helpful?" A "No" vote helps an organization improve communication with donors. This feedback is similar to many other online reputation systems such as Amazon's, except that we direct the discussion to be around the report, not the organization. Donors hesitate to criticize an organization, but will provide useful feedback about a specific report.

Aggregating this feedback into a measure of reputation has been impractical due to insufficient comments, but community feedback through our Kenya storytelling pilot study shows that community members are eager to talk about local organizations. Sorting out whether there is self-reporting bias in this feedback can be challenging, but it is possible by looking for patterns in narratives (i.e., clusters of feedback through just a few individuals, stories with identical elements, and insider knowledge about projects).

As we become able to improve the quantity and reliability of feedback, we intend to incorporate this signal into our project ranking system. Ultimately, we plan to broaden the scope of feedback to partners and beneficiaries, which will provide a 360-degree view of the organization's work, make rankings harder to game, and distinguish those organizations willing to open themselves up to feedback as organizations signaling a commitment to transparency and learning.

Postcards and Neighborly Advice

We recently introduced a "visitor postcards" program, which allows third-party travelers and volunteers who visit a project to report on what they saw and heard during their visit. The postcard format is narrative, brief (fewer than 750 words), and in the traveler's own voice—like an actual postcard. We hypothesize that informal reports from nonprofessionals carry more weight with individual donors than formal reports.

It is important to note that if asked, most donors would *say* that formal evaluations carry more weight with them (Gilbert et al. 2009; Reinhardt 2009). A recent survey found that 85 percent of affluent donors care about NGO performance, yet only 30 percent of them do any research before giving (Hope Consulting 2010). Reinhardt's survey in Brazil found that organizations that received third-party audits attracted more than double the funds of their competitors (Reinhardt 2009), showing that funding organizations do value audits. However, we find that—like affluent donors in the survey—the vast majority of people do not actually read the supplemental documentation on the project page, including formal evaluations.

When actual usage of reports is included in the equation, the cost-benefit ratio of providing formal evaluations may not warrant the added value. It would be far more beneficial to increase the number of brief eyewitness accounts posted for each project by visitors, and eventually by community members themselves. (By tracking the social network of community members posting these reports, we believe we can detect and eliminate "gaming" of the system.)

Likewise, organizations themselves do not value extensive reports if they know that the reports generated will not influence future funding. In 2000, Light wrote that NGOs expressed "some concern that scarce resources are being used more to jump through the hoops than actually serve clients" (Light 2000). Postcards strike a balance between effective oversight and effective donor engagement. More often than not, visits are such a rewarding experience that nearly all visitors desire the opportunity to spread the good news about the project, so we have a very low drop-off rate between those who confirm a visit and those that follow up by sending a postcard.

The postcard tool is based on the "power of neighborly advice" (Gilbert et al. 2009; Epley and Dunning 2000). Research has shown that people are more apt to make smart decisions when they rely on the opinion of a person who has firsthand knowledge of the situation than when they are provided with a complete summary of the facts. This effect is especially pronounced when the question of whether to trust another individual is involved (Bolton, Katok, and Ockenfels 2005). People choose the trustworthy stranger more often when first given the chance to talk to a third party who has met the stranger than when provided with a report or other proxy index of trust (Gilbert et al. 2009).

This "neighborly advice" effect has ramifications for international philanthropy in two ways. First, it emphasizes the importance of third-party reports in helping donors make smart decisions. Second, it explains why the majority of successful fund-raising depends on a single determinant: whether donors are asked to give by a known, trusted person. The power of neighborly advice is also surprising because several authors conclude that people who make smart decisions based on neighborly advice still express a lack of belief that such advice is as reliable as a set of facts, or formal evaluation (Gilbert et al. 2009).

Bad News?

So how do organizations respond to postcards that contain negative comments? This remains a complex issue to resolve. For a charitable organization, the purpose of joining GlobalGiving is to increase fund-raising, and negative comments undermine the organization's goal.

In the few cases where comments have a critical tone, we encourage organizations to respond with a follow-up report on how they plan to address the issues raised by the unimpressed visitor. Our goal is to create a visual representation of each organization's social network, support, and daily activities, so that those obviously trying to help stand out from the shams. We hypothesize that organizations that respond well to external criticism are also likely to incorporate the preferences of communities they serve, increasing community appreciation of (and therefore increasing community involvement with) the effort. Our ongoing efforts aim to test this hypothesis by finding new ways to gather feedback from beneficiaries in real time via SMS and the web.

A greater challenge than managing negative reports is the tendency of most visitors to self-censor negative information from postcards. In many cases, the postcard sender will email a private note raising concerns he or she does not wish to present publicly, despite clear directions to be completely honest about all aspects of the project. Complete honesty actually improves the trustworthiness of the report because readers tend to regard exclusively positive or negative reports with suspicion. Groups of donors appear to discredit reports based on what they lack, as well as what they contain. They can sift through the conversation between project leaders and other donors and reach conclusions about the trustworthiness of the organization. Thus, three important criteria for the emergence of an effective reputation system are: creating the space for the conversation, maintaining an open discourse, and encouraging honesty.

Filtering is also possible with Twitter. GlobalGiving has encouraged Kenyan organizations to adopt Twitter and use it to build rapport with prospective donors. It was instructive to discover that one project leader—who would later emerge as an individual having a very poor relationship with the youth he served in his community—was unable to turn his Twitter monologue into a conversation. At least five other Kenyans new to Twitter in the same period naturally started to form an interactive social network, but this one problem individual was always 100 percent "on message." (Despite its power to broadcast, people who use Twitter exclusively as a broadcast rather than an interactive communications channel ultimately fail to capture the full value of Twitter, because they are recognized as individuals who are not really interested in hearing from others—they might as well have been paying for ads on TV.) In fifty messages, he never mentioned another staffer, friend, or beneficiary by name and never discussed any aspect of his own life outside of the project. Moreover, many of his messages had heuristic similarities to spam or phishing. The individual asked for money in nearly every message, but failed to recognize the importance of building relationships first.

Elements of an Effective Reputation System

Comments by donors and votes on project reports are active forms of feedback and as such have limitations on reliability due to factors like inherent biases and information constraints (Wierzbicki and Nielek 2008). Use of complementary passive feedback mechanisms can enhance the reliability of information from active feedback. For example, our system aggregates donor behavior and project performance into its search ranking algorithm, so that projects with better reputations appear toward the top of search results and thus gather greater support.

From our point of view, the most important challenge for us to address is the challenge of client (or beneficiary) feedback. Client feedback shortcuts the principal-agent problem we identified earlier in this chapter among donors, NGOs, and clients. It redresses the asymmetry of power that is implicit in the donor-NGO-client chain and extends voice to the client part of the chain that has traditionally been the most silent. Because client voice has traditionally been underrepresented, amplifying it has the most potential for innovation, change, and dynamism—the history of business and technology has shown that innovation often emerges from the periphery and that such innovation has the biggest potential to disrupt business as usual.

The evidence from our pilot activities around beneficiary feedback suggests that there is a challenge of scale—in particular, a challenge of finding a low-cost solution that will gather sufficient community feedback to provide a realistic view of community-based organizations. Technological advances (Short Message Service—SMS) and technological penetration (six in ten people in the world have cell phones) are making new forms of interaction available, but there will have to be an accompanying shift in behavior to ensure sufficient, ongoing, and real-time feedback flow.

Real-time online gaming societies like World of Warcraft may suggest one approach to this challenge. They have become useful learning environments for trust research; addictive activities generate more data (Donath 2007; Bainbridge 2007). As feedback loops begin to directly benefit the participants, maintaining a reputation system becomes easier.

The evolution of GlobalGiving's reputation system for NGOs may reflect some general stages in the evolution of any reputation system. We began with a small network of sponsoring organizations in which every organization was vouched for by a trusted partner. Eventually, we transitioned to an open system in which we could work with any organization that met a set of benchmarks. In lieu of a chain of trust, we turned to vetting the social network willing to support the new partner. We examined its funders, referral sources, and the size of its donor support base as part of the vetting process.

Emerging organizations with an insufficient support base are sequestered and offered capacity training; they are not part of the website. The next phase will incorporate local community feedback, allowing organizations to both demonstrate local support and receive valuable dashboard data with which to design and improve their activities. This feedback will also provide them with a means of establishing a reputation that can help them attract financial support at a greater rate. In the longer term, making use of reputation systems in philanthropy can motivate more and smarter giving and suggest lessons for the introduction of reputation systems into other areas of society.

References

Arumi, A. M., R. Wooden, J. Johnson, S. Farkas, A. Duffett, and A. Off. 2004, December 31. The charitable impulse: Those who give to charities and those who run them talk about what's needed to keep the public trust. *Public Agenda*. Retrieved from: <http://www.publicagenda.org/reports/charitable-impulse>.

Bainbridge, W. S. 2007. The scientific research potential of virtual worlds. *Science* 317 (5837): 472–476.

Bolton, G. E., E. Katok, and A. Ockenfels. 2005. Cooperation among strangers with limited information about reputation. *Journal of Public Economics* 89 (8): 1457–1468.

Brown, L. D., and M. H. Moore. 2001. Accountability, strategy, and international nongovernmental organizations. *Nonprofit and Voluntary Sector Quarterly* 30 (3): 569–587.

Dixon, C. R. 2008. *The complete guide to writing successful fundraising letters for your nonprofit organization*. Ocala, FL: Atlantic Publishing Company.

Donath, J. 2007. Computer science: Virtually trustworthy. *Science* 317 (5834): 53–54.

Epley, N., and D. Dunning. 2000. Feeling "holier than thou": Are self-serving assessments produced by errors in self- or social prediction? *Journal of Personality and Social Psychology* 79 (6): 861–875.

Gilbert, D. T., M. A. Killingsworth, R. N. Eyre, and T. D. Wilson. 2009. The surprising power of neighborly advice. *Science* 323 (5921): 1617–1619.

Handy, F., and E. Katz. 1999, May 13. CharityVillage® research: Are nonprofits getting more by paying less? Retrieved from: <http://www.charityvillage.com/cv/research/rcar6.html>.

Hope Consulting. 2010. Money for good: The U.S. market opportunity for impact investments and charitable gifts from individual donor and investors. Retrieved from: <http://www.hopeconsulting.us/pdf/Money%20for%20Good_Final.pdf>.

Light, P. C. 2000. *Making nonprofits work*. Washington, DC: Brookings Institution Press.

Muttart Foundation. (2006). Talking about charities 2006: Tracking Canadians' opinions about charities and the issues affecting them. Retrieved from: <http://www.muttart.org/sites/default/files/downloads/TAC2006-03-CompleteReport.pdf>.

Pallotta, D. 2008. *Uncharitable: How restraints on nonprofits undermine their potential.* Lebanon, NH: Tufts University Press.

Reiner, T. A., and J. Wolpert. 1981. The non-profit sector in the metropolitan economy. *Economic Geography* 57 (1): 23–33.

Reinhardt, G. Y. 2009. Matching donors and nonprofits: The importance of signaling in funding awards. *Journal of Theoretical Politics* 21 (3): 283–309.

Schimmelpfennig, S. 2009, May 20. Good intentions are not enough: Charity ratings based on administration costs can do more harm than good [web log post]. Retrieved from: <http://informationincontext.typepad.com/good_intentions_are_not_e/2009/05/emphasis-placed-on-the-percent-charities-spend-on-administration-can-actually-lead-to-increased-wast.html>.

Vogele, S. 1992. *Handbook of direct mail: The dialogue method of direct communication.* Englewood Cliffs, NJ: Prentice Hall.

Wierzbicki, A., and R. Nielek. 2008. Fairness emergence through simple reputation. In *Proceedings of TrustBus '08: Proceedings of the 5th International Conference on Trust, Privacy, and Security in Digital Business*, ed. S. Furnell, S. Katsikas, and A. Lioy, 79–89. Berlin, Heidelberg: Springer-Verlag.

IV SUPPORTING SCIENCE

10   The Measurement and Mismeasurement of Science

Michael Nielsen

The public has a natural desire to maximize its return on investment for science funding, which has made reputation measures for scientific research increasingly influential. Michael Nielsen warns of the dangers of overreliance on any single metric of success, suggesting instead a more diverse approach to deciding which risky endeavors to support collectively—a perspective with implications beyond science.

Albert Einstein's greatest scientific "blunder" (his word) came as a sequel to his greatest scientific achievement. That achievement was his theory of gravity—the general theory of relativity—which he introduced in 1915. Two years later, in 1917, Einstein ran into a problem while trying to apply general relativity to the universe as a whole. At the time, Einstein believed that on a large scale, the universe is static and unchanging. But he realized that general relativity predicts that such a universe can't exist: it would spontaneously collapse in on itself. To solve this problem, Einstein modified the equations of general relativity, adding an extra term involving what is called the *cosmological constant*, which— roughly speaking—is a type of pressure that keeps a static universe from collapsing.

Twelve years later, in 1929, Edwin Hubble discovered that the Universe isn't static and unchanging, but is actually expanding. Upon hearing the news, Einstein quickly realized that if he'd taken his original 1915 theory seriously, he could have used it to predict the expansion that Hubble had observed. That would have been one of the great theoretical predictions of all time! It was this realization that led Einstein to describe the cosmological constant as the "biggest blunder" of his life.

The story doesn't end there. Nearly seven decades later, in 1998, two teams of astronomers independently made some very precise measurements of the expansion of the universe and discovered that there really is a need for the cosmological constant (Perlmutter et al. 1999; Riess et al. 1998). Einstein's "biggest blunder" was, in fact, one of his most prescient achievements.

The point of the story of the cosmological constant is not that Einstein was a fool. Rather, the point is that it's very, very difficult for even the best scientists to accurately assess the value of scientific discoveries. Science is filled with examples of major discoveries that were initially underappreciated. Alexander Fleming abandoned his work on penicillin. Max Born won the Nobel Prize in physics for a footnote he added in proof to a paper—a footnote that explains how the quantum mechanical wave function is connected to probabilities (Pais 1982). That's perhaps the most important idea anyone had in twentieth-century physics. Assessing science is hard.

The Problem of Measuring Science

Assessing science may be hard, but it's also something we do constantly. Countries such as the United Kingdom and Australia have introduced costly and time-consuming research assessment exercises to judge the quality of scientific work done in those countries. In just the past few years, many new metrics purporting to measure the value of scientific research have been proposed, such as the *h*-index (Hirsch 2005), the *g*-index (Egghe 2006), and many more (Van Noorden 2010). In June 2010, the journal *Nature* ran a special issue on such metrics (Nature 2010). Indeed, an entire field of scientometrics is being developed to measure science, and there are roughly 1,500 professional scientometricians (Braun 2010).

There's a slightly surreal quality to all this activity. If even Einstein demonstrably made enormous mistakes in judging his own research, why are the rest of us trying to measure the value of science systematically and even organizing the scientific systems of entire countries around these attempts? Isn't the lesson of the Einstein story that we shouldn't believe anyone who claims to be able to reliably assess the value of science? Of course, the problem is that although it may be nearly impossible to evaluate scientific work accurately, as a practical matter we are forced to make such evaluations. Every time a committee decides to award or decline a grant or to hire or not hire a scientist, they are making a judgment about the relative worth of different scientific work. So our society has evolved a mix of customs and institutions and technologies to answer the fundamental question: how should we allocate resources to science?

The answer we give to that question is changing rapidly today, as metrics such as citation count and the *h*-index take on a more prominent role. In 2006, for example, the UK government proposed changing its research assessment exercise so that it could be done in a largely automated fashion using citation-based metrics (Gilbert 2008). The proposal was eventually dropped, but the UK proposal is nonetheless a good example of the rise of metrics.

In this chapter, I argue that heavy reliance on a small number of metrics is bad for science. Of course, many people have previously criticized metrics such as citation count or the *h*-index. Such criticisms tend to fall into one of two categories. In the first category are criticisms of the properties of particular metrics—for example, that they undervalue pioneer work or that they unfairly disadvantage particular fields. In the second category are criticisms of the entire notion of quantitatively measuring science.

My argument differs from both these types of arguments. I accept that metrics in some form are inevitable—after all, as I said previously, every granting or hiring committee is effectively using a metric every time they make a decision. My argument instead is essentially an argument against homogeneity in the evaluation of science: it's not the use of metrics I'm objecting to, per se, but rather the idea of a relatively small number of metrics becoming broadly influential. I shall argue that it's much better if the system is instead very diverse, with all sorts of different methods being used to evaluate science. Crucially, my argument is independent of the details of what metrics are being broadly adopted: no matter how well-designed a particular metric may be, we shall see that it would be better to use a more heterogeneous system.

As a final word before we get to the details of the argument, I should briefly mention my own prejudice about the evaluation of science. This is the perhaps not very controversial view that the best way to evaluate science is to ask a few knowledgeable, independent, broad-minded people to take a really deep look at the primary research and to report their opinion, preferably while keeping in mind the story of Einstein and the cosmological constant. Unfortunately, such a process is often not practically feasible.

Three Problems with Centralized Metrics

I'll use the term "centralized metric" as a shorthand for any metric that is applied broadly within the scientific community. Examples today include the *h*-index, the total number of papers published by a scientist, and total citation count. I use this terminology in part because such metrics are often imposed by powerful central agencies—recall the UK government's proposal to use a citation-based scheme to assess UK research. Of course, metrics can also become broadly used across science, even without being imposed by any central agency, which is happening increasingly with the *h*-index and has happened in the past with metrics such as the number of papers published and the number of citations. In such cases, even though the metric may not be imposed by any central agency, it is still a central point of failure, so the term "centralized metric" is appropriate. In this section, I describe three ways centralized metrics can inhibit science.

Centralized Metrics Suppress Cognitive Diversity

Over the past decade, complexity theorist Scott Page and his collaborators have proved some remarkable results about the use of metrics to identify the "best" people to solve a problem (Hong and Page 2004; Page 2008). Here's the scenario that Page and company consider. Suppose that you have a difficult creative problem you want solved—let's say, finding a quantum theory of gravity. Let's also suppose that there are a thousand people worldwide who want to work on the problem, but you have funding to support only fifty people. How should you select those fifty? One way to do this is to design a metric to identify which people are best suited to solve the problem, and to then pick the fifty highest-scoring people according to that metric. What Page and company showed is that it's sometimes actually better to choose fifty people at random. That sounds impossible, but it's true for a simple reason: selecting only the highest scorers suppresses cognitive diversity that might be essential to solving the problem.

Suppose, for example, that the pool of a thousand people contains a few mathematicians who are experts in the mathematical field of stochastic processes, but who know little about the topics usually believed to be connected to quantum gravity. Perhaps, however, unbeknownst to us, expertise in stochastic processes is actually critical to solving the problem of quantum gravity. If you choose the fifty "best" people according to your metric, it's likely that you'll miss that crucial expertise. But if you pick fifty people at random, you've got a chance of picking up that crucial expertise. Richard Feynman made a similar point in a talk he gave shortly after receiving the Nobel Prize in physics:

If you give more money to theoretical physics, it doesn't do any good if it just increases the number of guys following the comet head. So it's necessary to increase the amount of variety . . . and the only way to do it is to implore you few guys to take a risk with your lives that you will never be heard of again, and go off in the wild blue yonder and see if you can figure it out. (Gleick 1993)

What makes Page and company's result so striking is that they gave a convincing general argument showing that this phenomenon occurs for any metric at all. They dubbed the result the *diversity-trumps-ability theorem*. Of course, exactly when the conclusion of the theorem applies depends on many factors, including the nature of the cognitive diversity in the larger group, the details of the problem, and the details of the metric. In particular, it depends strongly on something that we can't know in advance: how much or what type of cognitive diversity is needed to solve the problem at hand. The key point, though, is that it's dangerously naïve to believe that doing good science is just a matter of picking the right metric, and then selecting the top people according to that metric. No matter what the metric is, it'll suppress cognitive diversity. And that may mean suppressing knowledge crucial to solving the problem at hand.

Centralized Metrics Create Perverse Incentives

Imagine, for the sake of argument, that the U.S. National Science Foundation (NSF) wanted to encourage scientists to use YouTube videos as a way of sharing scientific results. The videos could, for example, be used as a way of explaining crucial but hard to verbally describe details of experiments. To encourage the use of videos, the NSF announces that from now on they'd like grant applications to include viewing statistics for YouTube videos as a metric for the impact of prior research.

Now, this proposal obviously has many problems, but for the sake of argument, please just imagine that it is being done. Suppose also that after this policy was implemented, a new video service came online that was far better than YouTube. If the new service were good enough, then people in the general consumer market would quickly switch to the new service. But even if the new service were far better than YouTube, most scientists—at least those with any interest in NSF funding—wouldn't switch until the NSF changed its policy. Meanwhile, the NSF would have little reason to change their policy until lots of scientists were using the new service. In short, this centralized metric would incentivize scientists to use inferior systems, and would therefore inhibit them from using the best tools.

The YouTube example is perhaps fanciful, at least today, but similar problems do already occur. At many institutions, scientists are rewarded for publishing in "top-tier" journals, according to some central list, and penalized for publishing in "lower-tier" journals. For example, faculty at Qatar University are currently given a reward of 3,000 Qatari riyals (approximately US$820) for each impact factor point of a journal they publish in (Qatar University Office of the Vice President for Research 2011). If this sort of incentive were broadly applied—and similar though less prescriptive schemes are used by many universities—it would create all sorts of problems. For instance, new journals in exciting emerging fields are likely to be establishing themselves and thus have a lower impact factor. So the effect of this scheme will be to disincentivize scientists from participating in new fields: the newer the field, the greater the disincentive! Any time we create a centralized metric, we yoke the way science is done to that metric.

Centralized Metrics Lead to the Misallocation of Resources

One of the causes of the financial crash of 2008 was a serious mistake made by ratings agencies (Roubini and Mihm 2010). The mistake was to systematically underestimate the risk of investing in financial instruments derived from housing mortgages. Because so many investors relied on the ratings agencies to make investment decisions, the erroneous ratings caused an enormous misallocation of capital, which propped up a bubble in the housing market. It was only after homeowners began to default on their mortgages in unusually large numbers that the market realized that the ratings agencies were mistaken, and the bubble collapsed. It's easy to blame the ratings agencies for this collapse, but this kind of misallocation of resources is inevitable in any system that relies on centralized decision-making. The reason is that any mistakes made at the central point spread out and affect the entire system.

In science, centralization also leads to a misallocation of resources. We've already seen two examples of how this can occur: the suppression of cognitive diversity, and the creation of perverse incentives. The problem is exacerbated by the fact that science has few mechanisms to correct the misallocation of resources. Consider, for example, the long-term fate of many fashionable fields. Such fields typically become fashionable as the result of some breakthrough result that opens up many new research possibilities. Encouraged by that breakthrough, grant agencies begin to invest heavily in the field, creating a new class of scientists (and granting agents) whose professional success is tied not just to the past success of the field, but also to the future success of the field. Money gets poured in, more and more people are drawn to the area, and students are trained and go on to positions of their own. In short, the field expands rapidly.

Initially, this expansion may be justified, but even after the field stagnates intellectually, there are few structural mechanisms to slow continued expansion. Effectively, there is a bubble in such fields, while less fashionable ideas remain underfunded as a result. Furthermore, we should expect such scientific bubbles to be more common than bubbles in the financial market, because decision making is more centralized in science. We should also expect scientific bubbles to last longer, because—unlike financial bubbles—there are few forces able to pop a bubble in science; there's no analog to the homeowner defaults to correct the misallocation of resources. Indeed, funding agencies can prop up stagnant fields of research for decades, in large part because the people paying the cost of the bubble—usually the taxpayers—are too isolated from the consequences to realize that their money is being wasted.

One Metric to Rule Them All

No one sensible would staff a company by simply applying an IQ test and employing whoever scored highest. And yet there are some in the scientific community who seem to want to move toward staffing scientific institutions by whomever scores highest according to the metrical flavor of the month. If there is one point to take away from this chapter, it is this: beware of anyone advocating or working toward the one "correct" metric for science. It's certainly a good thing to work toward a better understanding of how to evaluate science, but it's easy for enthusiasts of scientometrics to believe that they've found (or will soon find) the answer, the one metric to rule them all, and that this metric should henceforth be broadly used to assess scientific work. I believe that we should strongly resist this approach, and aim instead both to improve our understanding of how to assess science and to ensure considerable heterogeneity in how decisions are made.

I'll conclude with one tentative idea I have that might help address this problem: to democratize the creation of new metrics and thereby encourage the development of a large number of different ways of measuring science. (See chapter 3 for a similar idea for financial ratings.) Today, it's difficult to create new metrics—only a limited number of organizations, such as Thompson Reuters (who run the Web of Knowledge), have access to the necessary data. But if open science (Nielsen 2008) becomes the norm, this may change. By making scientific results openly accessible online and easily machine-readable, it should become much easier for a broad range of people and organizations to develop new metrics. That development will in turn lead to a healthy proliferation of different ideas about what constitutes "good science." Of course, if open science really does take hold, then I expect it will lead to a certain amount of "metric fatigue" as people develop many different ways of measuring science, and there will be calls to settle on one standard metric. I hope those calls aren't heeded. If science is to be anything more than lots of people following the comet head, we need to encourage people to move in different directions, which means valuing many different ways of doing science.

Acknowledgments

Thanks to Jen Dodd and Hassan Masum for many useful comments.

References

Braun, T. 2010. How to improve the use of metrics. *Nature* 465:870–872.

Egghe, L. 2006. Theory and practice of the *g*-index. *Scientometrics* 69 (1): 131–152.

Gilbert, N. 2008, December 18. Quality of UK research assessed. *Nature*.

Gleick, J. 1993. *Genius: The life and science of Richard Feynman.* New York: Vintage.

Hirsch, J. E. 2005. An index to quantify an individual's scientific research output. *Proceedings of the National Academy of Sciences of the United States of America* 102 (46): 16569.

Hong, L., and S. E. Page. 2004. Groups of diverse problem solvers can outperform groups of high-ability problem solvers. *Proceedings of the National Academy of Sciences of the United States of America* 101 (46): 16385–16389.

Nature. 2010, June 16. Assessing assessment (editorial). Special issue on science metrics. *Nature* 465:845.

Nielsen, M. 2008. *The future of science* [blog post.]. Retrieved from: <http://michaelnielsen.org/blog/the-future-of-science-2>.

Page, S. E. 2008. *The difference: How the power of diversity creates better groups.* Princeton: Princeton University Press.

Pais, A. 1982. *Subtle is the lord: The science and the life of Albert Einstein.* Oxford: Oxford University Press.

Perlmutter, S., G. Aldering, G. Goldhaber, R. A. Knop, P. Nugent, P. G. Castro, S. Deustua, et al. 1999. Measurements of omega and lambda from 42 high-redshift supernovae. *Astrophysical Journal* 517:565–586.

Qatar University Office of the Vice President for Research. 2011. *The research reward program.* Retrieved from: <http://www.qu.edu.qa/offices/research/academic/research_reward_program.php>.

Riess, A. G., A. V. Filippenko, P. Challis, A. Clocchiatti, A. Diercks, P. M. Garnavich, R. L. Gilliland, et al. 1998. Observational evidence from supernovae for an accelerating universe and a cosmological constant. *Astronomical Journal* 116 (3): 1009–1038.

Roubini, N., and S. Stephen Mihm. 2010. *Crisis economics: A crash course in the future of finance.* New York: Penguin.

Van Noorden, R. 2010. Metrics: A profusion of measures. *Nature* 465:864–866.

11   Usage-Based Reputation Metrics in Science

Victor Henning, Jason Hoyt, and Jan Reichelt

Citations are a valued currency in research as an easily measurable proxy for the attention of professional peers and the impact of scholarly work. However, the excessive use of citation-based metrics for judging research and researchers themselves has been criticized by many. Victor Henning, Jason Hoyt, and Jan Reichelt propose complementary usage-based metrics, which could measure how articles are actually read and used.

Problems with Journal Impact Factors and Modern Citation Systems

Citation-based reputation metrics such as the journal impact factor (JIF, the average number of citations per article and per year for a given journal) and the h-index and g-index (which measure the distribution of citations for a given author) play an ever-increasing role in modern science (reviewed in Egghe 2006; Garfield 2006; Hirsch 2005). As seemingly objective measures of academic impact and performance, they are used to determine career progression, postdoctoral positions, tenure, and grant funding.

Pressure on scholars to perform well according to these metrics has mounted. So has the criticism leveled against such metrics. It has been argued that they lead researchers to adopt undesirable strategic behaviors such as targeting high-impact "vanity journals," writing as many bite-sized papers as possible, and timing publications according to grant renewal or career progression needs (instead of submitting work when it is ready). It is likewise charged that these metrics can lead to academics engaging in citation bartering; gratuitous authorship; and a general increase in aggressive, exploitative, and self-promotional behavior (Lawrence 2008). Citation-based metrics are also thought to tempt journal editors into gaming the system using techniques that inflate their JIF, by methods including accepting only papers expected to receive a higher number of citations, encouraging self-citations, and publishing review articles in place of research articles.

From a methodological perspective, the critics point out that citation counts are context-free; that is, a citation is counted as positive even if a paper was cited in a negative context. Moreover, the Gini coefficient of the citation distribution is extremely high: a small fraction of papers garner the majority of all citations and the majority of papers are never cited at all (Weale, Bailey, and Lear 2004). This statistic also implies that a single highly cited article could inflate a JIF. As such, high JIF does not necessarily indicate that each article published in a particular journal is of equally high quality.

Another problem for JIFs is the arbitrary two-year window within which citations are measured, which favors fast-evolving disciplines. The *h*-index, similarly, is arbitrarily bound by the number of papers a researcher has published, so a young researcher with a few high-impact publications will still have a low *h*-index. Finally, there is evidence that only 20 percent of all papers cited have actually been read by the authors citing them (Simkin and Roychowdhury 2003).

In this chapter, we examine the idea of alternative, usage-based reputation metrics. We start by describing various usage-based metrics. We then discuss the potential of usage-based metrics for overcoming the limitations of citation-based metrics and examine their possible (intended and unintended) consequences on science and research. We close with a look at the practical difficulties of achieving usage-based metrics. In this final section, we make an analogy to Last.fm (a social music service that is largely based on such metrics) and describe Mendeley.com, which is a project implementing usage-based metrics for academic research.

What Are Usage-Based Metrics?

Usage-based metrics could be described as "Nielsen TV ratings for science." To obtain journal usage reports and make purchasing decisions, librarians currently use a system known as COUNTER (Counting Online Usage of Networked Electronic Resources, <http://www.projectcounter.org>; Brody et al. 2009). Because we are not scientometricians by trade, we will discuss only the raw data that could form the basis for usage-based metrics and will stop short of suggesting more sophisticated indices based on this data. That said, we do believe that if researchers were given more raw data, they would be able to develop such indices.

A starting point for usage-based metrics would be to first track the *pervasiveness* of research papers. The pervasiveness of a paper can be measured by whether it is present on the computers of a wide-ranging, distributed sample of academics or is present only on the computers of a small group of "experts" in a specific discipline. This metric would be a measure of the popularity or awareness that a paper is enjoying in a certain group of researchers. By aggregating paper pervasiveness data, the popularity of the authors, publication journal, and research topic can be quantified.

A second, more fine-grained usage metric would be the actual *time spent reading* each research paper (on screen, e.g., in a PDF reader such as Adobe Reader) and the *number of repeat readings* or *annotations* per paper. This metric would be a measure of the intensity with which the paper (its author, publication journal, research topic) is being examined—did readers only skim through a paper, or did they peruse it in detail? One could also track how often a paper is shared among collaborators and the level of group annotation that is occurring.

Finally, these metrics could be augmented with reader's *relevance ratings* and *tags*. These help to differentiate mere measures of attention from explicit quality judgments. Relevance of a paper to a particular reader could be tracked alongside that reader's discipline to suggest potential interdisciplinary audiences for a paper.

Taken further, relevance and tags can be used to reveal hidden topics within each paper. The relevance of these topics can be tracked and trends followed as a function of time, which can help answer questions such as, "Is a topic gaining or losing popularity within a field of research?"

Tags need not be formal keywords in the way that author-supplied keywords describe the document. Rather, tags describe feelings toward a document or how the document might be used. Tags such as "essential," "questionable," or "terrible" each provide valuable clues in capturing individual subjective feelings, whereas tags like "extract references" or "project XYZ" indicate how the document may be used. User-defined tags can both categorize papers and provide subjective emotive statements. These indicators can then be aggregated to define the overall "feeling" of a tagged paper.

Advantages of Usage-Based Metrics: Methodology

Let us consider whether the problems associated with citation-based metrics can be alleviated through usage-based metrics. We assume that the sample on which the usage-based metrics are based is sufficiently large and that usage can be captured by an automated system.

In terms of measurement theory, usage-based metrics exhibit several advantageous properties. If the goal is to assess a paper's (or researcher's) impact on the scientific community at large, citation-based metrics would be considerably enriched by a combined measure of pervasiveness, reading time, repeat readings, and relevance ratings. In combination, these would more completely represent the construct of scientific impact.

Moreover, because "usage" is a multi-item construct rather than a single-item measure as citations are, its convergent validity can be assessed. Because all three measures—pervasiveness, reading time, and relevance ratings—are supposed to capture the same construct—namely, scientific impact—they should correlate positively and significantly. If pervasiveness, reading time, and relevance do not correlate for an individual paper, this might be an indicator for gaming. If pervasiveness and reading time are low and relevance is high, this might be an indicator for a hidden gem. Of course, measuring the correlation between citation-based and usage-based metrics would be equally instructive.

Finally, because the three proposed usage measures operate on continuous scales rather than a binary (cited versus not cited) scale, they would add a contextual dimension and allow for a more fine-grained weighting of what a paper actually *meant* to a scholar who dealt with it.

Advantages of Usage-Based Metrics: Implementation

Methodologically, usage-based metrics would help to overcome the extreme skewness of the citation (and thus reputation) distribution: given that the selection of papers a researcher will cite is necessarily a subset of the papers that he or she is aware of, and given that citations are binary whereas usage is not, a usage distribution curve necessarily has a much longer tail and a much lower Gini coefficient than a citation distribution curve. Whereas many journals have started to limit the allowed number of citations per paper (or per page), the number of papers a scholar can read is in practice limited by his or her time; similarly, in practice, an author will usually read a number of different papers on a specific subject, but cite only one or two of them. Usage-based metrics would also deflate the problem of authors citing papers they did not actually read.

On a normative-behavioral level, due to the more distributed nature of measurement, usage-based metrics would be more difficult to game by authors and editors through citation-bartering or self-citations and could thus discourage such practices. The practice of gratuitous authorship, however, would likely remain unchanged; the effect of usage-based metrics on other aspects of authors' behavior (selection of target journals, packaging research into publication-sized papers, publication timing according to funding and career needs) would have to be seen.

In our opinion, the biggest advantage of usage-based metrics is that they would be available immediately on a per-article basis. Currently, due to the time required to write an article and take it through the peer review process (usually in multiple review rounds), it takes months until citations of a paper start to appear and years until they are included in impact factor indices. Usage-based metrics would let authors track how readership of their individual papers is evolving in real time, and the article's impact could evolve independently of the journal and its impact factor. If demographic information could be collected alongside the usage metrics, pervasiveness, reading time/repeat readings, and relevance ratings could be differentiated among geographic regions, academic disciplines, junior and senior faculty, and so forth.

Due to their immediacy, authors might also be able to quantify the impact of recent media coverage, speaking engagements, or conference presentations. Researchers would be able to retrieve the "hottest" papers for each topic (as marked by user-generated tags assigned to papers or by number of recent additions to users' libraries). They could similarly find the "hottest" tags in each academic discipline (to spot emerging research trends) or track up-and-coming authors with the highest percentage growth in readership in the past month. By looking at longitudinal trend data, scholars might be able to spot whether a paper, topic, or theory is steadily gaining followers, is subject to sudden "hype," or is already on the decline and is cooling off. In short, postpublication literature analysis and research would become more dynamic and up to date.

Recommendation Engines and Collaborative Filtering

An aggregate pool of solid usage data would be the basis for developing recommendation engines based on collaborative filtering principles. It has been argued that citations already act as reading recommendations, and recommendation models based on co-citations or citation networks ("localized citation graph search") have been developed (McNee et al. 2002). Collaborative filtering recommendations, however, have additional potential.

First, they could promote interdisciplinary research because they may be better in uncovering parallels between academic disciplines than citation networks. For example, when doing research on the psychology of emotion, a researcher might have read papers on emotion published in adjacent fields (philosophy, literature, linguistics, neurophysiology), and they may have tagged all of them with "emotion" in their reference management library. However, due to space constraints and immediate relevance, they might limit their citations to papers published in psychology journals. Picking up such patterns, collaborative filtering recommendations could help researchers to discover literature that could be of interest to them, even though it is not found in the citation network of their existing library. With the increasingly interdisciplinary nature of scientific research, highlighting interdisciplinary impact could become a major feature of a usage-based reputation system.

Collaborative filtering would also enable researchers to identify people with similar research interests (based on their personal libraries) and thus foster collaboration and academic networking, which could help younger researchers find experts in their fields more quickly. A first year PhD student today has practically no chance of quickly finding other PhD students who might have just started working on a similar research topic (or have just finished their thesis). Contacts and collaborations today are typically formed via conferences and through reading literature of related researchers. Although conferences have been and will continue to be an effective means of finding collaborators, the resources available to early-career academics to attend such conferences may limit the extent of networking by junior researchers.

Collaborative filtering is not bound in such a way and may also enable potential collaborations between researchers who have just started down a new research path and have yet to publish.

Among the researchers participating in the aggregate pool of usage data, a trust-based recommendation network can be established in which researchers can be recommended literature already in a colleague's library. It has been argued that when combined with other citation sources, trust-based recommendations can help to isolate controversial papers otherwise buried within a glut of mainstream literature (Hess and Schlieder 2008). Examples of trust-based recommendations are easy to find. Two clear examples are Netflix, which has a friend-based movie recommendation system, and Facebook, which has a friend recommendation tool.

Supplementing with Other Resources Adds Value

No single metric —or even a suite of metrics from a single source—will be able to fully determine an article's impact. With the use of modern API tools, this situation can be partially mitigated by "pulling in" additional sources of authority, such as COUNTER download statistics from publishers, database vendors, and university libraries. Citing postpublication reviews or discussions from blogs are examples of making an article dynamic. Enabling trackbacks, which display where a document has been hyperlinked on the web, can help measure pervasiveness. APIs from postpublication peer review sites such as F1000.com and citation information from databases such as Scopus, Web of Science, or PubMed would add even more value to the corpus of usage.

There has been some question as to the value of using article download statistics in predicting future citation numbers, and models have been built to address this (Jahandideh, Abdolmaleki, and Asadabadi 2007). In one report, the editors of *Laboratory Investigation* found that the top five downloaded PDF research papers in 2005 varied widely in terms of citation numbers from time of publication through 2007 (Ketcham 2008). This finding suggests that popularity and reading do not correlate well with document citation. In contrast, there are many fields with just a handful of researchers or experts. Usage-based metrics can still be used in these instances by normalizing the readership and comparing the data to similar papers in those fields. Expert reviews could supplement this normalized data to provide additional value.

Reading an uncited article could be just as valuable and influential as reading an article that is eventually cited. However, influential yet uncited literature does not help the authors of that paper if that information isn't recorded somehow. For the field as a whole, that downloaded, annotated, uncited paper contains data and conclusions that may remain unnoticed by the wider community. Downloaded data from publishers could be a valuable and corrective supplementary metric.

Limitations to Overcome

There are a number of problems to be overcome if we want to turn usage-based metrics into reality.

First, the privacy of sensitive information contained in the usage data needs to be preserved. Specifically, usage statistics and the associated demographic information need to be aggregated and presented in a way that makes it impossible to deduce the identity of individual researchers as readers of a given paper. Not doing so could result, for example, in attempts to piece together a picture of a competing researcher's literature library in order to gain insights into their research strategy and scoop them on publications.

Second, there is a possibility that the existing "success breeds success" effect of citation rankings (highly cited papers are more visible and thus attract even more citations) could be exacerbated by real-time, hype-driven "popularity" rankings. We believe that this concern could be addressed by making raw usage data available to the academic community at large in order to allow each discipline to develop its own domain-specific bibliometric rankings. In addition, as outlined previously, the personal nature of usage data could form the basis for recommendation engines, which would in turn divert researchers' attention away from universally popular articles to the articles most personally relevant to each researcher. In other words, recommendation engines could amplify usage (and thus reputation) of articles in the long tail of the usage distribution curve.

Third, as with any metric, safeguards against gaming and misuse would have to be established. As pointed out earlier, the distributed nature of measurement makes gaming usage-based metrics relatively difficult but not impossible. Algorithms and IP address trackers that flag potentially suspicious activity—in combination with community self-policing as used by Wikipedia—are likely to be effective answers to this problem.

Fourth, existing usage data sets are relatively isolated and inaccessible. We previously mentioned COUNTER as a supplementary source for download statistics, but this international standard currently suffers from two problems. Although COUNTER statistics are provided to libraries, publishers usually do not make them publicly available. Also, COUNTER statistics are isolated datasets that are not aggregated across publishers. At the article level, very few outlets present transparent usage metrics alongside online articles. When data are available for articles, they are limited at best. Although journals hosted by Stanford University's HighWire Press do factor paper usage into their website's information, HighWire presents a ranked list of only the most-downloaded or most-cited articles without any actual data.

The *Journal of Vision* and *Public Library of Science* (PLoS) are exceptions. They provide raw data counts and download rates. *Frontiers in Neuroscience* has even gone as far as to track online reading time for its articles. Overwhelmingly, though, publishers are reluctant to share anything beyond citation data, if they share anything at all. At this point, Open Access publishers such as PLoS are leading the way. The development of future APIs from subscription-based publishers partly hinges on whether PLoS demonstrably benefits from this practice, for example, by increasing the visibility and impact of their journal in news outlets and the academic community and by serving as an incentive for top authors to publish their papers with PLoS in order to receive more insight into the usage of their articles.

It should be noted that there have been several academic websites that have attempted to assign a quality rating system to academic papers, just as users rate books on Amazon. PLoS allows registered users to rate papers on three categories with a five-star system. It has been observed that fewer than one person per article uses this feature and that articles are indiscriminately rated with five stars (Binfield 2009). These systems appear to have failed due to a lack of incentive to participate in public ratings. After researchers have rated a number of papers, the ratings are of little further use to them, as the researchers cannot store papers alongside their own research paper collection as a sorting tool.

The fifth and perhaps biggest problem in scaling usage-based metrics lies in overcoming social hurdles rather than technical ones. How might we convince scholars to take part in generating and accepting usage-based metrics? In our opinion, the answer is that doing so must confer some type of utility to scholars beyond the idea of contributing to a fuzzy "greater good of science." More specifically, the tool that does the measuring on the researchers' computers should collect this data only as a secondary purpose and must have some other primary usage value.

Existing Models: Last.fm, Mendeley, PLoS, CiteULike, and ResearchScorecard

A successful example of usage-based metrics in a different setting is Last.fm, which bills itself as a "social music service." Last.fm's Audioscrobbler software tracks ("scrobbles") music listening behavior on the user's computer. Based on the user's listening profile, Audioscrobbler enables him or her to receive a personalized radio stream and music recommendations from Last.fm's collaborative filtering system, as well as to discover other users with a similar taste in music. Last.fm, in turn, is able to generate usage-based metrics (pervasiveness of songs, number of repeat plays, and tags) for songs, bands, and genres of music. With this model, over a period of five years, Last.fm has built one of the world's biggest music databases.

The research service we are building, Mendeley, tries to apply Last.fm's principles to the area of research and reference management, but with far more extensive privacy protection. The desktop software has the primary value of providing its users with a tool for managing, tagging, sharing, searching, and citing research papers. The companion website can be used for backing up research papers, creating a public re-search profile, and connecting to like-minded researchers. The website already displays the pervasiveness of research papers, authors, journals, and tags as measured by the desktop software, and we are currently working on measures of reading time and rel-evance ratings, as well as collaborative filtering recommendation mechanisms.

Another service that captures some form of pervasiveness is CiteULike.org, a social bookmarking service for academics. In its "CiteGeist" statistics, it displays the research papers that are most frequently bookmarked by its members. CiteULike also feeds data into Mendeley's usage statistics.

Among publishers, one of the leaders in providing open data is PLoS, which began an article-level metrics campaign in March 2009. PLoS provides a section for each ar-ticle that is devoted to how often it has been bookmarked on social sites, mentioned in blog posts, and cited (as determined by Google Scholar, PubMed, and CrossRef). PLoS has also begun to show download data from its servers to gauge an article's popularity and will augment its article pages with usage data via an API from Mendeley.

Closely related to article-level metrics are researcher metrics that try to quantify sci-entific expertise to find collaborators or new faculty. One such site, ResearchScorecard.com, uses data mining techniques to quantify and rank researchers based on grant funding and authorships and subsequently normalizes researcher rankings against peers in their field or university. By making relevant APIs available, such information could be used to supplement usage-based metrics, as previously discussed.

Conclusions

Usage-based metrics can add value to the academic world by providing additional information that is helpful for evaluating real-time academic impact at the article, researcher, and journal levels. They can also help to overcome many of the normative-behavioral and methodological problems that plague traditional citation-based impact metrics. They can complement citation data and deliver a much richer picture of re-searchers' interaction with academic content.

Because an increasing number of working papers are being published in (and down-loaded from) preprint archives such as arXiv.org, RePec.org, and SSRN.com, their us-age could be tracked as well. The practice of counting citations to preprints already exists in particle physics (SPIRES and its successor, INSPIRE)—and if pervasiveness, reading time, and relevance ratings already indicate that a preprint paper has achieved a very positive reputation in a wide academic audience, why still submit it to a peer-reviewed journal? In our view, it is likely that usage-based metrics will come to be accepted as a necessary complement to the added value of peer review. For instance, peer review gives expert insight into additional experiments that should be included or conclusions drawn that usage metrics cannot replicate. We should also caution that popularity does not necessarily indicate validity of the underlying research. Here, peer review again plays an important role to distinguish between hype and fact.

The major limitation to citation-based recommendations is that they provide little information as to why a document has utility. Usage-based metrics solve this problem through a more granular view on how a paper is being used, after which recommendations can be computed. Obtaining usage-based metrics, getting publishers to open up data streams, and dealing with privacy concerns will be among the primary challenges to such a system. By utilizing the power of reference management software and turning academic papers into "social objects" to measure usage, we believe that these limitations can be overcome.

References

Binfield, P. 2009. PLoS ONE: Background, future development, and article-level metrics. In *Proceedings: ELPUB2009 Conference on Electronic Publishing*, Milan, Italy.

Brody, T., R. Gedye, R. MacIntyre, P. Needham, E. Pentz, S. Rumsey, and P. Shepherd. 2009. PIRUS: Publisher and institutional repository usage statistics. Retrieved from: <http://www.jisc.ac.uk/whatwedo/programmes/pals3/pirus.aspx>.

Egghe, L. 2006. Theory and practise of the g-index. *Scientometrics* 69 (1): 131–152.

Garfield, E. 2006. The history and meaning of the journal impact factor. *Journal of the American Medical Association* 295 (1): 90–93.

Hess, C., and C. Schlieder. 2008. Trust-based recommendations for documents. *AI Communications* 21 (2): 145–153.

Hirsch, Jorge E. 2005. An index to quantify an individual's scientific research output. *Proceedings of the National Academy of Sciences of the United States of America* 102 (46): 16569–16572.

Jahandideh, S., P. Abdolmaleki, and E. B. Asadabadi. 2007. Prediction of future citations of a research paper from number of its internet downloads. *Medical Hypotheses* 69 (2): 458–459.

Ketcham, C. M. 2008. The proper use of citation data in journal management. *Archivum Immunologiae et Therapiae Experimentalis* 56 (6): 357–362.

Lawrence, P. A. 2008. Lost in publication: How measurement harms science. *Ethics in Science and Environmental Politics* 8:9–11.

McNee, S. M., I. Albert, D. Cosley, P. Gopalkrishnan, S. K. Lam, A. M. Rashid, J. A. Konstan, et al. 2002. On the recommending of citations for research papers. *Proceedings of Computer Supported Cooperative Work* 2002:16–20.

Simkin, M., and V. Roychowdhury. 2003. Read before you cite! *Complex Systems* 14:269–274.

Weale, A., M. Bailey, and P. Lear. 2004. The level of non-citation of articles within a journal as a measure of quality: a comparison to the impact factor. *BMC Medical Research Methodology* 4 (1): 14.

12 Open Access and Academic Reputation

John Willinsky

Open access aims to make knowledge freely available to those who would make use of it. High-profile open access journals like PLoS (Public Library of Science) have demonstrated a viable model: researchers pay a one-time fee upon publication so that the public at large can access this research without barriers. John Willinsky considers the effect that open access is having on reputation in academia and research publication.

While others wrestle with how to best establish authority, reliability, and trustworthiness within online business environments, I will speak to the academic equivalent by observing that the honing of the review-and-recommendation management of reputations has been a focus of academic life for many centuries. Academic life has always been subject to patronage, whether of the court, church, academies, universities, or the state (Moran 1991). Scholarly patrons trade in reputations by investing in the reputation of scholars, as well as artists, musicians, and poets—and seeking, by way of return on investment, an enhancement of their own reputation. The scholarly community has a claim, then, to being part of the original reputation society.

To give the briefest taste of that history, German philosopher-administrator Johann Justi wrote in 1760 of how "in the Republic of Letters, the academic ware is publicly vended for money. I mean 'academic money' there. One needs to know that the Republic of Letters mints a sort of coin called 'fame.' In the learned tongue, this minting means to cite someone else with much credit" (cited by Clark 2006, 373). A further historic indication of just how much reputation matters to academic life is found in Robert K. Merton's observation of "the great frequency with which the history of science is punctuated by disputes, often sordid, over priority of discovery" (Merton 1957, 635).

Reputation is precisely the asset or value that scholars have to offer, whether on the faculty job market or a journal's editorial board, as an expert witness, or as a reference for a colleague. The university contracts, in effect, to "rent" scholars' reputations for the duration of their careers. In a classic study on "communication" as the "essence of science," William D. Garvey refers to the "complex matter of institutional pride," in which an institution's "continued healthy existence depends on acknowledged scientific productivity" to attract outstanding scientists, good students, and the support of funding agencies (Garvey 1979, 17).

In addition, the university provides faculty with incentives to increase their reputational assets, as part of what Partha Dasgupta and Paul A. David term "the collegiate reputation-based reward system" (1994, 490). This academic form of life can be said to be underwritten by a reputation economy. To borrow from the classic definition of economics, reputation in academic life controls the production, distribution, and consumption of this public good known as research and scholarship.

One would think that scholars and universities, having long trafficked in finely calibrated measures of reputation, should have little trouble navigating this new digital realm—a realm that is staking its future on "the distributed formation of reputations, and consequent increased ability to distinguish better from worse," as Masum and Zhang describe in their "Manifesto for the Reputation Society" (2004). Yet for all of the academy's experience with reputation management, it is the Internet that has radically altered the distribution side of this economy. The Internet is enabling research articles to reach far beyond the circulation figures of any given print subscription and approach universal access, otherwise known as "open access" (Willinsky 2006).

Current debates about the viability of open access as a distribution principle for scholarly communication reveal tensions between the interests of researchers and publishers. Notwithstanding these tensions, open access holds considerable promise for improving the standing—or reputation—of research and scholarship more broadly.

I do not mean to imply that scholars are unduly self-interested or egomaniacal in their work. It is rather that reputation serves as the currency within the republic of letters, determining the work's exchange value. Given the technical and highly specialized nature of academic work, most people (even within the academy) are not able to evaluate a contribution on its own terms, although they may well be able to learn from it.

Those who work within the academy become very skilled at judging the stuff of reputations: where has the person's work been published, what claims of priority in discovery have they established, how often have they been cited, how and where reviewed, what prizes won, what institutional titles earned, and what organizations led. Even the blind review process—designed to ensure that the selection of articles is not susceptible to the influence of past achievements—ensures the reputational currency of both journal and author. Yet academic reputation also involves a person's degree of generosity with colleagues and his or her mentorship of students and junior faculty. It includes his or her spirit of collaboration and openness with data and methods and his or her helpfulness in reviewing, refereeing, and editing, along with all the other forms of support and leadership that the scholar provides.

The question I consider here is the impact of open access in relation to questions of researchers' reputations. (Parallel developments, including open source software

[Weber 2004] and the open data movement [King 2007], draw on and impact reputational aspects of academic and professional life.)

The initial reaction to the realization that research could freely circulate through open access was to dismiss any such work—and anyone associated with it—as lacking credibility. During the 1990s, it was common to hear faculty members say that although they were fine with it all, their colleagues (especially their colleagues on tenure and promotion committees) would judge it as reputation-damaging to post work online, publish in journals that appeared online, or otherwise step outside of the print tradition in any sort of digital fashion. This stance had a bemusing double twist to it, as it held that not only did placing work online reduce its (reputational) value to zero, but it was then likely to be stolen as well.

Yet for all of these conservative attitudes within the academy, the majority of journals moved online with the dawning of the twenty-first century and the majority of researchers soon favored online access to these materials over visiting library stacks to photocopy materials or make notes on index cards from copies of print journals. As the academic community began to realize not only the convenience of online access but its potential for circulating work worldwide, scholarly publishers sought to transpose the print subscription business model to the Internet in the belief that the circulation of academic work would continue to be restricted to subscribers—and that subscription price increases, with a slight "print-plus-online" boost, would continue unabated into the new century.

A number of researchers saw the Internet differently. Beginning in the 1990s, they began to post their work, making it freely available before, during, and after it was published, in a form that has become known as *author self-archiving*. Other researchers experimented with new forms of open access publishing that managed to align researcher interests in providing universal access to their work with the value (in terms of improving both reputation and the article) of having work peer-reviewed. This alignment led to the publication of *open access journals*, of which there are now thousands (Directory of Open Access Journals 2010).

These two approaches involved a minority of researchers. Those of us who feel some impatience over this seeming failure of our colleagues to take full advantage of the digital era would do well to remember that the universities were by no means the first to figure out that the printing press might be an excellent means for supporting student learning—Oxford University did not become involved in printing until 1584, well over a century after the introduction of the press (Carter 1975, 1). For most faculty members, it is fair to say that the digital era has changed little except the ease with which they access the literature and the speed with which they correspond with colleagues and journals.

This limited effect may yet change, for reasons that have to do with the nature of the reputation economy, which depends on how widely one's work is read and cited.

It is thus worthwhile understanding how open access has already affected academic practices.

To take a leading instance of a field transformed by the digital era, scientists working in high energy physics began in the 1990s to place early drafts and published versions of their work online, thanks to the initiative of far-sighted physicist Paul Ginsparg. In this repository, papers could be freely shared in what has since become arXiv. The scientists continued to send their research articles to *Physics Letters* or *Physical Review*, where they were peer-reviewed and published, but only after the work had been circulating for months—if not years—in arXiv.

With physicists logging into arXiv each day to see what is new and current in their field, rather than turning to the journals, they are dealing directly with the unregulated literature, which in principle may include anything from a Nobel Prize breakthrough to a perpetual-motion proposal. The papers they are reading may have yet to be submitted to a journal, or may be currently under review at a journal, or may have been accepted or published in a journal. An article is just as likely to be in all four states, in that order, with the progress noted in different iterations of the article that is uploaded to arXiv. arXiv is now used by several disciplines in addition to physics and holds in excess of half-a-million papers across physics, math, nonlinear science, computer science, computational biology, quantitative finance, and statistics.

So what has happened to the physics journals as a result of so much of the field's literature being available earlier and free online? The publishers reported no decrease in subscriptions over the first decade or so that arXiv was in operation (Swan 2005). The average price of a physics journal is still among the highest for any discipline, costing libraries well over $3,252 annually, although this figure represents all of physics (Van Orsdel and Born 2009). Price increases in this field exceeded 350 percent from 1990 to 2009, roughly the period during which arXiv became a major source of papers for physicists in a number of areas (Hooker 2009).

The journals still play an important role in authorizing and distinguishing the quality of papers for the physics community, but this aspect of the reputation economy is now largely disengaged from the circulation and direct utilization of knowledge by physicists. That is, the journals are still contributing to reputation making and as such are being used for tenure, promotion, and merit-pay purposes, at most once a year when reputation is cashed in. But for the daily work of these physicists, the currency, speed, and universality of access provided by arXiv outweighs the screening and authority value of the leading journals. They would rather search through it all and make their own calls.

The popularity of arXiv among researchers has generated the paradigmatic paradox that besets scholarly communication today: the journal remains indispensable for institutional reputation setting—even as, in a number of fields, it is no longer the principal point of knowledge exchange and circulation for those who actually produce and consume the research at issue. Furthering their innovative approach to scholarly communication, the particle physics community has launched an experiment by the name of SCOAP³ (Sponsoring Consortium for Open Access Publishing in Particle Physics) that seeks to effect "a global conversion of the main corpus of [particle physics] journals to the open access model" (SCOAP³ Working Party 2007, 3). The group has calculated that with a $15 million payment to publishers (which is less than is being paid by libraries in total subscription fees for the six relevant journals in which more than 80 percent of this literature appears), open access to the entire field of particle physics could be purchased (Mele, Dallman, Vigen, and Yeomans 2006).

In a clear sign of a market in transition between publishing media, university libraries find that they must subscribe to certain academic journals mainly to sustain the peer review and editorial judgment that are provided by the author's colleagues in the field. The economic inefficiencies are further exacerbated by commercial publishers running up journal prices to the point where their titles are many times more expensive than the much higher-ranked journals published by scholarly societies, as has been documented by Ted Bergstrom (2001) for journals in the field of economics. This misalignment between reputation value and price had already taken hold during the latter half of the twentieth century, as Bergstrom's work shows.

What this new publishing medium offers is a chance to explore new models that recognize, for example, how researcher interests in universal distribution and access can run contrary to traditional publishers' business models that are based on restricting access to journal content. It needs to be recalled that the intellectual property at issue in this reputation economy is a sponsored public good, which may distinguish it from the intellectual property marketed by large publishing houses or record labels (for which restricting access can be in the interests of both author/musician and publisher).

The reputation of research as a public good was recognized by those researchers who posted published versions of their work online. Many journal publishers have, as a concession to the open access movement, instituted author self-archiving policies. These policies offer a trade-off by restricting authors to posting their final draft (following peer review), with some publishers requiring a delay of twelve months after publication. (This second-class status for archived copies has become, in turn, the standard for the National Institutes of Health's Public Access Policy, required of all research published as a result of its considerable grants program.)

Meanwhile, interest in archiving grows among faculty members. As a result, many departments—and, in some cases, entire institutions—have instituted open access policies under which faculty have agreed to make sure everything that they publish is immediately posted in an open access archive, if only in a draft version (ROARMAP 2010). Archiving is augmenting the reputation of research as a body of work that is increasingly open, public, and universally available.

When it comes to open access journals, the case for reputation has been made by the Public Library of Science (PLoS). Directed by leading scientists, PLoS set out to establish that publishing with an open access journal did not have to cost anyone their reputation. They attracted funding that made it possible to publish on a very professional basis, while charging authors to publish their work, following the "page charges" model that had long been used by subscription journals to supplement their finances (where articles beyond a certain length cost the author an additional charge per page). PLoS has gone on to publish seven journals. What it established—almost from the beginning—is that open access is changing the reputation dynamics of journal publishing.

Within two years of its launch, *PLoS Biology* was able to achieve the highest journal impact factor (JIF) in the field of biology (Kennison 2005). (JIF is based on number of citations per article, and is perhaps the most widely regarded measure of journal reputation; it is calculated by the ISI Web of Science in the Journal Citation Reports.) A new journal similar to *PLoS Biology* would not have been able to attract the necessary readership if it had not been open access. *PLoS Biology* subsequently dropped its print edition, further demonstrating how far we have come since a decade ago, when the common advice to young faculty members was to stay away from electronic journals. Even among the most traditional of subscription journals, open access is having an influence—the highly ranked *New England Journal of Medicine* now makes much of its content free online six months after publication.

To gain a sense of what archiving or publishing one's work in an open access format can do for a researcher's reputation, one would do well to consult the annotated bibliography maintained by Steve Hitchcock (2009). It lists the studies that delve into the impact of open access by examining the difference open access makes to how often a work is read and cited as a result of it being made freely available online. To take but one of many examples, Gunther Eysenbach's study of the *Proceedings of the National Academy of Sciences* found that those articles that were made open access within the *Proceedings* were twice as likely to be cited in the first four to ten months after publication, with that ratio rising to almost three times as likely by ten to sixteen months after publication (Eysenbach 2006).

On the other hand, Philip Davis and colleagues (2008) failed to find a citational advantage for open access articles in the first twelve months in an extensive study of the biomedical field, but revealed a pattern of greater readership for work using this new approach, suggesting that reputations might well have been affected. Studies have found that the impact of open access differs across fields, with it being far lower in philosophy compared to political science (Antelman 2004). Other studies have found increased use of open access articles in developing countries, regardless of whether the articles were archived by their authors or published in open access journals; well over twice the usage was found in Chile and Bulgaria and somewhat greater than that in Brazil and Turkey (Evans and Reimer 2009).

This open access advantage, in terms of one's work attracting more citations than it would if the work had not been made open access, is a "limited-time offer" to researchers who archive their work and publish in open access journals. As funding agencies such as the Wellcome Trust and the National Institutes of Health as well as institutions such as Harvard and Stanford pass policies in support of open access, there will come a point when open access to research and scholarship is commonplace.

By that point, I speculate that the advantages of this greater accessibility will translate into an improved reputation for research as a whole. Research will play a greater role among professionals, policy makers, and interested members of the public (including Wikipedians). Signs of this interest in research are already emerging with the whole "evidence-based" movement in medicine and health (Sackett et al. 1996) and policy making in general (Pawson 2006), as well as with the educational focus on undergraduate research (Russell, Hancock, and McCullough 2007). Whether this enhancement of research's public reputation will translate into greater public support at all levels for research and scholarship can be only a hope at this point.

Certainly, one of the things that open access affords is the building of researcher reputations on a global scale, especially for researchers who previously had no reputation. The work of the Public Knowledge Project, with which I am involved, has provided journals in developing countries with an open source, free means of publishing their journals online. This online publication allows the journals' contents to become globally visible, enabling it to show up in Google Scholar search pages alongside other better-known work on the same topic. This level of visibility simply wasn't afforded by print, given the limits of both subscriptions and indexing.

But appearing on the same search result page is only part of this shift. Participating in the global research culture and having universal access to its literature is bound to help spread common research standards—something the Public Knowledge Project tries to support by using software to structure peer review, indexing, and other journal conventions. The Public Knowledge Project's software, Open Journal Systems, is used by approximately 1,500 journals in developing countries. It works in conjunction with the International Network for the Availability of Scientific Publications, which engages in the training of editors and the establishment of regional journal hosting and indexing services.

It is common to hear concerns expressed over the proliferation of research, as if somehow curtailing the global pursuit of knowledge in order to simplify one's own inquiry were a good thing. However, as the web grows, so do innovations for dealing with this ever-expanding body of information. Foremost among them are freely available search engines that allow one to sort through and find more of exactly what one is looking for. The U.S. government, for example, provides PubMed (life sciences) and Education Resources Information Center. When searching through these services, one can privilege journal articles over other materials but still be made aware of related materials by the same author, which enhances an individual's ability to judge for him- or herself the quality of research—or, at the very least, the reputation of the author. Google Scholar takes this a step further, allowing for a ready check of how often a work has been cited, by whom, and in what context.

Open access extends rather than derails the academy's reputation economy, opening it up to a wider and more global population. Still, risks abound and discernment is necessary. This new publishing medium is no less susceptible to deception and duplicity than print has been. As I write, there is news of a scientist fabricating data (Meier and Wilson 2009), a dubious open access publisher being tricked into publishing a fake article (Cooney 2009), and a highly respected subscription publisher being caught issuing fake journals sponsored by a pharmaceutical corporation (Grant 2009). It is not yet clear, this early into the history of the new medium, how scholarly publishers—who still retain ownership over the better part of this knowledge—are going to protect, if not continue to increase, their revenue streams in ways that do not conspicuously sacrifice the interests of scholars in seeing their work circulate as widely as possible.

What can be concluded at this point is that the academic community will continue to exploit the Internet in advancing the circulation of knowledge as a public good. This activity will continue to be underwritten by the reputational economy of public and private patronage. It is my belief that all of this bodes well for sharing knowledge and learning.

References

Antelman, K. 2004. Do open-access articles have a greater research impact? *College and Research Libraries* 65(5): 372–382. E-LIS. Retrieved from: <http://hdl.handle.net/10760/5463>.

Bergstrom, T. C. 2001. Free labor for costly journals? *Journal of Economic Perspectives* 15(4): 183–198. Retrieved from: <http://www.econ.ucsb.edu/~tedb/Journals/jeprevised.pdf>.

Carter, H. 1975. *A history of the Oxford University Press*, vol. 1. Oxford: University of Oxford Press.

Clark, W. 2006. *Academic charisma and the origins of the research university*. Chicago: University of Chicago Press.

Cooney, E. 2009, June 12. Fake paper tests peer review at open-access journal [web log post]. *White Coat Notes*. Retrieved from: <http://www.boston.com/news/health/blog/2009/06/phony_paper_tes.html>.

Davis, P. M., B. V. Lewenstein, D. H. Simon, J. G. Booth, and M. J. L. Connolly. 2008. Open access publishing, article downloads, and citations: Randomised controlled trial. *British Medical Journal* 337:a568.

Dasgupta, P., and A. David. 1994. Toward a new economics of science. *Policy Research* 23:487–521.

Directory of Open Access Journals. 2010. Retrieved from: <http://www.doaj.org>.

Evans, J. A., and J. Reimer. 2009. Open access and global participation in *Science*. *Science* 323 (5917): 1025.

Eysenbach, G. 2006. Citation advantage of open access articles. *PLoS Biology* 4 (5): e157.

Garvey, W. D. 1979. *Communication, the essence of science: Facilitating information exchange among librarians, scientists, engineers, and students*. Oxford: Pergamon.

Grant, B. 2009, May 7. Elsevier published six fake journals [web log post]. *The Scientist*. Retrieved from: <http://www.the-scientist.com/blog/display/55679>.

Hitchcock, S. 2009. The effect of open access and downloads ("hits") on citation impact: A bibliography of studies. Unpublished manuscript. *Open Citation Project*. Retrieved from: <http://opcit.eprints.org/oacitation-biblio.html>.

Hooker, W. 2009, April 19. Scholarly (scientific) journals vs. total serials: Percent price increase 1990–2009 [web log post]. *Open Reading Frame*. Retrieved from: <http://www.sennoma.net/main/archives/2009/04/scholarly_journals_vs_total_se.php>.

Kennison, K. 2005, June 23. The first impact factor for PLoS Biology [electronic mailing list message]. Retrieved from: <http://blog.lib.umn.edu/scholcom/accessdenied/029163.html>.

King, G. 2007. An introduction to the Dataverse Network as an infrastructure for data sharing. *Sociological Methods and Research* 32 (2): 173–199.

Masum, H., and Y. Zhang. 2004. Manifesto for the reputation society. *First Monday* 9 (7). Retrieved from: <http://firstmonday.org/article/view/1158/1078>.

Meier, B., and D. Wilson. 2009, June 5. Discredited research study stuns an ex-army doctor's colleagues. The New York Times. Retrieved from: <http://www.nytimes.com/2009/06/06/business/06surgeon.html>.

Mele, S., Dallman, D., Vigen, J., and Yeomans, J. 2006. Quantitative analysis of the publishing landscape in high-energy physics. *Journal of High Energy Physics* 12. Retrieved from: <http://www.scoap3.org/files/jhep122006S01.pdf>.

Merton, R. K. 1957. Priorities in scientific discovery: A chapter in the sociology of science. *American Sociological Review* 22 (6): 635–659.

Moran, B. T., ed. 1991. *Patronage and institutions: Science, technology, and medicine at the European court, 1500–1750*. Rochester: Boydell Press.

Pawson, R. 2006. *Evidence-based policy: A realist perspective*. Thousand Oaks, CA: Sage.

Registry of Open Access Repository Material Archiving Policies (ROARMAP). 2010. Retrieved from: <http://www.eprints.org/openaccess/policysignup>.

Russell, S. H., M. Hancock, and J. McCullough. 2007. Benefits of undergraduate research experiences. *Science* 316 (5824): 548–549.

Sackett, D. L., W. M. C. Rosenberg, J. A. M. Gray, R. B. Haynes, and W. S. Richardson. 1996. Evidence-based medicine: What it is and what it isn't. *British Medical Journal* 312:71–72.

SCOAP³ Working Party. 2007. Towards open access publishing in high energy physics. CERN, Geneva. Retrieved from: <http://scoap3.org/files/Scoap3WPReport.pdf>.

Swan, A. 2005. Self-archiving: It's an author thing. Paper presented at the Southampton Workshop on Institutional Open Access Repositories, University of Southampton, Southampton, UK. Retrieved from: <http://www.eprints.org/jan2005/ppts/swan.ppt>.

Van Orsdel, L. C., and K. Born. 2009, April 15. Reality bites: Periodicals price survey 2009. *Library Journal*. Retrieved from: <http://www.libraryjournal.com/article/CA6651248.html>.

Weber, S. 2004. *The success of open source*. Cambridge, MA: Harvard University Press.

Willinsky, J. 2006. *The access principle: The case for open access to research and scholarship*. Cambridge, MA: MIT Press.

V   IMPROVING POLICY

13 Reputation-Based Governance and Making States "Legible" to Their Citizens

Lucio Picci

A prerequisite to effective citizen engagement in governance is making government behavior transparent and understandable, or "legible," to its citizens. Lucio Picci shows how legibility can enable reputation-based governance and improve the accountability and incentives of governments and other large organizations.

Imagine a scenario in which citizens assess policies online, these assessments form the basis for reputational measures of public officials and other actors of governance, and these measures in turn influence governance decisions—for example, by determining bureaucrats' promotions and the choice of policies. Such a scenario can lead to *reputation-based governance*, which hinges on the ability of citizens to assess the outcomes of public policies, so that the administrators who are responsible for them may build a reputation (Picci 2011). With effective reputation-based governance, policies would be better attuned to people's needs and carried out more efficiently and effectively.

This chapter considers the issue of *legibility*, a term borrowed from James Scott (1998). Legibility has been used to refer to the ability of the state to "read" society—to understand the populace's collective abilities, biases, constraints, and desires in order to enable better governance. Yet there exists a parallel problem of *legibility of the state to its people*—an issue that should be seen as central in governance, especially forms of governance in which reputational incentives play a key role.

Within reputation-based governance, measures of reputation affect incentives; a high score, for example, eases the ascent up the career ladder. For this to happen, citizens should be able to understand easily what it is that they are assessing. For reputational measures to be computed, the responsibilities of the actions that are assessed should be unambiguously attributed—to public administrations, to individual administrators, and possibly to politicians.

In market applications of reputational systems, the identification of the relevant object and the tracking of responsibilities happens almost naturally. When buying on eBay, or when going to a restaurant, it is usually clear what it is that may be assessed (the product or service) and who the person or organization is whose reputational measure is being computed (the seller).

However, in the public sphere, the situation is quite different. Public governance today is complex and almost invariably multilevel: the overall action of the state is balkanized into countless policies and programs that almost invariably interact among themselves; boundaries are often blurred, and responsibilities for success or failure are not straightforward to attribute. This situation generally imposes a heavy cognitive load on citizens and opens the door for strategies of obfuscation of various types—unwarranted attribution of credit or blame, spin, bureaucratic delays, and downright propaganda. The necessary information may be available—indeed, thanks to the Internet, *lots* of information is available—but making sense of it is challenging.

What we face is a problem of *legibility of the state*—the task of gathering and decoding the vast array of information that communicates the state's overall actions. Before tackling this problem, we first consider the concept of legibility as James Scott (1998) originally introduced it: not of the state by society, which is what is needed for reputation-based governance to work, but legibility of society by the state, which is what states have long striven for.

Legibility of Society and Control

The concepts of legibility and of control of society go hand in hand. There are plenty of examples of control of society by the state. Video cameras in public spaces, we may think, are spying on us. It is compulsory in many countries to carry proof of personal identity. Even in the United States, where there is a deep-rooted resistance to forms of individual identification, the attacks of September 11, 2001, brought about greater compulsory identification before boarding an airplane. In Europe, where people are more nonchalant in this respect, national identity cards and automatic voting registration are the norm.

The state exerts a degree of control over its citizens. If we look at the issue from today's perspective, control arguably leads to more security—for example, vis-à-vis the terrorist menace. However, we are advised to take a broader historical view. Two necessities of the state go a long way in explaining its deep-seated tendency to control society. First, the requirement to levy taxes assumes the ability to identify persons and to eventually knock at their door should they not voluntarily pay their dues. Second, conscripting an army benefited historically from the capability of identifying persons.

There are societies in which this kind of control would be quite difficult. A nomadic tribe, for example, is difficult to tax or conscript. Persons who do not have a surname also constitute a problematic case. If John were "from the mountain," his identity might be perfectly clear within a small community. But if that John went to the plain, possibly to escape the occasional tax collector, then he would become one

John among many and—from the point of view of the state—a needle in a haystack. For such reasons, states do not like nomadic populations, and they also much prefer their subjects to have stable surnames, especially if they are linked to a unique numeric code. In modern societies, the friendlier face of the state's power also benefits from a legible society: infant vaccination programs and universal social services, for example, represent a positive achievement for humanity.

For society to be controllable, the state has to have means of "reading" it with ease. Society has to be legible, and the state has an interest in transforming society so as to make it such. In fact, Scott (1998) argues that many early initiatives of modern states may be interpreted as attempts to make society more legible. The introduction of surnames was a step in this direction, as was the imposition of a common national language, which allowed the immediate intelligibility of all written records produced without the need to interpret. Many agricultural reforms, by defining regular plots of land and easy ways of extracting any surplus in production, contributed to the goal of legibility. Overall, Scott summarizes, a "society that is relatively opaque to the state is . . . insulated from some forms of finely-tuned state interventions, both welcome (universal vaccinations) and resented (personal income taxes)" (1998, 77–78).

Legibility of the State and Accountability

We now consider the parallel problem of legibility of the state to its people, which is important in governance and central within reputation-based governance. Legibility of the state is needed for it to be accessible to its citizens: participation in state affairs and in the democratic process is facilitated by the ease with which the state and its activities can be deciphered. The legibility of the state, moreover, goes hand in hand with the possibility of holding it accountable for its actions.

Just as the state desires its citizens to be easily identifiable, so the citizens—in order to be able to hold the executors of policies accountable—should wish that the overall actions of the state be legible. Imagine a situation in which by feeding into one's mobile phone the unique identifier for a given policy, a wealth of information on that policy's characteristics, costs, and expected outcomes could be accessed. Further, under reputation-based governance, one could rate the policy's outcome, observe a summary of other people's assessments, and read the reputation measures of the administrators involved. So, policies should be well-identified and responsibilities clearly attributed: legibility and accountability are two sides of the same coin.

The wealth of information on policies, their outcomes, and the assessments that they receive could be harnessed in different ways. Of particular interest would be the comparison of the data available on similar initiatives that are carried out by different administrations. For example, such an information system could allow comparison of the cost of a kilometer of a new road with the average of similar works carried out elsewhere. Certainly, observing that the cost per kilometer of a length of road was 50 percent above the national average would not constitute a conclusive proof that something went wrong in its construction. There could be reasons to explain such difference: a more expensive road could be of better quality, or the terrain it covers could be more rugged. These differences could be taken into consideration by computing comparisons that are conditional on a host of external factors that may be relevant in determining costs.

Such average or "standardized" costs, if they could be computed, would aid in monitoring the execution of policies. In particular, they would assist in controlling one of the great plagues of governance: corruption. The very high economic and social costs of corruption go beyond the immediate diversion of public funds, as it has been demonstrated that corruption is accompanied by a series of distortions in the behaviors of public administrators, politicians, and firms, all of which add to corruption's damage (Lambsdorff 2006). Corruption affects some countries more than others, but it is a potentially serious problem everywhere. In many places, and particularly in relatively poor countries, the economic and social costs of corruption constitute a real tragedy.

The wealth of information available on policies under reputation-based governance would be quite helpful in this respect. The government could direct its auditing activities toward cases that look more suspicious because, for example, their unit cost significantly exceeds a measured average. Citizens, individually or through civil society organizations, could take advantage of the availability of well-organized data to hold their administrators and politicians accountable. For this to happen, the raw data should be freely available to all, so that any social actor could decide how to represent them. In this respect, Robinson and colleagues invite the U.S. government "to require that federal websites . . . use the same open systems for accessing the underlying data as they make available to the public at large" (2008, 160). (Note that exclusive control of the raw data by a single actor, by permitting the selection of *what* is publicly represented and *how*, would result in agenda-setting prerogatives within public discourse.)

Issues of Governance Design

Researchers interested in Internet-enabled forms of political participation sometimes have an exceedingly optimistic view of what the people want, believing that citizens are naturally interested in participating in politics and that—should the technological and organizational means be available—they would automatically turn into the engaged, net-enabled citizens of advanced forms of participatory democracies. Certainly, at times we observe dramatic examples of political participation. However, most of the time, people would arguably rather mind their own business and enjoy the company of their friends or lovers rather than participate in political activities. Researching the attitudes of American citizens to their government, Hibbing and Theiss-Morse summarize this reality with the disheartening conclusion that people "do not want to make political decisions themselves; they do not want to provide much input to those who are assigned to make these decisions; and they would rather not know all the details of the decision-making process." They conclude that "the last thing that people want is to be more involved in political decision making" (2002, 1).

This view may err on the side of pessimism, but it has the merit of alerting us to the importance of adopting forms of governance that make participation as easy, inexpensive, and enjoyable as possible for citizens. Lowering the cognitive obstacles to (and in general the cost of) political participation should be a priority. Unfortunately, notwithstanding some meritorious attempts at simplifying regulations and reducing the complexity of the tax system, the issue has rarely figured high among the preoccupations of public administration reformers.

Consider the so-called New Public Management reforms, which were fashionable during the 1980s and part of the 1990s. Dunleavy and colleagues remind us of the case of New Zealand, whose "pioneering [New Public Management] structural changes have left a country of 3.5 million people with over three hundred separate central agencies and forty tiny ministries, in addition to local and health service authorities" (Dunleavy, Margetts, Bastow, and Tinkler 2006, 470). In such a balkanized governance landscape, one wonders how citizens are supposed to figure out responsibilities or simply to remember the names of all the relevant institutional actors. New Zealand is probably an extreme case, and New Public Management styled reforms had—at least in some cases—a degree of success, but the anecdote shows a general tendency. It is striking to note how little attention has been dedicated to the cognitive problems of making sense of complex structures of governance. Of particular interest is the implication such difficulty has for the accountability of rulers and for popular participation in politics.

Today's Internet technologies can help in this respect. First, the Internet disseminates useful information cheaply. A citizen wishing to file a complaint, following a bad encounter with a government organization, in many cases may quickly learn from the organization's website who is in charge and to whom the letter should be addressed. At a more sophisticated level, we are witnessing the spread of so-called mashup applications, whereby different services are used in conjunction to represent policy-related data intelligently—and intelligibly. For example, information on public expenditures may be geocoded and then visualized in programs such as Google Earth.

The ability to visualize and make sense of large amounts of data opens up very interesting possibilities. However, technology alone does not solve the problem of legibility, because today's technological tools can only be applied within an already legible context. I'll make this point by considering a concrete example in the following section.

The Case of International Aid

In March 2010, the report of the United Nations Somalia Monitoring Group found that as much as half the food aid sent to Somalia was diverted from the intended beneficiaries to a web of corrupt contractors, militants, and local United Nations staff members. According to the same reference, "if the details of each contract and each transaction had been publicly available from the outset, it would not have been possible for these abuses to have taken place: transparency would pre-empt a good deal of this kind of abuse. The publication of broad summary totals for each project does not provide sufficient information to enable this kind of accountability or to prevent abuse" (Aidinfo 2010, 7).

In the world of delivering international aid to developing countries, there is a consensus that transparency should be increased. Aid projects typically involve many organizations acting in different and remote locations, so exercising control over projects is intrinsically difficult. The institutional context also matters because the projects often benefit countries that are characterized by high levels of corruption. Although the people who illegally benefit from such a system may be quite happy with the way it works, both donors and recipient countries have an interest in increasing the effectiveness of whatever resources are dedicated to international aid. As an expression of this convergence of interests, in September 2008, high-level delegations from all over the world met in Accra, Ghana, to address this and other issues related to international aid. The Accra meeting launched the International Aid Transparency Initiative (IATI), whose goal is "to make information about aid spending easier to access, use and understand" (IATI 2010a). To meet this broad goal, several interlocking initiatives are currently being undertaken.

We should note that for the most part, the problem is not one of creating new information from scratch, as much of the desired information already exists in the archives and institutional knowledge of the many organizations involved. In principle, a dedicated fact finder could ask particular organizations to disclose financial and other desired information on the aid project they are involved with. However, this would be no easy task. First of all, the names and addresses of such organizations would be needed. Those organizations would in turn find it costly to collect the desired information. The information coming from the different organizations would likely be provided in different formats and hence could be reconciled only with effort; verification would also be a concern. Again, we face a problem of legibility: the information may be available in principle, but finding, collecting, and making sense of it would require much work.

One obvious way to solve the problem would be to build a database into which all the interested parties could input the necessary information using a web interface. However, this possibility was discarded for several reasons, the foremost being that duplicating information that may already exist is costly and, as such, would hinder the adoption of the proposed solution and potentially cause its failure (Development Initiatives 2010). IATI chose an alternative route: brokering an agreement among the many stakeholders involved to adopt a common format to present the needed information, but leaving them otherwise free to publish it where they wish (IATI 2010b). Choosing a common format means agreeing on a series of standards and rules. First, there must be a system in place that can unambiguously identify each project and all of the organizations involved. Second, the information should be presented together with appropriate accompanying data (or metadata), clarifying what it is about. Third, the veracity and quality of the data made available should be verified by a third party.

The desired information would reside in many different locations, such as the web-sites of the organizations involved; these sites would have to be recorded into a common registry. Overall, the information would be machine-readable, in the sense that appropriate software could be written to collect it and automatically process it in desired ways. It is true that data scraping techniques (i.e., parsing of unstructured data) can in many instances permit the transfer of data that are not appropriately structured or designed to be machine readable. Although the collaborative use of data-scraping tools opens up interesting possibilities of increasing legibility of public governance "from below," such a solution can be only partial, due to its cost, partial applicability, and dependence on the availability of the desired data.

With structured and machine-readable data, anybody would be able to access the raw information that is made available, to process and visualize it as desired. Mashup applications, aimed for example at representing geocoded information on a map, would be straightforward to create. A similar setup would allow the introduction of reputational mechanisms in the management of aid projects. Once each project is clearly identified, the people who should in principle benefit from the project could evaluate its outcome. A clear knowledge of the chain of responsibilities in the execution of each project would in turn allow for the use of the assessments to compute suitable measures of reputation, not unlike what is done in many current Internet-based reputational systems such as eBay. These measures would likely be considered by donors deciding how to invest their resources. Organizations involved in delivering aid projects, as a consequence, would have a clear incentive to develop a reputation for responsibility, skill, and effectiveness. (See chapter 9.)

For such a concept to succeed, many important issues should be addressed. There should be a patient effort to work out bugs in reputation measures, and parallel field-work with real aid recipients to understand how to get valid and useful recipient evaluations. Also, many—if not most—actors will have incentives to skew the system and metrics to their advantage. In Picci 2011, the presence of incentives in gaming the system is considered explicitly; here it suffices to recognize that in governance, any set of incentives brings about attempts at bending them to serve one's needs, often in disaccord with the public good. These worries should be explicitly and carefully addressed in practical implementations.

The Road to Legibility of the State

In the case of international aid, the requirement of transparency could have been achieved by obliging all concerned organizations to publish on the web a set of relevant information on the projects to which they contribute. This requirement would have been a valuable step forward, but not in itself enough to guarantee legibility, which has to do with the possibility of easily making sense of the information available. Transparency is a necessary condition for legibility, but not a sufficient one.

The example story in particular shows that technology alone is not enough to solve problems of legibility. If IATI is successful in making international aid more legible, it will not be simply because more information is available, or because it will have hammered clever code into computers. It will also be because IATI will have built consensus among many stakeholders on a set of definitions, standards, and practices. Only when this intrinsically political goal is accomplished will the community of stakeholders of international aid be able to tap into the power of information technologies to increase both transparency and accountability.

In this respect, we observe an important difference from the private sphere. Legibility is easier to obtain in markets; an easily understandable description of what is traded is a prerequisite for market functions. The process of international harmonization of accounting practices certainly contributed, for example, to a situation in which the activities of public enterprises display—at least in principle—a high degree of transparency and legibility, while not being sufficient to prevent serious forms of corporate dishonesty. On the other hand, within the public sphere, legibility is often a matter of contention between a state and its citizens, with each one resisting the desire that the other has of control or accountability. Over the last century, a "struggle toward openness" (Fung, Graham, and Weil 2007, 24–29) has brought about, in the United States and elsewhere, an increased degree of transparency from which the people have benefited. And a struggle it was, with the state often fighting back—witness, in the United States, the general retrenchment in public access to government information under President George W. Bush (Fung, Graham, and Weil 2007).

The advantages that the adoption of reputation-based governance would bring to public governance add extra motivation to make the state more legible. Inevitably, reforms would be needed. In Picci 2011, it is argued that a way to tackle the legibility problem is to structure the actions of public administrations as easily identifiable policies that citizens could monitor and assess. The result would be a policy space more modular in nature, that is, one that is formed by clearly distinguishable modular building blocks.

Such organizational changes could be obtained only with public administration reforms, and would need a firm political will to carry out. This political will would be the result of the dialectic encounter between the state and the people. The former might try to defend in various ways its prerogatives and privileges, and to make arguments against adopting unproven new systems too quickly. As for the people, the potential benefits of introducing reputation-based governance might constitute an argument in favor of positive change.

Acknowledgments

I thank Hassan Masum, Mark Tovey, and Fabio Vitali for thoughtful comments on a preliminary version of this chapter.

References

Aidinfo. 2010. Show me the money: IATI and traceability. Briefing paper. Retrieved from: <http://www.aidtransparency.net/wp-content/uploads/2009/10/Show-me-the-money-IATI-and-aid-traceability.pdf>.

Development Initiatives. 2010. Implementing IATI: Practical proposals. Final draft. Retrieved from: <http://www.aidtransparency.net/wp-content/uploads/2009/06/Implementing-IATI-Jan-2010-v2.pdf>.

Dunleavy, P., H. Margetts, S. Bastow, and J. Tinkler. 2006. New Public Management is Dead—Long Live Digital-Era Governance. *Journal of Health Economics* 27 (5): 1201–1207.

Fung, A., M. Graham, and D. Weil. 2007. *Full disclosure: The perils and promise of transparency*. Cambridge: Cambridge University Press.

Hibbing, J. R., and E. Theiss-Morse. 2002. *Stealth democracy. Americans' beliefs about how government should work*. Cambridge: Cambridge University Press.

International Aid Transparency Initiative (IATI). 2010a. IATI home page. Retrieved from: <http://www.aidtransparency.net>.

International Aid Transparency Initiative. 2010b. Consultation on IATI Standards: Parts 1 (Scope), 2 (Definitions), and 3 (Data format). Retrieved from: <http://www.aidtransparency.net/wp-content/uploads/2009/06/Consultation-Paper-for-Data-Definitions-and-Format.doc>.

Lambsdorff, J. G. 2006. Causes and consequences of corruption: What do we know from a cross-section of countries? In *International Handbook of Economic Corruption*, ed. Susan Rose-Ackerman, 3–51. Cheltenham, UK: Edward Elgar.

Picci, Lucio. 2011. *Reputation-based governance*. Stanford, CA: Stanford University Press.

Robinson, D., H. Yu, W. Zeller, and E. W. Felten. 2008. Government data and the invisible hand. *Yale Journal of Law and Technology* 11:160–175.

Scott, J. C. 1998. *Seeing like a state*. New Haven: Yale University Press.

14   Trust It Forward: Tyranny of the Majority or Echo Chambers?

Paolo Massa

If reputation systems weight all perspectives similarly, they may devolve into simple majority rule. But if they give each user reputation scores that take only other similar users' opinions into account, they may become "echo chambers" in which like-minded people reinforce each others' views without being open to outside perspectives. Paolo Massa discusses design choices and trust metrics that may help balance these two extremes, and the broader implications for our future societies.

Trust Is a Key Element for Society

Trust is a key element for society. Without trust, society could not exist (Fukuyama 1995). We rely on trust when we walk out in the street, when we talk to somebody, when we buy something—in our every action.

Even the very act of reading this contribution is based on trust: you, the reader, have some degree of trust in the editors of the book, and in the authors of the contributions and their ability to collectively provide an insightful and interesting book.

The *Oxford English Dictionary* defines trust as "the firm belief in the reliability, truth or ability of someone or something" (1990b). In fact, the concept of trust is not new and has received much attention from scholars for centuries (Locke 1680). As trust is a multifaceted concept, thinkers from disciplines as diverse as economics, philosophy, psychology, sociology, anthropology, and political science have attempted to formalize it and to understand the importance trust has for our societies (de Tocqueville 1840; Putnam 1995; Mill 1859; Sunstein 1999).

Influential research has analyzed how trust correlates with basic features of communities and nations. The World Values Survey project is an ongoing research effort that is trying to assess the state of social, cultural, and moral values in different countries of the world. Every year, in each country, at least 1,000 citizens answer about 250 questions during face-to-face interviews. Some questions are related to general trust, such as, "Generally speaking, would you say that most people can be trusted?" These data give a detailed picture of values across time in the world. For example, in 1999, 61 percent of people in Norway said others in their country are trustworthy (the highest percentage in the survey), whereas only 6.6 percent of people in Brazil said others are trustworthy (the lowest). This finding suggests that different societies have a different default expectation of the trustworthiness of others.

These data have been used to demonstrate correlations between general trust and many features of societies and countries. For example, trust has been shown to be positively correlated with economic growth, well-being, and happiness, and negatively correlated with crime and corruption. Greater ethnic diversity was found to be correlated with less trust by one author (Putnam 1995), though this may depend on the society in question. The influential book *Bowling Alone* (Putnam 1995) also comments on the decline of social capital and general trust in America in the past twenty-five years as something that must be fixed from a public policy point of view. One study has shown the default level of trust to increase with education (Toshio 2001). Trust can be considered and studied as a basic constituent of a human society, and it correlates with what we might have in mind as a healthy society (Fukuyama 1995).

Trust 2.0: Society Moves Online

Social network sites (SNSs) are web-based services that allow individuals to construct a public or semipublic profile. Users can generally upload their picture, add a textual description of themselves and their interests, and have this information shown in their user profile, usually with an overview of recent activity performed by the user. Users can also be "friends" with other users or express other social relationships (boyd and Ellison 2007).

Examples of this new paradigm range from entertainment-oriented sites such as Facebook or Orkut.com to e-marketplaces such as eBay. They range from opinion-sharing sites such as Epinions or Essembly.com to activity-sharing sites such as Flickr.com or Delicious.com and to business networking sites such as LinkedIn (Massa 2006).

In all these settings, the social relationships and connections users can express are different and have different meanings. As boyd and Ellison (2007) note, "The nature and nomenclature of these connections may vary from site to site." Here we want to provide a unifying view about these online social relationships: they can be considered as expressions of trust, that is, as trust statements.

We use an operational definition of trust from Massa. Trust is defined as "the explicit opinion expressed by a user about a target user, regarding the perceived quality of a certain characteristic of the latter" (Massa 2006, 55). The term "trust statement" is used with the same meaning. For example, in some systems quality refers to the ability to provide reliable and interesting product reviews (as in Epinions). In other systems, it refers to the ability to be a good friend for the user (as in Facebook). In yet others, it is the ability to find interesting new websites (as in Delicious.com). This is called the *trust context*, and it is the characteristic of the target user that is evaluated by the user who emits the trust statement.

Of course, in different trust contexts, a user can express different trust statements about the same target user. For example, the subjective trust expressed by Alice of Bob about his professional skills (the trust context of LinkedIn) may not be correlated with the trust expressed by Alice of Bob about his quality of being an honest seller online (the trust context of eBay). In this chapter, we interpret the social relationships expressed on SNSs as trust statements. It should be noted that, at present, in only a few SNSs is there explicit mention of the term "trust"—for example, on Epinions the list of favorite users is called the "Web of Trust" (Epinions, n.d.).

Bloggers commonly include a list of blogs they read in their "blogroll," which often represents their trusted sources of information. The web itself can be considered as a giant trust network. Considering links between web pages as trust statements was precisely the clever intuition exploited by algorithms such as Google PageRank (Page et al. 1998) for inferring authority of web pages. Although links, citations, and other mentions can be negative as well as positive, the basic intuition works well enough in practice to be useful.

In the future, even more of our relationships may leave electronic trust trails, especially if current trends continue toward most people being always connected with powerful mobile devices.

Representing Trust

Trust is a relationship between two users. A formal example of a trust statement is "I, Alice, trust Bob as 0.8 in the range [0,1] about the trust context of pleasant violin playing."

Reputation is closely related to trust. In general, reputation summarizes what a community as a whole thinks about a certain user in a certain trust context. The *Oxford English Dictionary* puts it this way: "reputation is what is generally said or believed about a person's or thing's character or standing" (1990a).

For computational purposes, both trust and reputation can be represented as normalized values in the range [0,1], with 0 as the minimum (no trust or no reputation) and 1 as the maximum (total trust or total reputation). Formally, we have $trust(A,B)\rightarrow[0,1]$ *and reputation(A)$\rightarrow$[0,1]* meaning that trust is personalized and reputation is not. (We discuss later the key difference between trust and reputation, especially as metaphors for key design choices of SNSs.)

Frequently, SNSs don't allow users to express weights on trust relationships, mainly in order to keep the system simple for the user to understand. An exception is represented by eBay, at which it is possible to leave positive, negative and neutral feedback—this can be mapped, for example, to the values (1, 0, 0.5). Another exception is Advogato.org, an SNS for open source developers, at which users can express their trust relationships in other programmers using four textual labels—Master, Apprentice, Journeyer, and Observer—which can be mapped, for example, to the values 1.0, 0.8, 0.6, and 0.4 (Massa et al. 2008).

Asking humans to represent trust explicitly and to make trust statements visible is already changing how we humans think about and rely on trust. Zak postulates that in our society "the decision to trust another human being is largely unconscious and utilizes the 'social brain'" (2006, 23). Making trust explicit seems likely to change how we as a society use it.

Another challenge that representing trust introduces is the disproportionately large fraction of positive trust statements with respect to negative ones that is common to find on SNSs. On eBay for example, more than 99 percent of the feedback has been positive (Massa 2006). Moreover, trust statements are often made public (for greater accountability and less forgeability). Especially in sensitive contexts such as job relationships, you may need to have courage and a strong reason to explicitly and publicly express *trust(Me,MyBoss)=0.1*—not many people may be willing to do this.

The interface and keywords used in describing a social relationship also play a key role. In many sites, everything is conflated under the abused term "friend," while others such as Essembly allow for more contextual labels such as "ally" and "nemesis" (Brzozowski et al. 2008).

Reasoning on Trust

In all the SNSs mentioned earlier, it is possible to interact with unknown people. "Unknown" means that one does not have any firsthand idea about their reliability or about how much trust to place in them. Reputation systems (Resnick et al. 2000, Ziegler and Lausen 2004) and trust metrics (Massa and Avesani 2007) are techniques for answering questions such as, "Should I trust this person?" Based on the answer, one can decide whether to interact with another user.

Once trust statements are represented electronically, it is possible to reason based on them. Reputation systems and trust metrics usually work in the following way: first they aggregate all or some of the trust statements expressed by the users in a global or partial trust network, and then they perform some computation in order to predict the reputation or the trustworthiness of all the users. The computation ranges from simple averages for computing a global reputation such as in eBay, to trust propagation over the trust network for computing a global reputation such as with PageRank (Page et al. 1998), to a personalized trust score (Golbeck, Parsia, and Hendler 2003; Massa and Avesani 2007; Ziegler and Lausen 2004), to formal trust algebra based on probability theory (Jøsang 1999). Philosopher John Locke already provided what we have called a trust metric:

Probability, then, being to supply the defect of our knowledge, and to guide us where that fails, is always conversant about propositions whereof we have no certainty, but only some inducements to receive them for true. The grounds of it are, in short, these two following: *First*, The conformity of anything with our own knowledge, observation, and experience. *Secondly*, The testimony of others, vouching their observation and experience. In the testimony of others is to be considered: 1. The number. 2. The integrity. 3. The skill of the witnesses. 4. The design of the author, where it is a testimony out of a book cited. 5. The consistency of the parts, and circumstances of the relation. 6. Contrary testimonies. (1680, 886)

One of the main concerns about reputation systems and trust metrics is the fact that they can be attacked and gamed. What are often called "malicious users" can hijack systems in order to get a personal advantage, such as increasing the reputation of an identity ("reputation boosting") or decreasing it ("reputation nuking"). Usually, reputation boosting is applied to a personal identity or the identity of a friend, and reputation nuking is perpetrated on the identity of a competitor or enemy. There have been different recommendations for addressing these threats and making a trust metric more attack-resistant (Levien, n.d.; Massa 2006).

A Change in Perspective: From Global to Local

We consider now a different conceptual approach, and claim that a system is attackable if the system is created with the assumption of a correct value of reputation for everyone. In this case, there will be incentives to try to game the system in order to influence this unique and global reputation value. Such a system is inherently attackable. If this assumption is dropped, the threat is weakened significantly.

What we are suggesting is to move from global trust metrics to local trust metrics (Massa and Avesani 2007). Global trust metrics compute a global reputation value for every single user, coming to conclusions such as "the reputation of Carol is 0.4." On the other hand, local trust metrics predict trustworthiness scores that are personalized from the point of view of every single user, coming to conclusions such as "Alice should trust Carol as 0.9" and "Bob should trust Carol as 0.1." The very same user Carol can be predicted as trustworthy from the point of view of Alice and as untrustworthy from the point of view of Bob.

Local trust metrics don't try to average differences of opinion but rather to build on them. The assumption of local trust metrics is that every opinion is worthy and there are no automatically wrong opinions. If someone happens to disagree with the large majority who think that "George is trustworthy," it may not be useful for society at large to consider his or her opinions as wrong or malicious. Playing on "one man's signal is another man's noise," we might say "one man's trusted peer is another man's untrusted peer" (Massa 2006).

Without moving into the contentious domain of political ideas, it is easy to provide an example from the debated domain of peer-to-peer (P2P) file sharing. In a P2P network, Alice might consider "good" a peer that shares a lot of leaked political documents or just-released copyrighted movies (i.e., trust that peer), yet Bob might consider the very same peer "bad" (i.e., distrust that peer). But there is no universally applicable trust statement. Each peer can believe what he or she prefers based on his or her own subjective belief system (though group norms and laws may constrain individual beliefs). Disagreements are a normal part of life and social groups and are often even productive. Without an overriding social concern, there may be no positive utility in trying to squash down differences of opinion.

Although the previous argument is anecdotal, we have offered an analysis of the Epinions trust network as evidence that trust statements are indeed subjective in a real world setting (Massa and Avesani 2007). Epinions is a website at which users write reviews about products and assign them a rating. Epinions also allows users to express their Web of Trust, that is, "reviewers whose reviews and ratings they have consistently found to be valuable" and their Block list, that is, "authors whose reviews they find consistently offensive, inaccurate, or in general not valuable" (Epinions, n.d.). These expressions correspond to issuing a positive trust statement such as $trust(A,B)=1$ and a negative trust statement such as $trust(A,B)=0$, respectively.

We found that on Epinions, it is common to have disagreements of opinion about the trustworthiness of other users; that is, it is common that someone places a certain user in their Web of Trust and someone else places the very same user in their Block List. Typically, these opinions are not wrong or malicious; they represent legitimate differences of evaluation. Simply put, there are users who are trusted by some and distrusted by others; we call these users *controversial users*. Surprisingly, in the Epinions dataset that we evaluated, more than 20 percent of users were controversial users (Massa and Avesani 2007).

For controversial users, global trust metrics are not effective by definition because global averages cannot predict correctly the very different trust statements received by this kind of user. However in Massa and Avesani 2007, we also performed an empirical comparison of local and global trust metrics that demonstrates our claim. Moreover local trust metrics can be attack-resistant (Golbeck, Parsia, and Hendler 2003; Levien, n.d.; Ziegler and Lausen 2004). For instance, if only the opinions of users directly trusted by the active user are considered, it is less easy for an attacker to influence the prediction that the active user gets. As long as the active user does not explicitly trust one of the bogus profiles (and the users whom he or she trusts don't do it either), the bogus profiles are not going to influence computations of trustworthiness values. The user is in control and can check which trusted users, if any, have been fooled into trusting a bogus profile.

Recently, SNSs have been moving toward emphasizing more locality. For example, Essembly, a "fiercely non-partisan social network," allows members to post "resolves" reflecting controversial opinions, such as "Overall, free trade is good for American workers" (Brzozowski et al. 2008, 1). Members can then vote on these resolves, using a four-point scale: Agree, Lean Agree, Lean Against, or Against. Users can vote once per resolve, and all votes are viewable by other members, forming an ideological profile. In this site, users can express three different social relationships: friend as "someone you know personally and have a friendship with in the real world," ally as "someone who you don't necessarily know, but . . . share a desire to make some change in the world," and nemesis as "someone who you don't agree with . . . their world view is just psychotically skewed." (Brzozowski et al. 2008, 2). A striking pattern seems to emerge: an enemy of an enemy seems to be a friend or ally. Similarly to Essembly, Lerman and Galstyan (2008) analyze social voting patterns of Digg users; at Digg, users' social networks are used to suggest personalized interesting stories.

Two Extremes of Possible Societies as Shaped by Trust Metrics

We would like to conclude by highlighting two extremes of society that can be induced by the basic assumptions behind the two different kinds of trust metrics: tyranny of the majority and echo chambers.

A system powered by a global trust metric, in effect, tends to assume that there are globally agreed-upon good users, and that people who think differently from the average are malicious. This assumption encourages herd behavior and penalizes creative thinkers, black sheep, and original and unexpected opinions.

We underline that there is a *tyranny of the majority* risk—a term coined in 1835 by Alexis de Tocqueville in his book *Democracy in America* (1840). Nineteenth-century philosopher John Stuart Mill in his book *On Liberty* (1859) also analyzes this concept with respect to social conformity. The term "tyranny of the majority" refers to the fact that the opinions of the majority within society are the basis of all rules of conduct within that society. On each specific issue, people will express themselves either for or against the issue, and the side with the largest number of supporters will prevail. Each minority has, by definition, opinions different from the majority (Massa and Avesani 2007), opinions with no "protection . . . against the tyranny of the prevailing opinion and feeling." (Mill 1859, 13).

The Wikipedia project tries to find a balance between what different people think about every single topic by asking the contributors to adopt a "neutral point of view" (NPOV). This approach seems to work well enough in most cases at present, possibly because the people who self-elect for editing Wikipedia articles largely share a similar "culture." However, the frequent "edit wars" evident on highly sensitive and controversial topics show that it is—and will be—hard to keep this global and theoretically unbiased point of view.

We believe that the minority's opinions should be seen as an opportunity and a point of discussion, and not simply assumed to be sources of "incorrect" (or "unfair") ratings, as they are often modeled in simulations in trust metrics research papers. Moreover, in digital systems such as SNSs, automatic personalization is possible, so there is in principle no need to make this assumption and try to force users to behave in the same way.

Research carried out by Salganik, Dodds, and Watts (2006) is enlightening in this regard. They created a music website at which users could rate and download songs by unknown bands. The home page also showed the top ten list, that is, the most popular songs (or, if you like, the songs currently appreciated by the majority). They assigned the users to eight different copies of the site with the same songs in them, without the users knowing it. The striking result was that in each of the site copies, the top ten lists determined by user ratings were different. Popularity was not primarily induced by some intrinsic quality of the songs, but by aggregated ratings activity and how it was displayed in the top ten list. This result suggests that an artist like Britney Spears, who is popular in our world, might have been a nobody in some other world. Different majorities, formed based on different and seemingly random patterns, imposed on the community and its minorities a certain top artist. This fact was unavoidable in the mass media era. But now that personalization is possible, is it necessary to constrain everybody into a global "best" (such as Britney Spears) when we can end up with many different local "bests"?

We can ponder the other extreme: total personalization. But there is a risk in this extreme as well that is caused by emphasizing too much locality in trust propagation by a local trust metric. This total personalization approach consists in considering, for example, only opinions of directly trusted users and not of the rest of the community constituents.

This risk has been called the *echo chamber* or "daily me" (Sunstein 1999). Sunstein notes how "technology has greatly increased people's ability to 'filter' what they want to read, see, and hear"(Sunstein 1999, 3). He warns that everyone with access to this technology has the ability to listen to and watch just what they want to hear and see—to encounter only opinions of like-minded people, and never be confronted with people with different ideas and opinions.

In this scenario, there is a risk of segmentation of society into micro groups that tend to adopt extreme views, develop their own culture, and not communicate with people outside their group. Sunstein argues that in order to avoid these risks, "people should be exposed to materials that they would not have chosen in advance. Unplanned, unanticipated encounters are central to democracy itself" and "many or most citizens should have a range of common experiences. Without shared experiences . . . people may even find it hard to understand one another" (Sunstein 1990, 9). Recent research published in the *Psychological Bulletin* shows that people are about twice as likely to select information that supports their own point of view (67 percent) as to consider an opposing idea (33 percent) (Hart et al. 2009).

These considerations are not new. As cited by McPherson, Smith-Lovin, and Cook (2001), in *Rhetoric* and *Nicomachean Ethics*, Aristotle noted that people "love those who are like themselves"; in addition, Plato observed in *Phaedrus* that "similarity begets friendship." McPherson, Smith-Lovin and Cook (2001) conducted a large analysis of *homophily* (the tendency to bond with others who are similar) in social networks and found that "homophily in race and ethnicity creates the strongest divides in our personal environments, with age, religion, education, occupation, and gender following in roughly that order." They conclude commenting how homophily limits people's social worlds in a way that has powerful implications for the information they receive, the attitudes they form, and the interactions they experience.

A society without some common shared culture cannot be defined as a society. The societal utility of "massification" is that we, as a society, can rely on some cultural artifacts that bond us together. Knowing we can rely on common culture is reassuring, and allows different people to feel some bonds as a group and as a society. When, or if, there are no more cultural elements capable of bonding us together because all have become singletons with their own peculiar and totally personalized cultures, the very existence of our society may be at risk (Sunstein 1999).

Conclusion

As we have seen, concerns about ways of trusting and the societies they induce are not new. What is new is that information and communication technologies are playing an increasing role in shaping our future societies.

We believe that in the near future, more and more people will increasingly rely on opinions formed based on facts collected through reputation systems and social network sites (Massa 2006). The assumptions on which these systems are constructed will have a fundamental impact on the kinds of societies and cultures they shape. Here we have offered "tyranny of the majority" and "echo chambers" as a way to think about the two extremes of a range of options toward which our society might evolve.

The final and very open question is, "Will we be able to mediate between the two extremes?" This is surely not an easy task. We hope this chapter can help modestly, by providing some starting points for a fruitful and ongoing discussion about issues which are important for our common future.

References

boyd, d. m. and Ellison, N. B. 2007. Social network sites: Definition, history, and scholarship. *Journal of Computer-Mediated Communication* 13: 210–230.

Brzozowski, M. J., T. Hogg, and G. Szabo. 2008. Friends and foes: Ideological social networking. *Proceeding of the twenty-sixth annual SIGCHI conference on human factors in computing systems* (CHI '08), New York, 817–820.

Epinions. n.d. Web of Trust FAQ. Retrieved November 7, 2010, from: <http://www.epinions.com/help/faq/?show=faq_wot>.

Fukuyama, F. 1995. *Trust: The social virtues and the creation of prosperity.* New York: Free Press.

Golbeck, J., B. Parsia, and J. Hendler. 2003. Trust networks on the semantic web. *Proceedings of Cooperative Information Agents* VII:238–249.

Hart, W., A. H. Eagly, M. J. Lindberg, D. Albarraccin, I. Brechan, and L. Merrill. 2009. Feeling validated versus being correct: A meta-analysis of selective exposure to information. *Psychological Bulletin* 135 (4): 555–588.

Jøsang, A. 1999. An algebra for assessing trust in certification chains. *Proceedings of the Network and Distributed Systems Security Symposium* (NDSS99), San Diego, CA.

Lerman, K., and A. Galstyan. 2008. Analysis of social voting patterns on Digg. *Proceedings of the ACM SIGCOMM Workshop on Online Social Networks.*

Levien, R. n.d. Attack-resistant trust metrics. Unpublished doctoral dissertation. Retrieved from: <http://www.levien.com/thesis/thesis.pdf>.

Locke, J. [1680] 1978. *An essay concerning human understanding.* Sussex, UK: Harvester Press.

Massa, P. 2006. A survey of trust use and modeling in current real systems. In *Trust in E-services: Technologies, Practices, and Challenges,* ed. R. Song, L. Korba, and G. Yee, 51–83. Idea Group.

Massa, P., and P. Avesani. 2007. Trust metrics on controversial users: Balancing between tyranny of the majority and echo chambers. In *International Journal on Semantic Web and Information Systems* (special issue on Semantics of People and Culture): 39–64.

Massa, P., Souren, K., Salvetti, M. and Tomasoni, D. 2008. Trustlet: Open research on trust metrics. *Scientific International Journal for Parallel and Distributed Computing,* 9 (4): 341–351.

McPherson, M., L. Smith-Lovin, and J. M. Cook. 2001. Birds of a feather: Homophily in social networks. *Annual Review of Sociology* 27:415–444.

Mill, J. Stuart. 1859. *On liberty.* McMaster University archive for the history of economic thought. London: J. W. Parker and Son.

Oxford English Dictionary. 1990a. Reputation entry. New York: Oxford University Press.

Oxford English Dictionary. 1990b. Trust entry. New York: Oxford University Press.

Page, L., S. Brin, R. Motwani, and T. Winograd. 1998. The PageRank citation ranking: Bringing order to the web. *Proceedings of ASIS98,* 161–172.

Putnam, R. D. 1995. Bowling alone: America's declining social capital. *Journal of Democracy* 6 (1): 65–78.

Resnick, P., K. Kuwabara, R. Zeckhauser, and E. Friedman. 2000. Reputation systems. *Communications of the ACM* 43 (12): 45–48.

Salganik, M. J., P. S. Dodds, and D. J. Watts. 2006. Experimental study of inequality and unpredictability in an artificial cultural market. *Science* 311 (5762):854–856.

Sunstein, C. 1999. *Republic.com*. Princeton: Princeton University Press.

de Tocqueville, A. [1840] 1966. *Democracy in America*, trans. G. Lawrence. New York: Doubleday.

Toshio, Y. 2001. Trust as a form of social intelligence. In *Trust in Society*, ed. C. Cook, 121–147. New York: Russell Sage Foundation.

Zak, P. J. 2006. Trust. *Journal of Financial Transformation* 4 (1): 17–24.

Ziegler, C. N., and G. Lausen. 2004. Spreading activation models for trust propagation. In *IEEE International Conference on e-Technology, e-Commerce and e-Service* (EEE '04),Taipei, Taiwan, 83–97.

15 Rating in Large-Scale Argumentation Systems

Luca Iandoli, Josh Introne, and Mark Klein

How can reputation enable more effective and collaborative deliberation? Luca Iandoli, Josh Introne, and Mark Klein describe how argument maps can be extended to intuitively highlight ideas of collective interest. They then report on applications in the areas of climate change and biofuels, and suggest that reputation-enabled online argumentation might help us to overcome systemic challenges.

Enabling Large-Scale Deliberation through Argumentation Technology

Dealing with systemic challenges—such as global terrorism, climate change, and ecosystem health—demands the effective synthesis of perspectives and expertise from hundreds or thousands of contributors with diverse bodies of knowledge. Existing approaches to group decision making are not well suited to these kinds of problems. Informal deliberation, such as might go on in a boardroom, has been shown to have many deficiencies (e.g., Nunamaker et al. 1991; Stasser, Taylor, and Hanna 1989). Technologically mediated processes may address some of these problems, but do not scale (e.g., DeSanctis and Gallupe 1987). And large-scale, socially mediated processes (e.g., government decision making) have been roundly criticized in the popular media for their inefficiencies.

In this chapter, we discuss an approach to grappling with large systemic challenges through mass collaboration enabled by the Internet. It has been demonstrated in recent years that the work of many volunteers can be combined to improve processes that previously could only be performed by a much smaller number of experts. For example, news aggregators (e.g., Slashdot, Google News) improve upon the functions of traditional media outlets by identifying news items of interest to a community or individual. Wikipedia is larger and more up to date than the *Encyclopedia Britannica*, and of comparable quality (Giles 2005) yet has been created in far less time.

Our approach to large-scale problem solving integrates community rating with large-scale argumentation systems to enable semistructured deliberation by very large groups. *Community rating* refers to the set of rules, practices, and tools through which the members of an online community evaluate online content or other users' behaviors and qualifications. Community rating can help users separate good content from bad or irrelevant content, spot inappropriate behaviors, and recognize trustworthy or expert members. Examples of community rating are the eBay system for evaluating seller or buyer reliability and the Slashdot voting system for identifying interesting comments on articles (discussed in more detail in chapter 7).

Large-scale argumentation systems are web-based systems in which large numbers of users (hundreds or more) use argument maps to deliberate on controversial topics. *Argument maps* allow for the presentation of relevant issues, together with each of the positions one might hold with respect to an issue, coupled with the arguments for (or against) such positions. Argument maps often use visual presentation techniques (e.g., tree diagrams, colors) to make these relationships clear.

Combining Argumentation with Community Rating

Instead of individual posts, argumentation systems involve chains of reasoning. Positions are supported or refuted by arguments, which may themselves be supported or refuted by other arguments.

The ratings for individual arguments may be combined or *aggregated*, which allows one to compute a rating for the position (and other arguments) to which the individual arguments connect. This approach ensures that highly rated positions are not simply popular, but are also well supported by compelling arguments.

The combination of community rating with argument maps has many potential benefits:

• Rating in argumentation systems enables the rapid and consistent evaluation of a chain of reasoning for or against a particular idea. If users see that a position they favor has what they consider to be an inappropriately low rating, it provides them with an incentive to enter more compelling arguments, which will (they hope) result in higher ratings for their favored position. This system drives the creation of a more complete map of possible solutions and their underlying rationales.
• Such maps can help people become aware of biases in their beliefs (e.g., when their evaluation for a position is inconsistent with their ratings for the underlying arguments) and can thus encourage people to evaluate posts based on reason, rather than bias.
• The structure and visual presentation of an argument map can make higher-level aspects of the overall deliberation obvious. For instance, rankings of arguments in any subtree can be analyzed to calculate the overall degree of consensus within that subtree. This information can be used to color the map, allowing areas of consensus and sources of conflict to be quickly identified.
• Argumentation systems provide more nuanced information about users and hence offer a powerful method for deriving and incorporating reputation scores. For instance,

a user that posts arguments or provides ratings that are inconsistent with one another may lack sound reasoning skills (or be deliberately contrarian) and should not be considered a reliable participant. On the other hand, a user who consistently posts arguments that generate large, contentious debates may have a better understanding of the important issues in an argument than others. In both cases, reputation scores can be used to modify the weight allocated to that user's posts and ratings within a map.

In the remainder of this chapter, we survey work to date on rating for argumentation systems, suggest relevant requirements and design techniques, and report empirical evidence to show how argumentation tools might improve online deliberations (Iandoli, Klein, and Zollo 2009; Introne 2009).

Requirements for Rating in Argument-Based Platforms

Online argumentation (also known as *computer-supported argument visualization*) has received considerable attention by scholars, particularly in the field of computer-supported cooperative work (Kirschner, Shum, and Carr 2003). Online argumentation structures users' contributions to a deliberative conversation, resulting in the creation of "argument maps" made up of issues, positions, and associated chains of pros and cons.

An argument map is often displayed as a tree diagram that starts with a single question or issue under debate. For example, a map might be rooted at the question, "What kinds of open computing approaches can increase productivity?" One or more positions are shown to descend from this question. These represent possible answers to the question—in this case, say, "wikis," "microblogs," and "web forums." Finally, chains of pro and con arguments may be attached to individual positions. For example, a chain of all "con" arguments attached to a given position would represent an extended discussion about some negative aspect of that position; in the example case, this might be a long discussion about how difficult it is to ensure quality in wikis. An argument can itself spawn further chains of arguments, and so on.

The visual presentation of the map makes some aspects of the argument easier to see. All arguments that share a common ancestor in the tree (either a position or another argument) concern that ancestor. Arguments that are related tend to be physically closer together in the map. The diversity of ideas about a position or argument is indicated by how many arguments it generates (i.e., by the number of arguments that descend from it in the tree).

Argumentation systems promise many potential benefits for collective deliberation (Conklin 2005). In an argument map, it is easy to see what has and has not been covered to date. All perspectives on an issue—regardless of the community the author comes from—are contained in the argument map with little redundancy. Additionally, the central role of positions and arguments encourages users to express the evidence for and the logic behind the ideas they favor.

Work on online argumentation has focused mainly on the development of effective formalisms for argument representation, and on implementing more effective user interfaces. However, systems to help *evaluate* the positions and arguments made in online platforms have been largely omitted, despite increasing attention to trust and reputation mechanisms in e-commerce, search engines, collaborative filtering, web forums, and so on (for a review, see Jøsang et al. 2007).

To meet the challenge of providing users with systems to evaluate the quality of ideas and arguments, we believe that an argument rating and aggregation system is a useful approach. Rating and aggregation systems (which combine ratings to compute support for a position or argument, as described previously) should exhibit the following characteristics:

1. *Minimal effort*   The use of ratings should be straightforward for users, and should not increase the users' cognitive burden.
2. *Transparency*   Users should be able to understand, at least somewhat, how judgments are aggregated—the computed scores should reflect users' intuitive expectations.
3. *Robustness*   The performance of a rating and aggregation system should handle incomplete and conflicting ratings and should degrade gracefully with attempts to manipulate the system.

Inspiration for the technical implementation of argument rating and aggregation in online argumentation can be found in existing decision support systems, which use "belief propagation" to aggregate subjective probability through a map of related variables (e.g., Neil, Fenton, and Nielson 2000). Many such systems employ Bayesian networks (Pearl 1988) as a core technology. Unfortunately, Bayesian networks are incompatible with criteria (1) and (3) in the previous list for several reasons. Bayesian treatments require an exhaustive specification of many conditional probabilities (i.e., relationships between connected variables); all states of a variable need to be known, and they do not allow for conflicting evidence on the same variable.

An alternative technique for aggregating uncertain information that addresses each of the previous limitations is the Dempster-Shafer theory of belief functions (Shafer 1976). Dempster-Shafer theory is more forgiving than Bayesian probabilities because it supports a natural representation of ignorance and does not require an exhaustive specification of states and probabilities. It also supports the expression of conflicting evidence on any variable. Dempster-Shafer theory has been used in a variety of decision-support applications (e.g., Das 2005; Beynon, Curry, and Morgan 2000; Straszecka 2006) and has recently been demonstrated as a rating aggregation technique in a web-based collaborative decision support application (Introne 2009).

In summary, Dempster-Shafer aggregation addresses each of the requirements stated previously as follows:

1. *Minimal effort* A judgment in Dempster-Shafer represents a user's level of confidence in the believability of an argument and can be interpreted as a subjective probability. The semantics of subjective probabilities is usually quite understandable to nonexperts, and users can rate whatever they want, when they want to.

2. *Transparency* Though the full understanding of Dempster-Shafer aggregation would require some knowledge of probability theory, it is intuitive in its behavior. For instance, rating an argument against a position highly will decrease that position's score and increase the score of the alternative position(s).

3. *Robustness* Dempster-Shafer aggregation does not require complete information about all variables, and handles conflicting information. It will ultimately succumb to manipulation, but requires the concerted efforts of many different raters operating on different arguments in a chain of reasoning—individual ratings have a small incremental impact on the aggregate rating, with a large enough body of users.

Empirical Evaluations

The authors have thus far conducted three empirical evaluations of the value of integrating rating algorithms into large-scale argumentation systems. We discuss these results in the following subsections.

The Deliberatorium
One evaluation occurred in the context of the Deliberatorium, an online argumentation tool designed for large-scale communities (Iandoli, Klein and Zollo 2009). The Deliberatorium was used by 160 participants over a 3-week period to deliberate about the possible uses of biofuels in Italy, creating what is to our knowledge the largest single argument map ever built (around 5,000 entries).

The results showed that users were able to quickly and comprehensively explore and map the debate, though substantial moderation was needed to ensure that the argument map was well-organized as users became accustomed to use of the argument formalism (Gürkan et al. 2010). Users were free to employ a five-point scale to assess the quality of arguments, but no mechanism for rating aggregation along the tree branches was available at the time. Notwithstanding the absence of an aggregation system, statistical analysis revealed that users who systematically utilized the rating functionality explored more of the map, developed a deeper understanding of the debate structure, and contributed to the improvement of the map contents significantly more than nonraters.

REASON
Introne (2009) examined the impact of Dempster-Shafer belief aggregation on the effectiveness of collaborative decision making using an online argumentation tool

called REASON. The study focused upon the *common knowledge problem*, which describes a well-documented tendency of groups to focus upon and assign disproportionate weight to information that more people share (Stasser, Taylor, and Hanna 1989). This phenomenon has troubling implications for large-scale deliberation, and has been cited as a reason for favoring voting over deliberation for collective decision making (e.g., Sunstein 2006).

The results of this study showed that participants using an argument formalism with rating aggregation not only made fewer errors than those using a map without rating aggregation but also overcame the common knowledge problem (i.e., they did not overvalue shared information). Thus, the information provided to collaborators via rating aggregation helped them to be less biased in their evaluation of the information they exchanged.

The Climate Collaboratorium

The Climate Collaboratorium is a system currently under development at the MIT Center for Collective Intelligence (Malone et al. 2009). The system uses an innovative combination of Internet-mediated interaction and climate models to help large and geographically dispersed groups systematically explore, evaluate, and come to decisions about how to address climate change challenges. At the core of the system lies an evolving collection of user-created plans for dealing with climate change. For instance, the actions in a plan might include reducing greenhouse gas emissions by a specified percentage, or implementing policies such as a carbon tax or a cap-and-trade system. Computer models are used to infer the impacts of these plans, such as the resulting atmospheric concentrations of carbon dioxide, temperature changes, and economic costs. Users can debate plans by entering arguments for or against their plausibility and desirability; users can also rate the credibility of such arguments and vote for the plans they prefer.

At the time of evaluation, the Collaboratorium user interface contained a list of the available plans. Each plan was presented as a position in an argument map rooted at the question, "What plan should be adopted at the U.N. climate talks in December 2009?" A tree of pro and con arguments was attached to each plan option; this tree was displayed both as a traditional message forum and as a bird's-eye-view map. Each user could rate any post up or down, and ratings were aggregated throughout the map using Dempster-Shafer aggregation. Users could also vote directly for a policy plan without expressing any judgment on single pros or cons; these direct votes were simply counted, and the outcome reported.

In the Climate Collaboratorium, each plan's calculated aggregate rating and number of direct votes were reported independently. The calculated aggregate ratings can be used as a proxy for the amount of *rational support* for a particular policy, given the available arguments and their associated belief scores. In contrast, the number of direct votes are a proxy for the plan's *popular support*. Because the two scores are obtained independently, it is possible to spot situations in which popular plans are supported by few and/or poor arguments.

In user testing, we found that aggregate ratings (rational support) and votes (popular support) often did not correspond precisely. If this finding is replicated in larger studies, it may offer an interesting lens upon the relative merits of deliberation versus voting. We hope to develop techniques that adapt to such misalignments—encouraging community members to either strengthen the popular plan by adding better arguments, or switch their votes to support the plans with higher aggregate ratings.

The previously mentioned experiments provide empirical evidence demonstrating the feasibility and potential benefits of large-scale argument mapping tools—in particular, those that are equipped with rating and aggregation systems. These results suggest that argument mapping systems can be scaled up to hundreds of users or more by adding moderation. The incorporation of rating and aggregation seems to improve use of argument maps, and can help users overcome significant problems with deliberation. Finally, our experiences with using the Climate Collaboratorium suggest that such systems may evolve to be viable tools for e-government and deliberative democracy.

We have not yet fully explored the use of rating and aggregation in argument mapping systems for the development of reputation systems. However, the availability of belief propagation procedures can be a useful basis for the development of better reputation systems. Of particular interest for future exploration are systems in which participant reputations—rather than being based simply on peer assessment—can be linked to the amount of rational support generated by their contributions.

Conclusion

The empirical findings we have presented are encouraging, and demonstrate the worth of combining argumentation technology with computational frameworks for rating and aggregation. Our current and future research directions include: (1) analyzing the impact of rating and aggregation on group decision-making pitfalls, such as information cascades or group polarization (Sunstein 2009); (2) developing improved metrics and aggregation techniques that better satisfy the three requirements outlined earlier; (3) designing additional measures that exploit ratings to provide feedback to users on such attributes as consensus, group activity, and user reputation based on rational as well as popular support.

Argumentation with rating and aggregation holds great potential for grappling with the information overload that we are faced with as a society. The Internet has engendered revolutionary ways of using distributed collaboration to accumulate knowledge at an unprecedented scale. Search engines can help us sift through information, but there are few tools to help organize, summarize, and evaluate it. For this reason, Internet skeptics often raise questions about the reliability and accuracy of online content, and about the detrimental effect such huge volumes of dispersed, unorganized, and possibly incoherent information can have on the quality of individual thinking.

As our world becomes more complex and interconnected, our need to make effective use of this information becomes ever more urgent. Large-scale online argumentation is a powerful tool in pursuit of this goal. Like Wikipedia, online argumentation could be used to produce vast knowledge bases through the collective efforts of many. Unlike Wikipedia, the incorporation of rating and aggregation supports the adaptive evaluation of the knowledge in the system, lays bare the conflicts and uncertainties that are part of the knowledge base, and makes rational structure and the rhetorical strategies behind competing positions clear. Contributors may be anonymous in such systems, but the force of their contributions depends upon their ability to produce sound and rational arguments. Ultimately, such a tool might help us to overcome our collective biases, to synthesize our increasingly balkanized social dialog, and to achieve the collective wisdom we need to solve the challenging problems we face today.

References

Beynon, M., B. Curry, and P. Morgan. 2000. The Dempster-Shafer theory of evidence: An alternative approach to multicriteria decision modelling. *Omega* 28 (1): 37–50.

Conklin, J. 2005. *Dialogue mapping: Building shared understanding of wicked problems.* New York: John Wiley and Sons.

Das, S. 2005. Symbolic argumentation for decision making under uncertainty. In *2005 8th International Conference on Information Fusion*, Philadelphia, PA, 1001–1008.

DeSanctis, G., and R. B. Gallupe. 1987. A foundation for the study of group decision support systems. *Management Science* 33 (5): 589–609.

Giles, J. 2005. Internet encyclopaedias go head to head. *Nature* 438: 900–901.

Gürkan, A., L. Iandoli, M. Klein, and G. Zollo. 2010. Mediating debate through on-line large-scale argumentation: Evidence from the field. *Information Sciences* 180:3686–3702.

Iandoli, L., M. Klein, and G. Zollo. 2009. Enabling on-line deliberation and collective decision-making through large-scale argumentation: A new approach to the design of an Internet-based mass collaboration platform. *International Journal of Decision Support System Technology* 1 (1): 69–92.

Introne, J. E. 2009. Supporting group decisions by mediating deliberation to improve information pooling. In *Proceedings of the ACM 2009 international conference on supporting group work*, Sanibel, FL, 189–198.

Jøsang, A., R. Ismail, and C. Boyd. 2007. A survey of trust and reputation systems for online service provision. *Decision Support Systems* 43 (2): 618–644.

Kirschner, P. A., S. J. B. Shum, and C. S. Carr. 2003. *Visualizing argumentation: Software tools for collaborative and educational sense-making.* London: Springer.

Malone, T. W., R. Laubacher, J. Introne, M. Klein, H. Abelson, J. Sterman, and G. Olson. 2009. *The Climate Collaboratorium: project overview.* CCI Working Paper No. 2009-03.

Neil, M., N. Fenton, and L. Nielson. 2000. Building large-scale Bayesian networks. *Knowledge Engineering Review* 15 (3): 257–284.

Nunamaker, J. F., A. R. Dennis, J. S. Valacich, D. Vogel, and J. F. George. 1991. Electronic meeting systems. *Communications of the ACM* 34 (7): 40–61.

Pearl, J. 1988. *Probabilistic reasoning in intelligent systems: Networks of plausible inference.* San Francisco: Morgan Kaufmann.

Shafer, G. 1976. *A mathematical theory of evidence.* Princeton: Princeton University Press.

Stasser, G., L. A. Taylor, and C. Hanna. 1989. Information sampling in structured and unstructured discussions of three- and six-person groups. *Journal of Personality and Social Psychology* 57 (1): 67–78.

Straszecka, E. 2006. Combining uncertainty and imprecision in models of medical diagnosis. *Information Sciences* 176 (20): 3026–3059.

Sunstein, C. R. 2006. *Infotopia: How many minds produce knowledge.* New York: Oxford University Press.

Sunstein, C. R. 2009. *Going to extremes: How like minds unite and divide.* New York: Oxford University Press.

VI THE REPUTATION SOCIETY

16   Privacy, Context, and Oversharing: Reputational Challenges in a Web 2.0 World

Michael Zimmer and Anthony Hoffman

When personal information is shared online, it may spread farther and faster than expected or inappropriately push intimate details to near-strangers. Michael Zimmer and Anthony Hoffman address the twin risks of information spreading beyond its intended context, and the oversharing of personal information.

People have always divulged personal information: we mention our salary during a conversation at dinner with a friend, or detail recent sexual activities over drinks, or send a letter to the editor of a local newspaper providing opinions on taxes or gun control. We also have always been compelled to provide personal information to authorities, much of which is a matter of public record: traffic violations, property taxes, voter registration data, political campaign donations. Yet as a matter of practice, all of these information disclosures remained separate and obscure: each was scattered across space and time and shared with select individuals, but rarely with very many people. One friend learned one piece of information about you, and a coworker learned something else. One government body had a file on you in an archive, and another had a record in a database across town. Although personal information was divulged and perhaps even publicly available, it was difficult to discover, collect, and aggregate. Thus, although various public disclosures were made, we maintained a semblance of privacy due to the obscurity of the pieces of data that were publicly available.

In our Web 2.0–driven era, however, this "privacy via obscurity" is eroding (see, generally, Zimmer 2008b). Powerful and innovative Web 2.0 tools and services have made our personal information—previously scattered and hard to locate—increasingly discoverable, visible, and linkable. Various Web 2.0 platforms have emerged that make visible personal information that was previously disclosed, but that until now has remained obscure.

Innovative uses of Google Maps include the detailed mapping of the geographic dispersion of campaign contributions during the 2008 U.S. presidential elections (Huffington Post 2010) and the locations of individuals appearing on sex offender registries (Riley 2007). Widgets enabling the sharing and streaming of content—a key feature of Web 2.0—provide an easy means of accessing and distributing personal information that was previously difficult to discover. For example, the online Wisconsin Circuit Court Access system that provides web access to certain public records of the circuit courts of Wisconsin also offers users the ability to subscribe to a certain case, so updates to a court case can be automatically fed to users who no longer need to visit the website to re-run their search query (Wisconsin Circuit Court Access, n.d.). And when website managers have not included such tools, custom toolbars and bookmarklets integrated into web browsers make it easy to share previously obscure web pages that might include personal data. As a result, one can search public tax records, minutes from PTA meetings posted online, or personal photos tucked away in folders of long-forgotten personal websites and easily post such information to Facebook and other social network accounts. What was previously obscure becomes immediately available to millions.

Some of the most popular Web 2.0 services—Facebook, Twitter, and Foursquare, for example—encourage users themselves to openly disclose personal information about their lives, their interests, and their location. Here, bits of information previously shared only within a physical network of friends now become digitally broadcast to multitudes of "Facebook friends" and other followers. Although most of this sharing remains voluntary, the power of Web 2.0 to allow these streams of personal information to be viewed across platforms, captured and archived, cut and pasted, data-mined, and mashed up makes apparent a striking contrast to sharing in the past. The privacy via obscurity previously enjoyed due to physical and practical limitations on the sharing and spread of personal data disappears once a person's Facebook status updates or uploaded photos are immediately indexed by search engines (Zimmer 2008b). Privacy via obscurity is similarly compromised when personal geolocational data are shared online (Tsai et al. 2009; Schonfeld 2010) or when obscure Twitter utterances become archived by the Library of Congress (Parry 2010). Further, we experience diminished obscurity when separate streams of information from individual online services are merged into a single feed, such as with the FriendFeed.com aggregation service, or accessed from a single interface, such as TweetDeck's ability to bring content from Facebook, Twitter, LinkedIn, and Foursquare into a single window on a user's desktop.

Each of these examples reveal how increasingly powerful Web 2.0 tools and services make it easier to share, visualize, aggregate, and access a variety of personal information streams. As a result, although users anticipate some visibility when sharing online, the growing power of web tools and services frequently exceeds the information visibility limits that people presume to exist.

Eroding Control over Information Flows

These concerns over how information shared online might exceed a user's expectations of where that information actually flows reveal an erosion in users' ability to control their information flows online. When sharing information on Web 2.0 platforms, a typical user might presume that his or her information exists only within that sphere: a status update on Facebook is visible only on the Facebook site, or a message on Twitter is available only to those who happen to follow his or her stream of tweets. Thus, some expectations of privacy might persist, with the presumption that information shared remains constrained to the originating platform. Yet the very nature of Web 2.0 is for platforms to be open and interoperable: Facebook status updates are now viewable on Twitter platforms, whether you "liked" a friend's link on Facebook is visible to people visiting the originating site (not only on Facebook itself), private Tweets can be publicly retweeted, and so on. As a result, users lose control over their information flows.

Although much of the sharing noted in the previous examples is intentional—and users should take steps to ensure they understand the nature of sharing across Web 2.0 platforms—the rapid evolution of these powerful tools makes it harder for users to control precisely what information is shared and with whom. Services frequently change their architecture and terms of service, resulting in sharing of information beyond what users initially anticipated. Facebook, for example, added the News Feed function publishing users' changes to their static profile pages as a stream of updates fed to each friend (Rosmarin 2006). This change threatened the privacy of users who previously assumed that only those friends who happened to visit their page would notice the changes; instead, any change made was automatically fed to all followers (Zimmer 2006). Facebook also frequently adjusts what information within user profiles is considered "permanently public" and restricts users' ability to control what is shared with whom (Zimmer 2009; Stone 2009). Similar privacy concerns have arisen related to Google's Buzz social networking service (Helft 2010), in which users had little control over who might receive the information they chose to share on the service. Without the ability to keep up with the rapidly changing Web 2.0 environment, users who participate in various social media environments and share personal information based on a certain set of system settings and promises made by service providers might suddenly find themselves sharing more than they thought with people they had not intended to be recipients. As a result, users lose the ability to control the flows of their personal information, and are threatened by privacy and reputational harms.

Web 2.0 and Leakage within Informational Contexts

Possible threats to privacy and resulting reputational harms as a result of the issues described in the previous examples are multiple and varied, but they typically share a common feature: personal information—although perhaps intended to be public and shared to a particular audience—was made visible beyond the expectations of the user. This issue can best be described as a leakage of personal data outside a particular informational context. When considered in these terms, we can gain a clearer understanding of potential privacy and reputational threats.

The concept of an informational context was developed by Helen Nissenbaum in her theory of privacy as "contextual integrity" (Nissenbaum 2004; Nissenbaum 2009). Rejecting the traditional dichotomy of public versus private spaces—and its related clean division between public and private information—Nissenbaum begins with the premise that the multitude of information-sharing activities take place in a "plurality of distinct realms," or contexts.

Within each of these contexts, norms exist—either implicitly or explicitly—that both shape and limit our roles, behaviors, and expectations. The root of Nissenbaum's theory is that people behave differently with different people in different situations in order to maintain privacy, which means that individuals expect information to flow differently depending on the particular context, and that certain contextual norms are presumed to exist when information is shared in a particular circumstance. Whether in discussions with a physician, purchasing items in a store, or simply walking through a public park, norms of information flow govern what and how much personal information is relevant and appropriate to be shared with others. The theory of contextual integrity is built around the notion that there are "no arenas of life *not* governed by *norms of information flow*" (Nissenbaum 2004, 137). These norms explain the boundaries of our underlying entitlements regarding personal information, and our privacy is invaded when the informational norms are contravened.

Rather than aspiring to universal prescriptions for what is public versus private information, contextual integrity works from within the normative bounds of a particular context. It is designed to consider how the introduction of a new practice or technology into a context—or across contexts—might affect or breach the governing informational norms. If the introduction of a new technology or practice is found to conflict with the standing informational norms, a red flag is raised, indicating that contextual integrity has been violated.

Viewing Web 2.0 through the lens of contextual integrity provides us with a better understanding of the privacy and reputational risks of these new information tools. Rather than simply accepting the rhetorical stance that just because users place personal information in a Web 2.0 service, they forego all expectations of privacy, contextual integrity helps us recognize that as information flows through and across contexts, informational norms might be violated, and thus recognizable privacy concerns emerge. Consider, for example, the reaction to the launch of new "feeds" on Facebook, discussed in the following section.

Contextual Integrity and Facebook Feeds

In September 2006, Facebook launched a set of new features: the News Feed, which appears on each user's Facebook home page, and the Mini-Feed, which appears in each user's profile (Sanghvi 2006). With the News Feed, each time users log into their Facebook page, they are greeted with a detailed listing of the activities of all their friends. The Mini-Feed is similar, but centered around one person. Both note when you wrote on someone's wall and when you commented on a photo, along with other details, such as your responses to event invitations, your new friends, what groups you recently joined, and what changes you made to your personal profile. Facebook said the changes were aimed at advancing the core mission of the site, which is to keep people abreast of their friends' lives: "What we wanted to create is a news ticker, if you will, of the activity of people's friends in their network" (Webster 2006).

The reaction, however, was explosive. Hundreds of protest "Groups" formed on Facebook, with tens of thousands of members objecting that every time you did anything on Facebook at that point, you issued a bulletin for all of your friends. Consider the thoughts of a commenter on Slashdot:

Let's say I break up with my girlfriend. Previously, I would simply change my relationship status to "single." Eventually, my closer friends would notice that my relationship status changed. Now, it is announced to the world as soon as it would happen. . . .

Just because we choose to disclose something does not mean we wish to draw attention to it when the situation changes. Even something as innocuous as an invitation to a party shows up; if I decline the invitation, everyone knows I just declined. (rlbond86 2006)

Summarizing the reactions best, social network scholar Fred Stutzman noted that "[Facebook's] users are stunned, reeling—the same way you'd behave if you found out that you had to share every minute detail of your life with everyone you know" (Stutzman 2006).

Facebook promptly responded to the rising criticism, with founder Mark Zuckerberg defending their changes and claiming nothing had really changed in terms of user privacy. (Zuckerberg 2006b). Although Facebook's response was technically accurate—no new information was made visible that was previously hidden—it failed to recognize how these changes had an impact on the existing norms of personal information flows and violated the contextual integrity of the social networking platform. Previously, users posted personal information to their profile page and invited "friends" to have access to that page. Occasionally, users would change their personal information, and a friend would have to happen upon their page at the right day and time to notice the change—they'd also have to have a good memory of the previous "state" of the page to notice whether anything changed. Some level of serendipity and recall was required to notice changes to a friend's personal information.

The introduction of the News and Mini-Feeds, which highlighted and transmitted changes to friends' profiles, violated these established norms. Although the visible information might have remained the same, the distribution had changed: serendipity and personal memory were no longer necessary ingredients, as the feed was automatically sent to every friend and provided precise details of each and every change to the user's profile. The norms of information flow changed. In short, by adding a feed for all changes to a particular user's profile, Facebook changed the way personal information flows within that context, and that did affect user privacy.

By viewing the Facebook feed incident through the lens of contextual integrity, we can recognize that notions of privacy still exist even in today's online world where open flows of personal information are increasingly the norm. Privacy is not just about keeping some facts secret and making others publicly known. Privacy is contextual. With the introduction and subsequent justification of the Feeds feature, Facebook showed a lack of understanding of the nuanced contexts of information sharing online. The concerns over how these feeds disrupted the contextual integrity of information flows on the social network forced Facebook to provide new tools—a mere two days after the initial launch—to allow users to better manage how their information flowed within the feed framework. The apologetic words of Facebook's Mark Zuckerberg reveal the contextual nature of sharing information online:

I wanted to create an environment where people could share whatever information they wanted, but also have control over whom they shared that information with. . . .

Somehow we missed this point with News Feed and Mini-Feed and we didn't build in the proper privacy controls right away. This was a big mistake on our part, and I'm sorry for it. But apologizing isn't enough. I wanted to make sure we did something about it, and quickly. So we have been coding nonstop for two days to get you better privacy controls. . . . (Zuckerberg 2006a)

In this statement, Facebook can been seen as acknowledging—implicitly, if not explicitly—the importance of context as it relates to information sharing on social networking and similar online platforms: people want to share, but only to certain people and under certain conditions. This is an important step, and as online services continue to expand both in their power and popularity, it will be vital for designers and users alike to recognize how information sharing is inherently contextual, and how any disruption of the intended contextual norms has implications for one's privacy and reputation (Solove 2007; Zimmer 2008b; Nissenbaum 2009).

Contexts and Oversharing Online

The previous discussion illuminated the privacy concerns implicit in the flow of personal information across contextual boundaries. Indeed, the recent history of the web is littered with examples of such contextual conflicts. Jobs have been lost over photos posted on Facebook in contexts assumed to have been private. Relationships have dissolved over blog postings. Public ridicule and shame has followed innocent YouTube videos gone viral. The harm done in these cases is often attributed to an Internet user's willingness to "overshare," a long-standing concept commonly understood as the divulgence of information excessive or inappropriate to a given context. Recently, however, the term has become practically synonymous with many of the most popular Web 2.0 applications, such as Twitter's microblogging service or Facebook's status updates—both of which allow users to constantly broadcast the details of their lives (graphic, mundane, or otherwise) to friends and family.

The concept of "oversharing" was made popular by Emily Gould, a blogger and online journalist who published an essay in *New York Times Magazine* that mused on blogging, online existence, and life in general. "One of the strangest and most enthralling aspects of personal blogs," Gould wrote, "is just how intensely personal they can be. I'm talking 'specific details about someone's S.T.D.'s' personal, 'my infertility treatments' personal." Unsurprisingly, she refers to the imparting of this level of detail as "oversharing." She continues, "There are nongynecological overshares, too: 'My dog has cancer' overshares, 'my abusive relationship' overshares" (Gould 2008, ¶ 9).

The increasing ubiquity of oversharing led *Webster's New World Dictionary* to make the term their 2008 Word of the Year. Defining it as "the name given to *TMI (too much information)* [emphasis original], whether willingly offered or inadvertently revealed," the dictionary explicitly states that

overshare [emphasis original] is a new word for an old habit made astonishingly easy by modern technology. It is yet another product of digital advances that allow people to record and transmit their lives—in words, videos, and graphics—to anyone with Internet access, friend or foe. (*Webster's New World Dictionary* 2008)

As this passage indicates, the rise of the term reflects the affordances of new web tools and is indicative of their challenges. However, the term is also an attempt to resolve some of these challenges: to label an expression an *overshare* (or a person an *oversharer*) is an effort to establish a context—to refocus the blurred lines—and posit the offending expression (or person) as inappropriate. In other words, it is an effort to normalize information-sharing practices online by assigning a label to modes of expression deemed outside the norm.

Like all normative expectations, however, those emerging around the practice of online information sharing reflect the values of the larger cultural framework from which they develop. Thus, being labeled an "oversharer" is an ideologically charged accusation. Critical analysis of the occurrence of the term in online venues reveals that oversharing is largely conceptualized as a negative social practice (Hoffmann 2009). Given this negative connotation, reputational harm can result from the divulgence of private information in a context that is seen as normatively inappropriate. Even for those who maintain control of their information flows online, this reputational harm could persist if the crossing of contexts results in labeling as an "oversharer" by those on the receiving end of the information flow.

Conclusion

The challenges presented by Web 2.0 are increasingly well documented (Solove 2007; Allen 2008; Zimmer 2008b). These technologies "[represent] a blurring of the boundaries between Web users and producers, consumption and participation, authority and amateurism, play and work, data and the network, reality and virtuality" (Zimmer 2008a). These blurred boundaries also blur the boundaries between public and private, between contexts, and between notions of normatively acceptable amounts of information sharing online. This chapter has illuminated some of the privacy and reputational challenges inherent in the growing power and popularity of online platforms, highlighting the diminishment of privacy via obscurity, the challenges of controlling one's information flows across contexts, and the dangers of being labeled an "oversharer."

Although we by no means suggest that Web 2.0 is inherently problematic or should be avoided, this chapter should serve as a critical warning in the spirit of cultural critic Neil Postman, who remarked in his book *Technopoly* on how "we are surrounded by the wondrous effects of machines and are encouraged to ignore the ideas embedded in them. Which means we become blind to the ideological meaning of our technologies" (1992, 94). The goal of this chapter has been to remove some of these "blinders" and to bring some clarity to the complexities of privacy, contexts, and reputation within these emerging information-sharing platforms.

With this clarity in mind, future information-sharing platforms and reputational systems can be better designed. Users should be provided with greater control over their personal information flows, with particular attention paid to the contextual nature of information sharing practices (see, for example, Barth et al. 2006, who attempt to formalize aspects of the theory of contextual integrity in a logical framework for use in information systems). Social networking sites should provide users with easier means to manage their identities across contexts, and provide users with visual feedback as to how far their information sharing might extend (Dwyer and Hiltz 2008). All this can mitigate the chance of oversharing beyond an intended context.

References

Allen, M. 2008. Web 2.0: An Argument against Convergence. *First Monday* 13 (3). Retrieved from: <http://firstmonday.org/htbin/cgiwrap/bin/ojs/index.php/fm/article/viewArticle/2139/1946>.

Barth, A., A. Datta, J. C. Mitchell, and H. Nissenbaum. 2006, May. *Privacy and Contextual Integrity: Framework and Applications.* Paper presented at the IEEE Symposium on Security and Privacy, Oakland, California.

Dwyer, C. A., and S. R. Hiltz. 2008. *Designing privacy into online communities.* Paper presented at the Internet Research 9.0 Conference, Copenhagen, Denmark.

Gould, E. 2008, May 25. Exposed. *New York Times Magazine*. Retrieved from: <http://www.ny times.com/2008/05/25/magazine/25internet-t.html>.

Helft, M. 2010, February 12. Critics say Google invades privacy with new service. *New York Times*, B1.

Hoffmann, A. 2009. *Oversharing: A critical discourse analysis*. Unpublished master's thesis. University of Wisconsin–Milwaukee, Milwaukee, WI.

Huffington Post. 2010. Campaign donors—fundrace 2010. Retrieved November 7, 2010, from: <http://fundrace.huffingtonpost.com>.

Nissenbaum, H. 2004. Privacy as contextual integrity. *Washington Law Review* 79 (1): 119–157.

Nissenbaum, H. 2009. *Privacy in context: Technology, policy, and the integrity of social life*. Stanford, CA: Stanford University Press.

Parry, M. 2010, May 7. Library of Congress, facing privacy concerns, clarifies Twitter archive plan. *Wired Campus: Chronicle of Higher Education*. Retrieved from: <http://chronicle.com/blogPost/ Library-of-Congress-Facing/23818>.

Postman, N. 1992. *Technopoly: The surrender of culture to technology*. New York: Vintage Books.

Riley, D. 2007. See all sex offenders in your neighborhood. *TechCrunch*. Retrieved November 1, 2010, from: <http://techcrunch.com/2007/08/25/sex-offenders-in-your-neighborhood>.

Rosmarin, R. 2006. Facebook's makeover. *Forbes.com*. Retrieved June 18, 2010, from: <http:// www.forbes.com/2006/09/01/facebook-myspace-internet_cx_rr_0905facebook.html>.

rlbond86. 2006, September 6. Re:Yeah, stalking IS supposed to be hard [website comment]. Slashdot: Facebook changes provoke uproar among users. Retrieved November 1, 2010, from: < http:// yro.slashdot.org/comments.pl?sid=195861&cid=16050447>.

Sanghvi, R. 2006. Facebook gets a facelift [web log post]. *The Facebook Blog*. Retrieved September 20, 2006, from: <http://blog.facebook.com/blog.php?post=2207967130>.

Schonfeld, E. 2010. Check-ins, geo-fences, and the future of privacy. *TechCrunch*. Retrieved June 1, 2010, from: <http://techcrunch.com/2010/05/27/geo-fences-privacy>.

Solove, D. 2007. *The future of reputation: Gossip, rumor, and privacy on the Internet*. New Haven: Yale University Press.

Stutzman, F. 2006. How Facebook broke its culture [web log post]. *Unit Structures*. Retrieved October 3, 2008, from: <http://chimprawk.blogspot.com/2006/09/how-facebook-broke-its-culture .html>.

Tsai, J. Y., P. Kelley, L. Cranor, and N. Sadeh. 2009, September 26. *Location-sharing technologies: Privacy risks and controls*. Paper presented at the Research Conference on Communication, Information and Internet Policy (TPRC). George Mason University School of Law, Arlington, VA.

Webster, G. 2006. Doug Jones sneezed. 1:23pm [web log post]. *Campus Progress*. Retrieved September 20, 2006, from: <http://www.campusprogress.org/articles/doug_jones_sneezed._123pm>.

Word of the Year. 2008. Overshare is Webster's New World Dictionary's 2008 Word of the Year. Retrieved April 3, 2011, from: <http://wordoftheyear.wordpress.com/press-release-overshare-is -word-of-the-year>.

Wisconsin Circuit Court Access. n.d. Wisconsin Court System RSS feeds. Retrieved November 1, 2010, from: <http://wcca.wicourts.gov/rss.xsl>.

Zimmer, M. 2006. More on Facebook and the contextual integrity of personal information flows. *MichaelZimmer.org*. Retrieved October 3, 2008, from: <http://michaelzimmer.org/2006/09/08/ more-on-facebook-and-the-contextual-integrity-of-personal-information-flows>.

Zimmer, M. 2008a. Preface: Critical perspectives on Web 2.0. *First Monday* 13 (3). Retrieved from: <http://firstmonday.org/htbin/cgiwrap/bin/ojs/index.php/fm/article/viewArticle/2137/1943>.

Zimmer, M. 2008b. The externalities of Search 2.0: The emerging privacy threats when the drive for the perfect search engine meets Web 2.0. *First Monday* 13 (3). Retrieved from: <http://first monday.org/htbin/cgiwrap/bin/ojs/index.php/fm/article/view/2136/1944>.

Zimmer, M. 2009. Facebook's privacy upgrade is a downgrade for user privacy [web log post]. *MichaelZimmer.org*. Retrieved June 10, 2010, from: <http://michaelzimmer.org/2009/12/10/face books-privacy-upgrade-is-a-downgrade-for-user-privacy>.

Zuckerberg, M. 2006a. An open letter from Mark Zuckerberg. *The Facebook Blog*. Retrieved September 20, 2006, from: <http://blog.facebook.com/blog.php?post=2208562130>.

Zuckerberg, M. 2006b. Calm down. Breathe. We hear you. *The Facebook Blog*. Retrieved September 20, 2006, from: <http://blog.facebook.com/blog.php?post=2208197130>.

17   The Future of Reputation Networks

Jamais Cascio

How will reputation systems evolve in practice? Jamais Cascio suggests a taxonomy of reputation systems, distinguishing them by how reputations are generated and whether participation is optional. He then offers a scenario-based exploration of each type of reputation system, showing how it might unfold.

What will the world look like as reputation networks become more commonplace? Although accurate predictions of the future are impossible, we can still think through some implications of choices we make today. A common tool for doing so is the *scenario planning process*, a structured method of teasing out likely consequences of significant—and uncertain—drivers. Scenario planning is used by governments, corporations, and NGOs around the world, but can be undertaken by small groups or even individuals.

One important aspect of scenario planning is the recognition that there is no one possible future; rather, we need to think about a diverse set of possible futures, with the goal of testing strategies and choices against different possible outcomes. There are plenty of questions that can be asked about the future of reputation systems. How are the networks accessed? Under what conditions? Can ratings be contested? Do reputation scores from different networks influence each other? Does the reputation network have any kind of official standing, or is it entirely "for entertainment purposes?" What happens if you face discrimination on the basis of the reputation result? Do the scores tie in with other social network functions?

But for me, in thinking about the evolution of reputation networks, two issues loom large above the others. The first concerns process: how are the reputation ratings generated? Do they come from other participants offering explicit ratings, or are they the result of analysis of factors that aren't solely reputation-related? The second concerns participation: whom do the networks cover? Is participation a choice, and what are the implications of opting out?

In the language of scenario planning, these crucial questions of process and participation are the "critical uncertainties." These uncertainties can be positioned as two ends of a spectrum of possible outcomes. For the question of whether ratings are given directly by participants or emerge from other factors, we could ask whether future reputation systems will be *direct* networks or *emergent* networks. For the question of whether future reputation systems will focus on people within narrowly defined communities or offer broad coverage across multiple communities, we could ask whether they'll be *constrained* networks or *universal* networks.

Direct networks are reputation networks built on direct ratings by participants (peers and/or affected parties). (The seller/buyer reputation system on eBay is an example of a direct reputation network—buyers and sellers can give each other positive or negative ratings.)

Emergent networks, conversely, are reputation networks based on algorithmic analysis of behavior, connections, and the like, not on direct rating by peers. (See chapter 7 in this volume.) Google's PageRank is an example of an emergent reputation network—a page's position in Google search results comes from analysis of factors such as which and how many sites link to that page, not from any "this page is better than that one" rating.

Constrained networks are reputation networks that offer a narrow reputation score within a particular community, or for a particular issue. Most present-day reputation networks are of this type.

Universal networks are reputation networks that attempt to provide a general reputation score across communities and areas of interest. It's unlikely that any single reputation rating will be interpreted equally by all groups, but the "universal" reputation would reflect a consensus, majority, or otherwise dominant view.

These two driving forces combine to offer four different scenarios describing the ways in which reputation networks could evolve. It's important to note that these four are by no means mutually exclusive, and are likely to coexist fairly broadly.

• **Direct-constrained** reputation networks involve direct ratings by a constrained community of people. These reputation networks closely match most of the reputation networks we see in the world today. These are reputation networks that rely on the direct, intentional ranking of peers within the community, on the basis of the concerns of the community. There may be ways to contest ratings, but all participants opt into the network by being part of the community.

One possible evolution of these systems would be toward greater consistency of language and meaning, so that participants have a better sense of what a positive or negative reputation means in the context of the community. This change would also allow someone who has a positive reputation to be able to communicate that with people outside of the community in a way that they could appreciate; similarly, a negative reputation could be used against a misbehaving community member in a way that would have meaning to those outside the community. Ultimately, a single utility may be used to follow reputation ratings across a variety of communities.

Consistent rankings would also open up the possibility of portability between reputation networks, in which the positive or negative ratings in one community could influence the ratings in another, otherwise unrelated community.

• **Direct-universal** reputation networks involve direct ratings given to a nearly universal community of people. These networks would be akin to a Facebook or Twitter on steroids—a general (non-issue-specific) social network with the added ability to give reactions to other community members. Depending upon the rules of the social network, those reactions may be based on something documented, allowed to be purely whimsical, or somewhere in between.

Such a system would be likely to include some kind of social filter, so that the weight given to the rating of someone outside of a user's direct experience is moderated by the rating given to any intermediaries. (For example, Alice looks up Bob—previously a stranger—and sees that he has a "possible problem" reputation. Alice is connected to Bob via Carol; Carol sees Bob as a "great guy, would meet with again," but Alice rates Carol with an "untrustworthy." Carol's view of Bob is weighted accordingly.)

The big question in such a system is transparency. Would a user be able to see exactly the rating given by a peer? Both "yes" and "no" present problems for accountability. If users can see ratings given by peers, lower-status peers may artificially increase the rating they give to higher-status peers in order to avoid trouble, or to trigger an improved rating in response. If users cannot see ratings given by peers, users have no way to respond to negative attacks or unfounded gossip.

• **Emergent-constrained** reputation networks produce a reputation score based on relevant factors within a particular community. The frequency with which a member's discussion responses are deemed positive or negative is a classic example—have too many comments rated down and take an automatic reputation hit; have a certain number rated highly and receive an automatic reputation boost.

More advanced forms of emergent-constrained systems would rely less on direct user rating of relevant factors and more on analysis of language. "XYZ Corporation sucks!" is a common refrain online; a language-analysis-based system would translate that into a more formal reputation score in aggregate with what other users have to say.

This kind of system could be a platform for the development of "metareputation" systems, wherein individual direct-constrained reputation ratings are aggregated to produce a metarating. Such a system would likely be best suited for combining thematically related sites; a metarating that crossed diverse subjects might not see enough duplication of people (whether participants or subjects of debate) to offer much value. Conversely, a metarating system that embraced antagonistic communities—an anti–digital rights management site and a pro–recording industry site, for example—

may see the same people, but with wildly divergent ratings. An individual scoring highly within both groups, however, might indicate someone worth paying closer attention to.

• **Emergent-universal** reputation networks would produce a reputation score based on relevant factors across a very wide community. These networks would offer the greatest overall utility, but would be by far the most difficult to construct. Such a system would have to combine a wide range of inputs from a diverse participant base, and do so in a way that would still provide meaningful results. This model of reputation network combines the challenges of both the emergent-constrained approach (e.g., limiting the scope of perspectives) and the direct-universal approach (e.g., deciding how much transparency is appropriate).

But the biggest dilemma of this kind of emergent-universal system would be the question of opting out. By its nature, an emergent-universal reputation network wouldn't need active acquiescence for someone to become subject to a reputation rating. The very act of identifying someone as having positive or negative aspects— whether done casually or formally, maliciously or carefully—would bring the subject into the network. Given similarities of names, misspellings, and the like, it's highly likely that an individual who wanted to opt out of the system would still find himself or herself continuing to receive ratings.

Such a problem becomes even more profound if the emergent-universal reputation system gains enough preeminence that serious economic and personal decisions hinge on a person's reputation rating. People without a reputation rating—or with an "opt-out" tag—could find themselves facing discrimination; they could easily be treated as if they had a markedly low reputation score.

The other issues raised about the future of reputation systems, from the technologies required to the potential for discrimination, will manifest in all four of these scenarios. But the scenario process doesn't stop with spelling out clear implications of the intersection of two critical uncertainties. Scenarios often include a short narrative element, describing life in each of the four future worlds.

Scenario 1, direct-constrained reputation: direct (explicit) ratings that apply only within a constrained community of people

Neighborhood Watch
Sarah and Ben looked at the screen glumly. The house was perfect—ideal, really—exactly what they wanted to start a family. Not too far of a walk from transit, lots of community gathering spots nearby, a park, even an old-style school, if they wanted that. The UN Climate Authority had identified this region as being unlikely to see disruptive changes over the next two decades. It was just perfect.

Except, apparently, for the neighborhood. Ben tapped through the tabs, hoping that something might be different this time. No. No luck. Where to begin?

There were the usual petty infractions and misbehaviors—the regularly-too-late-with-child-support guy, the teenager who has been known to listen to goth music, the missed car payments, the lower-than-average credit rating—but these were the kinds of things you'd find just about anywhere. What Ben and Sarah saw on the report was much more troubling.

The local water district identified three of the homes on this block as being serial over-waterers, and started raising rates on the whole block on the argument that peer pressure usually worked better than fines and formal policing. Usually. The block had a real mix of ages and subcultures, though, so the water-savers didn't have enough leverage over the reputations of the water-wasters to get them to change their ways.

Although there weren't any officially reported incidents, the presence of a couple of neighbors on a Party Circle network meant that there were likely to be loud parties at least a few times a year.

The most recent new addition to the neighborhood seemed pretty quiet, but apparently was active in a local evangelical church. Not a problem in and of itself, but the neighbor was also highly regarded in a loose network calling itself the "Conversion Commandos." A recent jump in this neighbor's reputation with that group suggested (at least according to the real estate agent's analysis software) that he was pretty active.

Worst of all, the older couple who owned the house next to the place that Sarah and Ben wanted had appeared on one of those guerilla "donor map" sites; the neighbors had given a decent amount of money to a political cause that Sarah and Ben had actively opposed. It wasn't a subject that was likely to come up in conversation, but they'd still know that the next-door neighbors were (in Sarah and Ben's view) bigots—and that they would probably see Sarah and Ben as shameful, in turn. All of the interactions they would have would be shaped by that awareness.

Not for the first time, the couple commented that just a decade earlier, they would have bought the house and discovered all this about their neighbors the old-fashioned way—through gossip, misunderstandings, and the occasional newspaper headline. As they looked again at the list of what they'd find living on this block, they wondered which way worked out better in the end.

Scenario 2, direct-universal reputation: direct (explicit) ratings that apply across a nearly universal community of people

Wildflowers

Alejandra stopped her work and cursed under her breath. This was the third ping on RepApp in ten minutes. She hadn't checked RepApp in at least a week—her reputation just didn't change all that often. Something must be happening, and she doubted it was going to be good.

She switched to the RepApp window and looked at the field of flowers. That was her preferred visual setting; like most people, she hated the default "yellow smiles and red frowns" visual. Most of the flowers were bright and open, waving in the "breeze" but still pretty close to the "ground"—a sign that her general reputation was pretty average. But a couple of the flowers over on the "wildflower" side had shot up high and opened exaggerated blooms, and many more had wilted entirely. As Alejandra looked over her reputation field, RepApp pinged again, and two more flowers wilted, while another one started to grow.

She tried to identify which reputation networks were showing this activity, but she didn't recognize the names. This was hardly unusual; RepApp pulled from thousands of "metanetworks"—reputation aggregators and sites that did free reputation analysis. She finally saw one where she had an account, and followed the link to get the reason for the change.

Apparently, a picture she'd taken and posted to Wikimedia had been used by a science blogger (okay, not a problem), and that article had been picked up by one of the biggest political news blogs (uh oh). That meant that thousands of smaller political blogs picked up the story, too . . . and it looked like about a third had used the picture she'd taken. Although she was getting a positive reputation surge from the political activists that agreed with the original political news site, she was getting a far bigger negative reputation hit from those who opposed it. That the big political news site didn't really represent Alejandra's views didn't matter; what mattered was that her work had been linked to it, and that was enough to set off a "hate cascade."

Alejandra remembered reading somewhere that sites like Wikimedia usually had some kind of "disassociation of use" form that could help in this kind of situation. It probably wouldn't be enough to reverse the reputation change, but it might keep it from getting worse.

At that moment, however, a tall flower over on the "tend your garden" side of the field—representing one of the photography groups she belonged to—started to wilt. Those were supposed to be nonpolitical groups. Great.

This was going to be a mess to clean up.

Scenario 3, emergent-constrained reputation: emergent (implicit) ratings that apply only within a constrained community of people

Reputation Ransom
Jeff swore at the display on his phone. He had just gotten a text message from SocialForge indicating that his "Forge Factor" had changed by more than 25 percent. That went with the alert from the contract work site he used informing him that his

sociability rating was approaching unacceptable levels, and the email from Chatter-Watch telling him that he was at risk of being booted from the system because of his dangerously low "trustability" score. That was just in the last couple of days—all of this had been happening now for over a month. And none of these sites could tell him why this was happening, only that the "reputation algorithms had responded to ongoing changes to his online profile."

What really drove Jeff crazy was that he hadn't done anything—he had just been working, going to the gym, and hanging out at home reading or watching movies. He hadn't dated in months (not since that disastrous split with his ex), and hadn't changed his routine in a long time. Suddenly, he was being told that his profile had changed so severely that it was killing his reputation. That wasn't just annoying—it could ruin his prospects for work.

Jeff got back to his flat and decided to forget the gym tonight. He was too distracted—and anyway, maybe a change in routine would help. As he got himself a drink, his phone buzzed again with an incoming message, and Jeff gestured to have the display routed to the TV on the wall. He nearly dropped the glass when he saw the subject line.

"Want your reputation back?" Damn it. He'd read about these scams, but never thought one would hit him. Did someone guess a password, overhear him—oh, of course. About two months ago, he thought he'd lost his smartID card at a job, but found it again later that day in a place he could swear he'd looked. Someone must have skimmed the data and used it to go after him.

Like most of these scams, whoever this was demanded money. Jeff set the message aside and started doing a wide-ranging search for any recent references to him. It didn't take him long to discover membership on sites he'd never heard of, entries by him on blogs he'd never seen, even videos uploaded to YouTube under his name. Some of it didn't even make sense, but it all had the right phrases and structure to trigger automated profile sniffers. Whoever ran this scam must have software agents setting all this stuff up. Jeff didn't even code, and he could think of a half-dozen ways to do it.

Well, he wasn't going to pay the ransom, that was for sure. He would, however, have to make a call he really didn't want to make. His ex was a cop, working on fraud—exactly the person he'd need to talk to. Jeff picked up his phone again, pulled up the old contact, and tapped it. "Hello, Tom?"

Scenario 4, emergent-universal reputation: emergent (implicit) ratings that apply across a nearly universal community of people

Augmented Relationships

Hiroko hated getting to the airport early, but her hosts had arranged for the taxi, and traffic was amazingly light. She stepped briskly around an older couple trying to figure out how to use the biometric check-in—"just walk through at a normal pace, guys"—and got in line for security. The airport security staff all wore augmented reality glasses that would identify people in line and pull up relevant data, monitor for microchanges to their facial expressions, and even run security cam searches to track their recent movements.

There were signs everywhere demanding that all augmented reality (AR) glasses, smartpads, and cameraphones be shut off. (People still use cameraphones? Yeah, probably that couple still stuck at check-in.) Nice. They get to see everything about us, but we don't get to see anything about them. How's that "transparent society" working out for you?

Hiroko amused herself while she waited by thinking about the supposedly ultrasecure, classified software the Transportation Security Administration AR systems ran. Cracked and available for download within a day. It was a nice bit of kit, though, even if not quite legal for her to use. Fortunately, the smartpad that still had the system loaded was at home.

She sailed through security, of course (although was startled, as she was putting her shoes back on, to see all of the TSA workers suddenly lift their heads and turn to look at the same guy—he must have tripped some rep flag, but whatever it was wasn't enough for him to be stopped).

Getting to her gate reminded Hiroko of the one advantage of early arrival: she could grab one of the open power plugs. Turning her AR specs back on, she gazed idly at the other passengers slowly filtering in, and waited for the market sim to load on her pad. Everyone had the same pre-jet-lagged look, even—hey!—that old couple. Guess they figured out how to check in.

She avoided staring, of course. If she looked for too long at someone's face, the specs would try to identify who it was, whether you had any connection to him or her, and then work out how you should feel about that person based on how other people in your social network respond to him or her. Sometimes useful, but also a bit rude—like you were looking for the right way to try to flirt. As a result, she didn't have anything more than the basic reputation watch app on her specs—frankly, she thought, the super-detailed rep systems were something for aging Gen Y'ers, training wheels for the no longer digitally hip.

The guy sitting down a couple of rows away caught her eye. He looked familiar, but she couldn't place him. Okay, just this once, she thought, and held her gaze. He looked up, and seemed to have a similar don't-I-know-her reaction. After a second, a light ring popped up around his face, along with his name (Michael Ahmadi) and the connection.

He used to date her sister. Her sister had told her all sorts of things about their relationship. Very, very detailed things. Too-much-information kind of things. As if on cue, the ring Hiroko's AR system displayed around Michael's face started pulsing bright red—"he's a hot one."

Hiroko's face went just as red and she quickly looked down, just as Michael's augmented reality system identified her. In an instant, he saw who she was, saw the connection, and guessed why she was blushing.

He started blushing, too, and quickly looked away.

Hiroko sighed quietly. This was going to be a long flight.

18 "I Hope You Know This Is Going on Your Permanent Record"

Madeline Ashby and Cory Doctorow

Cory Doctorow was one of the first speculative fiction authors to portray a reputation-based future society. Fellow author Madeline Ashby sets the stage for a Doctorow excerpt portraying an unusual university environment. Ashby then gives a provocative scenario of how reputation systems could influence another educational arena.

It is August 2009, and Cory Doctorow is watching his daughter play on a secluded beach. Cory's visits to Toronto always feel like long and involved status updates: a high-pressure stream of information and opinion laced with jokes and stories and hugs. The man is a whirlwind, picking up people and spinning them around in the centrifuge of his seemingly boundless energy. But in this moment, he appears restful. I'm sitting a little behind him, digging my toes in the sand, when one of Cory's friends from way back comes up and asks me how I know him. "Well, he published my first big story."

Instantly, Cory twists to face me. "Really? That was your first story?" He claps his hands together. "Ha! I'll dine out on that one for years!"

Reputation is everything, in our business. You're only as good as your last project. And although there are ways in which the fiction community measures reputation (inbound links, Amazon ratings, bestseller lists, awards), none of them render changes in real time, and none of them translate into meaningful currency. Our social capital has no stock ticker. And even if it did, there's a big leap between measuring that capital and using it in place of cash, as the characters of Cory's first novel do.

In that novel, *Down and Out in the Magic Kingdom*, new technologies (including virtu- ally limitless energy and life extension) have put human society on easy street, creating a fascinating social experiment called the "Bitchun society" (Doctorow 2003). A strik- ing innovation of the Bitchun society is a reputation-based currency called *Whuffie*, which functions both as a universal metric of personal reputation and as the method of monetary exchange (see foreword and chapter 2 in this volume). With the institu- tion of Whuffie, in other words, you literally pay for the things you want by debiting your reputation score, at whatever value it is currently assessed. Reputation is cash. But one of cash's greatest virtues lies in its relatively untraceable nature, and it's hard to support a politically unpopular cause with Whuffie when your neighbors and colleagues have a heads-up on your spending. A reputation-based economy that required all our transactions to be traced would also necessitate either a fundamental shift in global morality and law, or the capacity for citizens to maintain multiple "accounts."

The possibility of maintaining multiple accounts more accurately reflects the status quo today. Online and off, we maintain multiple identities, each of which has its own attendant reputation. Who we are at work is different from who we are at home, and those two identities are different from the person role-playing at Comic-Con or the person speaking to our in-laws. This reality of human experience—the fracturing of the self into disparate masks, each of them contextually appropriate—is nothing new. What is new is the knowledge that each of those subjectivities can now be graded and marked in very real and potentially lasting ways. Relatives and supervisors may furrow their brows when you express an opinion they disagree with, but your friends online can vote you up and down, give you hearts or stars or gold, or nix you from their friends list. This is the charm of reputation economies. They codify the currents that once flowed invisibly beneath the surface of our conversations and transactions.

Reputation and its assessment have long provided fodder for fiction. Near the end of *Les Liaisons Dangereuses*, the Marquise de Merteuil flees the city when two letters exposing her duplicitous nature become public; her health declines and she is left literally scarred by the sudden fall of her reputation (de Laclos and Stone 1782). In a world in which we may carry our online karma through multiple stages of our lives, the story remains resonant. Our friends may forget our sins, but Google never will. The record of our failures will be there when our grandchildren's fingers itch for the stories we refuse to tell. Our reputations will not merely precede us; they will outlive us and everyone else who helped us establish them.

In other cases, our reputations survive unscathed despite our best efforts to the contrary. In an interview given in April 2010, Cory acknowledged the inequity endemic to the economy he had imagined: "I think Whuffie is primarily one of those systems that rewards you for having gotten lucky or doing something good some time ago, and then continues to reward you for that forever at the expense of other people" (Canavan 2010). This situation is far from ideal. As Cory noted in response to utopian interpretations of Whuffie, "A properly Utopian system is one in which you have something that's a lot like merit, not like circumstance—where people are rewarded based on how great they are, not based on how great they used to be" (Canavan 2010).

It is with these words in mind that I wrote the second scenario of this chapter. The first scenario is an excerpt from *Down and Out in the Magic Kingdom*. In it, the main character recalls the first days of Whuffie. To employ Jamais Cascio's helpful terminology from chapter 17, Whuffie is a direct-universal system, global in reach and almost free of contextual framing. Everyone in the story uses it, taking stock of their rankings through heads-up displays—in some cases, these are built right into their eyes. In many ways, this ranking is more pervasive, resilient, and meaningful than any other metric of identity. The characters may cast aside families, beliefs, and citizenships, but Whuffie is forever.

I sought to invert these paradigms in my own scenario. I wanted to write about a direct-constrained or emergent-constrained system that depended heavily upon context. I hoped to create a local, merit-based system whose metrics still translated to meaningful gains and losses despite the relatively small contextual frame. But what limited context could possibly exude such vast power over so many interlocking systems, joining them together into one very important but ultimately impermanent score?

Naturally, I wrote about high school.

Scenario 1, excerpt from *Down and Out in the Magic Kingdom* by Cory Doctorow

Bitchun wars are rare. Long before anyone tries a takeover of anything, they've done the arithmetic and ensured themselves that the ad-hoc they're displacing doesn't have a hope of fighting back.

For the defenders, it's a simple decision: step down gracefully and salvage some reputation out of the thing—fighting back will surely burn away even that meager reward.

No one benefits from fighting back—least of all the thing everyone's fighting over. For example:

It was the second year of my undergrad, taking a double-major in not making trouble for my profs and keeping my mouth shut. It was the early days of Bitchun, and most of us were still a little unclear on the concept. Not all of us, though: a group of campus shit-disturbers, grad students in the Sociology Department, were on the bleeding edge of the revolution, and they knew what they wanted: control of the Department, oustering of the tyrannical, stodgy profs, a bully pulpit from which to preach the Bitchun gospel to a generation of impressionable undergrads who were too cowed by their workloads to realize what a load of shit they were being fed by the University.

At least, that's what the intense, heavyset woman who seized the mic at my Soc 200 course said, that sleepy morning mid-semester at Convocation Hall. Nineteen hundred students filled the hall, a capacity crowd of bleary, coffee-sipping time-markers, and they woke up in a hurry when the woman's strident harangue burst over their heads.

I saw it happen from the very start. The prof was down there on the stage, a speck with a tie-mic, droning over his slides, and then there was a blur as half a dozen grad students rushed the stage. They were dressed in University poverty-chic, wrinkled slacks and tattered sports coats, and five of them formed a human wall in front of the prof while the sixth, the heavyset one with the dark hair and the prominent mole on her cheek, unclipped his mic and clipped it to her lapel.

"Wakey wakey!" she called, and the reality of the moment hit home for me: this wasn't on the lesson-plan.

"Come on, heads up! This is not a drill. The University of Toronto Department of Sociology is under new management. If you'll set your handhelds to 'receive,' we'll be beaming out new lesson-plans momentarily. If you've forgotten your handhelds, you can download the plans later on. I'm going to run it down for you right now, anyway.

"Before I start though, I have a prepared statement for you. You'll probably hear this a couple times more today, in your other classes. It's worth repeating. Here goes:

"We reject the stodgy, tyrannical rule of the profs at this Department. We demand bully pulpits from which to preach the Bitchun gospel. Effective immediately, the University of Toronto Ad-Hoc Sociology Department is *in charge*. We promise high-relevance curriculum with an emphasis on reputation economies, post-scarcity social dynamics, and the social theory of infinite life-extension. No more Durkheim, kids, just deadheading! This will be *fun*."

She taught the course like a pro—you could tell she'd been drilling her lecture for a while. Periodically, the human wall behind her shuddered as the prof made a break for it and was restrained.

At precisely 9:50 a.m. she dismissed the class, which had hung on her every word. Instead of trudging out and ambling to our next class, the whole nineteen hundred of us rose, and, as one, started buzzing to our neighbors, a roar of "Can you believe it?" that followed us out the door and to our next encounter with the Ad-Hoc Sociology Department.

It was cool, that day. I had another soc class, Constructing Social Deviance, and we got the same drill there, the same stirring propaganda, the same comical sight of a ten-ured prof battering himself against a human wall of ad-hocs. Reporters pounced on us when we left the class, jabbing at us with mics and peppering us with questions. I gave them a big thumbs-up and said, "Bitchun!" in classic undergrad eloquence.

The profs struck back the next morning. I got a heads-up from the newscast as I brushed my teeth: the Dean of the Department of Sociology told a reporter that the ad-hocs' courses would not be credited, that they were a gang of thugs who were totally unqualified to teach. A counterpoint interview from a spokesperson for the ad-hocs established that all of the new lecturers had been writing course-plans and lecture notes for the profs they replaced for years, and that they'd also written most of their journal articles.

The profs brought University security out to help them regain their lecterns, only to be repelled by ad-hoc security guards in homemade uniforms. University security got the message—anyone could be replaced—and stayed away.

The profs picketed. They held classes out front attended by grade-conscious brown-nosers who worried that the ad-hocs' classes wouldn't count toward their degrees.

Fools like me alternated between the outdoor and indoor classes, not learning much of anything.

No one did. The profs spent their course-times whoring for Whuffie, leading the seminars like encounter groups instead of lectures. The ad-hocs spent their time bad-mouthing the profs and tearing apart their coursework. At the end of the semester, everyone got a credit and the University Senate disbanded the Sociology program in favor of a distance-ed offering from Concordia in Montreal.

Scenario 2, *I Hope You Know This Is Going on Your Permanent Record* by Madeline Ashby

"It would be a real boost to your score," Okiayu had reminded her. "And the more exams you take, the more you counterbalance your current score. So next year, when you take the exams for real, you might be accepted to your first choice school."

The prep school pimps had taken her out to a Choco Cro. Mid-afternoon, it wasn't busy. Megumi stared at her espresso and croissant on its plate. It was still too hot; chocolate would ooze out if she bit into it now. They used to serve the croissants in cardboard cones for exactly that reason, but there was a law now about disposables. She'd met a guy once who collected the cones. He'd feathered them across his walls, orange and yellow and green, muted like the colors in a 35mm film. His score, like hers, was low. Not just low. Marianas Trench low.

"Please don't underestimate this opportunity," Horie said. When Megumi attended the cram school, Horie had just been the girl taking attendance. Had it really been that long?

"We would of course pay your exam fees and travel costs," Okiayu said.

"Including meals?"

"Including meals."

Belatedly, Megumi checked the school's rankings with her mood ring. It was the last vestige of her old life, and she kept it tuned to an academic channel. The tiny LEDs buried in its core glowed a warm, healthy pink when in the presence of a high score, and shifted to green around newbies. She turned it three times around her finger to activate it. A faint blue light answered her: a score submerged below baseline.

Now their offer made sense. The students at their cram school probably weren't acing entrance exams like they used to. The scores were slipping just enough so that the school couldn't quite justify its standard percentage increase in tuition fees this year. The entrance exam cycle started two months from now. In all likelihood, everyone else on the cram school's list of potential score-skewers had refused this offer.

"I want a bonus, too," she said. "I'd be studying over the holidays, and that means missing overtime pay."

"We'll pay you a temp's wages for the exam days, with bonuses for high scores."

To make any money at all, Megumi would have to take all the exams possible and do very well, thus boosting the school's total score. Watching Okiayu bite into his croissant, she had a feeling he'd planned it this way. For the first time in a long time, she pointed the ring at herself. Its light sputtered out and died.

* * *

At home, Megumi reviewed her total reputation score. If she searched far back enough, she could find the very first data point: an early education specialist's assessment of which preschool would suit her best, based on fifteen minutes of supervised playtime at the ward park. Other inputs trickled in over the years, from traffic cams that told the system whether she held hands with the other kids as she crossed the street, to vending machines that tattled whenever she bought too much sugar, to baseline things like her grades and her participation in clubs. She'd once had the kind of score that made people recheck their displays. She watched their eyes veer sharply to the upper right corner of their glittering spectacles, or caught them scanning her face with their phones under pretence of waving hello. In junior high, the entrance counselors at her first-choice high school said they would enroll her based on her reputation arc alone. She took the exams anyway.

Other countries, ones that weren't still climbing out of the economic wreckage left by the quake, organized their university entrance process differently. But in Japan, getting into the public universities was everything. This too was a function of reputation: everyone knew that the private universities were for-profit corporations where you paid for a piece of paper that meant nothing about your ability to do real work. During the financial deep freeze, competition for entrance to public universities spiked. So the entrance exam system, once designed to catch and keep the best students, reorganized itself to start keeping the majority of students out. The first step was creating reputation points.

Megumi had older cousins who argued against the system. What did it matter if they frequented karaoke rooms, if they got their homework done? Why should a percentage of their total grade be based on whether they smiled during presentations or opened doors for older teachers? But the Ministry of Education praised the system as a return to traditional values: good behavior at home meant good behavior at school meant good behavior at work. And as the most cynical former students told Megumi, the system didn't change anyone's perceptions of student behavior so much as it quantified what everyone was already thinking. The outsiders in the school had understood the role reputation played in their academic life. They knew what the teachers thought about them and their hobbies, and how those thoughts influenced the grading process. Now the smart kids knew it, too.

Megumi worked the system like a pro until she slept with her math teacher.

Hattori was a young teacher, only nine years older than Megumi. He was married. His wife was pregnant. Every day, he had a funny story to tell about the pregnancy, usually involving the toilet's estrogen meter. The laughter that bubbled up out of her during these stories was the most natural part of Megumi's day. It was the only reaction she didn't have to perform. She liked him. They worked well together planning math team study sessions and fundraisers. They painted the club fair booth together. The last day before summer break, he gave her the mood ring. He'd won it from a capsule toy machine while playing for an RFID pacifier intended for his baby.

But when the students returned, the baby stories didn't. Hattori's wife had miscarried. "I didn't just lose the child," he told her later. "I lost *her*."

It happened in Hokkaido, where the math team was staying for the national competition. They won, but with the preparation and travel and explanations of each problem, Megumi lost her voice. Noticing this, Hattori invited her up to his room after the celebratory dinner, claiming to have a packet of lozenges that would ease the pain in her throat. His wife liked them best, he said. Then he started to cry. He cried silently, crumpling in on himself, until Megumi wrapped an arm around his shoulders and pulled him close.

When it all came out, he tried telling the principal that he'd taken advantage of her. But it had happened the other way, and Megumi said so. Strategically, this was a bigger mistake than sleeping with Hattori. The admission called all of her previous grades into question. The school mounted an inquiry. Her score plummeted. Senior year, she didn't even bother with her university entrance exams.

* * *

That January, Megumi blazed through the exams. She had learned the new testware online via practice exams, not wasting her time on memorization or studying. Even back then, Megumi had never spent much time on memorization. In every subject except English, she considered the persona of the one designing the exam, and thought about what they would like to hear, then clicked accordingly. The only process that could teach her how to inhabit these personae was taking test after test. It helped that the other students—they looked so young!—took note of her score and sat far away, as though they feared catching her decrepitude. This gave her the space she needed to stretch and yawn and scratch and do all the things she'd never dared to do while in a classroom. Her partial scores, when they appeared onscreen after each exam, were not as good as her old ones had been. But they rose.

She started receiving messages from her old classmates through the reputation system's attendant social network. The account came with her kindergarten registration. She once boasted hundreds of friends. Then Hattori happened, and they disconnected in droves. Now they merely lurked, peeping her partial scores and occasionally leaving anonymessages. After the second week, when she'd done ten tests and her academic ranking spiked, the fans arrived. They dug up her story and her pictures and the old posts written about her. Junior high schoolers, usually one from every major school, they wanted help with their high school entrance exams, and with their own crushes. When they had tricky questions about math or science, she helped them. This was her only traditional attempt at studying. As a result, her reputation rose among a group in which she was not really a member: an active group, still in school and still dynamic. The effects of this on her score were unexpected, but for Megumi, not entirely unwelcome.

* * *

She completed her final exam in Hokkaido, at the same hotel where she and Hattori had first slept together. It was under new management, and featured revamped décor. Without recognizing the name, she might never have known. Even the room where they had stayed was now a lounge. She grabbed a drink there, afterward. It was on the house. "My daughter follows you," the bartender said. "She looked you up after she heard you were connected to this place. She worked as a maid here last summer."

"I'm not sure I'm the kind of person your daughter should look up to."

"Even smart people make stupid mistakes," he said. "You were seventeen, right? Back when I was seventeen, that's what being seventeen was for."

"I tried to tell the student council that, too."

"Well, seems you've smartened up since then. You gonna try again for university?"

"I don't know," Megumi said, because she honestly didn't.

"Well, you're done your exam, you're in Hokkaido—where are you headed now?"

"That's easy. The bath. I always take one after a test."

"That's a good habit. Clears your mind. You seem like you haven't lost your smarts. You didn't really lose it, did you, between then and now?"

"Oh, I lost it, all right." Megumi finished her drink. "I'm just wondering if I'll get it all back."

* * *

In the bath, she considered her words. The bartender was right. She *was* smart. She still had the knack for exams, and at one time she'd had the hang of the system. But between her first night in this hotel and her second, she'd seen other systems. She'd been part of the Midorep community, assessing the environmental sustainability of products and giving them a rep. It was how she'd met the Choco Cro carton man, saving the cardboard from the recycler raccoons and their trash-laden bikes. At one time, she had read manga based on whether the artists' reps had high scores for allowing freedom of use: unless they allowed fans to make their own derivatives, she wouldn't pick up the title. But these were only fractions of life, not the sum total of it. Megumi no longer believed that the sum total of any person could be calculated by a horde of outsiders. Not when the people closest to you had no idea who you were or what you might do.

She watched the steam rising from her bath and wondered where Hattori had gone. What was his score, now? Did he still allow himself to be graded? Did he still grade others? Briefly, she wished that all mistakes had a homeland they could return to, so she could visit her mistakes and ask them if they remembered events the same way she did.

Once, she had known the smart thing to do. She had the script memorized. It was easy, even comforting, to let other people tell her how good she was. But being herself was harder, and so was being her own judge. You had to set your own baseline, select your own metric. Invent your own system.

Under the water, she twisted her ring three times. It glowed lilac, somewhere between the drowning blue and the living pink. Carefully, she placed it on the lip of the tub, and lifted herself free of the water.

References

Canavan, G. 2010, April 26. Trying to Predict the Present: An Interview with Cory Doctorow [web log post]. *Writing the future*. Retrieved from: <http://sites.duke.edu/writingthefuture/2010/04/26/trying-to-predict-the-present-an-interview-with-cory-doctorow>.

Doctorow, C. 2003. *Down and out in the magic kingdom*. New York: Tor Books.

de Laclos, C. and P. W. K. Stone. [1782] 1961. *Les liaisons dangereuses*. Harmondsworth, Middlesex, England: Penguin.

Contributors

Madeline Ashby is a science fiction writer and graduate student of the Strategic Foresight and Innovation program at the Ontario College of Art and Design. Her work has been published in *Nature*, Flurb, Escape Pod, Tor.com, Worldchanging Canada, and io9.com.

Jamais Cascio writes about the intersection of emerging technologies and cultural transformation, focusing on the importance of long-term, systemic thinking. He speaks around the world on issues including the global environment, technological transformation, and political change. His work appears in publications such as *Atlantic Monthly*, the *Wall Street Journal*, and *Foreign Policy*. He was featured in a National Geographic TV documentary on global warming, *Six Degrees*. Cascio serves as a Research Fellow at the Institute for the Future and as Senior Fellow at the Institute for Ethics and Emerging Technologies. In 2009, *Foreign Policy* magazine listed him as one of their "Top 100 Global Thinkers." Cascio's past work on reputation includes a major section of the "Transhuman Space" science fiction game, covering the evolution of a future reputation system, exploratory essays at multiple foresight-oriented websites, and a multimedia presentation at South-by-Southwest 2008 entitled "The Chorus."

John Henry Clippinger is codirector of the Law Lab at Harvard University Berkman Center for Internet & Society, a multidisciplinary research laboratory to explore the role of law in facilitating self-governance, privacy, and institutional innovation. Clippinger was a Senior Fellow at the Berkman Center, where he cofounded and supported the development of an open source, interoperable identity framework called Project Higgins to give people control over their personal information. He is the author of *A Crowd of One: The Future of Individual Identity* and author/editor of *The Biology of Business: Decoding the Natural Laws of Enterprise*. Clippinger is a graduate of Yale University and holds a PhD from the University of Pennsylvania. He is a frequent participant at the Highlands Forum, the Aspen Institute, the CEO Leadership Institute of Yale School of Management, World Economic Forum, Kauffman Foundation, the Gruter Institute, Creative Leadership Summit, Fortune Brainstorm, and the Santa Fe Institute Business Network.

Chrysanthos Dellarocas is an associate professor at the Boston University School of Management. He holds PhD and SM degrees in computer science from MIT and was previously an associate professor at MIT's Sloan School of Management and an associate professor at the Robert H. Smith School of Business at the University of Maryland. His highly cited research examines the implications of consumer-generated content and social web technologies on business and society. He has been quoted in the *New York Times*, the *Wall Street Journal*, *Business Week*, the *Washington Post*, CNN, and the *Financial Times*. He has brought in more than $2 million in research funds from Google, DARPA, NSF, and other funding agencies and received the prestigious NSF CAREER award. Before joining academia, Dellarocas worked for Andersen Consulting (now Accenture) and McKinsey & Co. He is an inventor with nine patents and is a board member of several Web 2.0 startups.

Cory Doctorow is a science fiction novelist, blogger, and technology activist. He is the coeditor of the popular weblog Boing Boing and a contributor to the *Guardian*, the *New York Times*, *Publishers Weekly*, *Wired*, and many other newspapers, magazines, and websites. He was formerly Director of European Affairs for the Electronic Frontier Foundation, a nonprofit civil liberties group that defends freedom in technology law, policy, standards, and treaties. He is a Visiting Senior Lecturer at Open University (UK); in 2007, he served as the Fulbright Chair at the Annenberg Center for Public Diplomacy at the University of Southern California. Cory's books include *For The Win*, a young adult book about videogames, labor politics, and economics; the *New York Times* bestseller *Little Brother*; *Overclocked: Stories of the Future Present*; *Down and Out in the Magic Kingdom*; *Makers*; and *Content: Selected Essays on Technology, Creativity, Copyright, and the Future of the Future*.

Eric Goldman is associate professor and director at the High Tech Law Institute of the Santa Clara University School of Law. In addition to a stint as general counsel of Epinions.com—a consumer review website now part of the eBay enterprise—Eric has provided legal or consulting advice to some of the other companies mentioned in his chapter (which is adapted from a talk at the Third Annual Conference on the Law and Economics of Innovation at George Mason University, May 2009).

F. Randall "Randy" Farmer coauthored *Building Web Reputation Systems*. He has been creating and organizing online communities for more than thirty years and coinvented many of the basic structures for both virtual worlds and social software. His firsts include: one of the first multiplayer online games; one of the first message boards; the first virtual world; the first avatars; the first online marketplace; the first user newsfeed/friend feed (in Yahoo! 360°); the first multipurpose reputation platform and grammar. For almost five years, Randy worked as the community strategic analyst for Yahoo!, advising on best practices for their online communities. Randy was the principal designer of Yahoo!'s global reputation platform and the reputation models that were deployed upon it. He is in high demand as a freelance community systems design consultant and public speaker, and his online publications and interviews are widely read and cited.

Victor Henning studied Business Administration at the WHU Koblenz, the Université Libre de Bruxelles, and the Handelshøyskolen BI Oslo, and graduated with an MBA in 2004. He went on to pursue his PhD on the role of emotions in decision making at the Bauhaus-University of Weimar, where he was also a lecturer in consumer research and in film industry economics. His research has been funded through a grant from the German Federal Ministry of Education and Research and a dissertation scholarship from the Foundation of the German Economy. His work has been published in journals such as the *Journal of Marketing* and *Media, Culture & Society*, and has won two Best Paper Awards at the AMA Summer Educators' Conference. Since October 2007, he has been the cofounder and director of Mendeley.

Anthony Hoffmann received his BA in English and Studies in Cinema and Media Culture from the University of Minnesota in 2005. Hoffmann earned a masters degree in Library and Information Science at the University of Wisconsin–Milwaukee in 2009 and is currently pursuing a PhD in Information Studies with a focus on information ethics and policy.

Jason Hoyt holds a PhD in genetics from Stanford University, where he worked under the direction of Michele Calos researching human gene therapy with site-specific nonviral vectors. Also amongst his direct research advisors were Gavin Sherlock, Anne Brunet, and Andrew Fire, 2006 Nobel Laureate in Medicine. While a graduate student at Stanford, Jason saw the need and opportunity to improve collaborative research through modern Internet concepts and technologies. This resulted in founding Ologeez.org (peer-review literature searching, recommendation engine, and group collaboration for academics and industry professionals). Since March 2009, he has been the research director of Mendeley.

Luca Iandoli is professor of business and economics at the University of Naples Federico II (Italy) and has been a Fulbright visitor researcher at the MIT Center for Collective Intelligence. His current research interests include online collaborative technologies and their applications to organizational learning, knowledge management, and collaboration in clusters of small firms.

Josh Introne is a research scientist at the MIT Center for Collective Intelligence. He received his PhD in computer science from Brandeis University in 2008. Introne's research has focused upon techniques for integrating intelligent support in collaborative systems. He is currently engaged in a number of projects that seek to leverage the representational work of web-based communities to improve their collective intelligence via the integration of artificial intelligence techniques.

Mari Kuraishi is president of GlobalGiving Foundation, an online donation marketplace that connects citizens to the causes and countries they care about. Mari heads up the internal operations of GlobalGiving, which she cofounded with Dennis Whittle. Before GlobalGiving, she worked at the World Bank, where she managed and created some of the Bank's most innovative projects, including the first ever Innovation and Development Marketplaces and the first series of strategic forums with the World Bank's president and senior management. Mari also designed a range of investment projects in the Russia reform program. In addition to her native Japanese, Mari also speaks Russian, Italian, and French. She has an undergraduate degree in history from Harvard University and did graduate work in Russian and Japanese history and politics at Harvard and Georgetown Universities. Mari also completed the Advanced Management Program at Harvard Business School.

Mark Klein is a principal research scientist at the MIT Center for Collective Intelligence, and an affiliate at the MIT Computer Science and AI Lab (CSAIL) as well as the New England Complex Systems Institute (NECSI). He has made contributions in the areas of computer-supported conflict management for collaborative design, design rationale capture, business process redesign, exception handling in workflow and multiagent systems, service discovery, negotiation algorithms, understanding and resolving emergent dysfunctions in distributed systems, and—more recently—collective intelligence.

Cliff Lampe is assistant professor in the Department of Telecommunication, Information Studies and Media at Michigan State University. He received his PhD in Information in 2006 from the School of Information at the University of Michigan. He studies large-scale online interactions and how sociotechnical tools can be used as architecture in online systems. He has studied sites like Facebook, Slashdot, NewsTrust, and Everything2 as part of this research agenda. Topics he studies include the use of recommender systems to socialize new members of online communities, the role that Facebook interaction has on the generation of social capital, and how users participate in sites over longer periods of time.

Paolo Massa is a researcher at IRST (Institute for Scientific and Technological Research) at Bruno Kessler Foundation (FBK) in Trento, Italy, where he leads the SoNet (Social Networking) research group. He received his PhD from ICT International Graduate School of University of Trento in March 2006, defending a thesis titled "Trust-aware Decentralized Recommender Systems." Paolo's research interests include trust and reputation, recommender systems, and commons-based peer production phenomena such as Wikipedia.

Hassan Masum is a researcher, author, and entrepreneur, and has been a foresight specialist, engineer, scientist, and global health innovator. He is Innovation Lead at the McLaughlin-Rotman Centre for Global Health, Affiliate Researcher at the Waterloo

Institute for Complexity and Innovation, and past team leader in the Ethical, Social, Cultural project of the international Grand Challenges in Global Health initiative. Hassan has published in *Nature, Nature Biotechnology, Innovations, Stanford Social Innovation Review, First Monday, BMC International Health and Human Rights, PLoS Neglected Tropical Diseases,* and other venues. He contributed chapters to the books *Worldchanging, Collective Intelligence,* and *Global Health and Global Health Ethics*. Hassan coauthored the well-known "Manifesto for the Reputation Society" and is coeditor of this volume. He is passionate about working with governments, innovative organizations, and change makers to tackle complex challenges and to disseminate effective sociotechnical solutions.

Marc Maxson is Manager of Impact and Innovation at the GlobalGiving Foundation. His role is to oversee trust, evaluation, and reputation systems that enable crowdsourcing to direct greater levels of support to organizations based on their performance in and their relationship with the communities they serve. Prior to GlobalGiving, Marc earned a PhD in Integrative Biosciences at Pennsylvania State University and did molecular neuroscience research at Tulane. As a Peace Corps volunteer, he trained staff and developed computer programs at several high schools in Gambia. As a Fulbright researcher in 2003, he visited several countries in West Africa to gauge the impact of computers and the Internet on education and culture in rural areas.

Craig Newmark is the founder of Craigslist.org, a site where people can help each other with everyday needs including housing and jobs. The site has a culture of trust, based on shared values like "treat people like you want to be treated." He currently works as a customer service rep, in no managerial role. Previous experience includes thirty years working with computers for IBM, GM, Charles Schwab & Co., and Bank of America. He's also working with a wide range of groups using the Internet to help each other out, such as DonorsChoose.org, the Iraq & Afghanistan Veterans of America, Kiva.org (microfinance), AllForGood.org, which is the "Craigslist for service," Consumer Reports, and the Craigslist Foundation. He's working on the advisory board of Wikipedia, considering customer service and trust issues. Craig is also actively engaged with government workers on multiple levels to use the Internet for superior public service and with the Sunlight Foundation for government accountability and transparency.

Michael Nielsen is one of the pioneers of quantum computation. Together with Ike Chuang of MIT, he wrote the standard text in the field. His research contributions include involvement in one of the first quantum teleportation experiments, which was named one of Science Magazine's Top Ten Breakthroughs of 1998. Michael was a Fulbright Scholar at the University of New Mexico and has worked at Los Alamos National Laboratory, as the Tolman Prize Fellow at Caltech, as Foundation Professor of Quantum Information Science at the University of Queensland, and as a Senior Faculty Member at the Perimeter Institute for Theoretical Physics. Michael left academia to write a book about open science and the radical change online tools are causing in the way scientific discoveries are made.

Lucio Picci holds a PhD from the University of California–San Diego. He is professor of economics at the University of Bologna. Between 2007 and 2009, he served as Senior Scientist at the Institute for Prospective Technological Studies (IPTS—part of the European Commission's Joint Research Centre) in Seville, Spain. His research interests are at the intersection between political economy, public governance, and the economics of innovation. He has published in journals such as the *American Journal of Political Science*, *Research Policy*, and the *Review of Economic and Statistics*. He is the author of *Reputation-Based Governance*.

Jan Reichelt studied Business Administration at the WHU Koblenz, the LUISS Rome, and the University of Bath School of Management and graduated with an MBA in 2004. He then commenced his PhD studies in information management at the University of Cologne, Germany. During this time, he was a lecturer in electronic business and information management and spent a research period at the Indian Institute of Management, Bangalore. Additionally, he worked as an advisor to a member of SAP's supervisory board until 2007. Since October 2007, he has been the cofounder and director of Mendeley.

Lior Jacob Strahilevitz is deputy dean and professor of law at the University of Chicago Law School. He received his BA in political science from the University of California at Berkeley in 1996, graduating with highest honors. He received his JD in 1999 from Yale Law School, where he served as executive editor of the *Yale Law Journal*. Following his graduation, he clerked for Judge Cynthia Holcomb Hall on the U.S. Court of Appeals for the Ninth Circuit. He then practiced law in Seattle before joining the University of Chicago faculty in 2002. He was tenured in 2006 and became deputy dean in 2010. His teaching and research interests include property and land use, privacy, intellectual property, law and technology, and social norms. He thanks the Morton C. Seeley Fund and the John M. Olin Fund for research support.

Alex Steffen cofounded Worldchanging and was executive editor there from 2003 to 2010. Worldchanging became one of the most widely read sustainability-related publications on the Internet, with an archive of over ten thousand articles by leading thinkers around the world. Steffen has spoken to audiences including Nike, Amazon, Ideo, Arup, Yahoo!, TED, Pop!Tech, Tallberg, and South by Southwest Interactive. Steffen's work has been the subject of stories in the *New York Times*, *USA Today*, the *L.A. Times*, the *Wall Street Journal*, the *San Francisco Chronicle*, *Wired*, the *Guardian*, the *Seattle Times*, the *Seattle Post-Intelligencer*, *Fast Company*, *Red Herring*, SEED, the Associated Press, CNN, CBC, NHK, NPR's *All Things Considered*, and others. His essays have been translated into German, French, Japanese, Portuguese, and Spanish and anthologized widely, including in the 2050 Project's book *Choosing Our Future*. He guest-edited the final issue of the *Whole Earth Review*.

Mark Tovey edited *Collective Intelligence: Creating a Prosperous World at Peace*, is coeditor of this volume, and was editor of Worldchanging Canada from 2006–2010. He did his PhD in Cognitive Science at Carleton University and is an affiliate researcher at the Waterloo Institute for Complexity and Innovation. Mark's passions lie in designing mass collaborative systems to solve global challenges. He is regularly invited to give talks or serve as a panelist at conferences, which have included the Quantum2Cosmos Festival, the O'Reilly Open Source Convention, the Canadian Creative Cities Summit, and Canada's Top 100 Green Employers.

John Whitfield is a science writer based in London. A former staff writer at the journal *Nature*, he has been freelance since 2004, and specializes in writing about evolution and ecology. He is the author of *In the Beat of a Heart: Life, Energy, and the Unity of Nature* and *People Will Talk: The Science of Reputation*.

John Willinsky is on the faculty of the Stanford University School of Education. Until 2007, he was the Pacific Press Professor of Literacy and Technology and Distinguished University Scholar in the Department of Language and Literacy Education at the University of British Columbia (UBC). He is a Fellow of the Royal Society of Canada. He is the author of *The Access Principle: The Case for Open Access to Research and Scholarship*, which won the 2006 Blackwell's Scholarship Award and the Computers and Composition Distinguished Book Award. He has also written *Empire of Words: The Reign of the OED*, *Learning to Divide the World: Education at Empire's End*, which won Outstanding Book Awards from the American Educational Research Association and History of Education Society, and the more recent titles *Technologies of Knowing* and *If Only We Knew: Increasing the Public Value of Social Science Research*. He retains a partial appointment at UBC, where he directs the Public Knowledge Project, which is researching systems that hold promise for improving the scholarly and public quality of academic research.

Yi-Cheng Zhang is a professor of theoretical physics at the University of Fribourg in Switzerland. He coauthored "Manifesto for the Reputation Society" with Hassan Masum, heads a research team that has produced many models of reputation and economic phenomena, and is the "Z" in the KPZ equation for nonlinear stochastic growth. He has published more than a hundred academic articles and is coauthor of *Minority Games: Interacting Agents in Financial Markets*.

Michael Zimmer is an assistant professor in the School of Information Studies at the University of Wisconsin–Milwaukee and codirector of the Center for Information Policy Research. With a background in new media and Internet studies, the philosophy of technology, and information policy, Zimmer studies the social, political, and ethical dimensions of new media and information technologies.

Index